TABLE OF CONTENTS

PHYSICAL EDUCATION REQUIRMENTS ... 3

PHYSICAL EDUCATION FORMS ... 4
Physical Education Log ... 5
Organized or Team Sports Verification Log ... 7

ESSENTIALS OF FITNESS ... 8
Health-Related Components ... 9
Skills-Related Components ... 9
Wellness-Related Components ... 10

FITT PRINCIPLE AND MORE ... 11

PLANNING AND PREPARING FOR EXERCISE ... 14
Warm-Up and Cool-Down ... 15
Weather Precautions Related to Exercise ... 16
Fitness Test ... 17
Performance Scorecard ... 19
Physical Education Performance Chart ... 20
Working With A Purpose: Goal Setting ... 21

HEALTH-RELATED FITNESS COMPONENTS ... 22
5 Components Of Health-Related Physical Fitness ... 23
Body Composition ... 24
Cardiovascular Endurance ... 26
Pulse and Target Heart Rate ... 26
Benefits of Cardiovascular Endurance Exercise ... 29
Flexibility ... 31
Muscular Strength ... 37
Muscular Endurance ... 41

PHYSICAL EDUCATION KITS ... 46
Physical Equipment Kits 6–8 ... 46
Electronic Movement Band ... 47
Grade 6 PE Equipment Kit ... 48
Grade 7 PE Equipment Kit ... 112
Grade 8 PE Equipment Kit ... 177

ANATOMY SECTION ... 233
Skeletal System ... 234
Muscular System ... 235
Circulatory System ... 236
Respiratory, Nervous, Digestive System ... 237

CAREERS ... 238

PHYSICAL ACTIVITY JOURNALS ... 240
Fitness Workout Journal ... 242
Physical Education Journal ... 243

GLOSSARY OF TERMS ... 244

STANDARDS ALIGNMENT INDEX PAGE ... 249

Copyright 2024 © Lincoln Learning Solutions. All rights reserved.

Welcome to the
PHYSICAL EDUCATION PROGRAM

MISSION STATEMENT

Physical Education is an integral part of the total education process. Our educators believe in a sound mind and a sound body at any ability level. Schools are responsible for teaching students to use skills in real-world settings. Our mission in Physical Education is to help students reach their maximum potential in order to ensure a healthy, productive life. Physical Education explains how and why the body moves, promoting students' mental and social development through performing physical activities. The course also provides students with the knowledge and skills to become healthy and active individuals. By participating regularly in a broad spectrum of activities, students—regardless of ability level—are able to meet physical challenges; develop essential motor skills; assess their individual abilities; appreciate the joy of human movement; and develop strategies for physical improvement.

PHYSICAL EDUCATION REQUIREMENTS

REQUIREMENTS FOR PHYSICAL EDUCATION

- Students in grade 6 should complete **36 hours** of Physical Education activities for a passing grade. This is an average of three hours per week for 12 weeks.
- Students in grades 7-8 should complete **72 hours** of Physical Education activities for a passing grade. In other words, you should average three hours of activity per week for 24 weeks.
- Your school will notify you if they require more or less required hours.
- You may begin documenting your hours from the first day of your school year until your completion date.
- Each week, record your hours and activities in the electronic Physical Education Log. Save the Physical Education Log in your user file on your computer.
- Record your activities by the day. Do not group activities by the week or month.
- Record no more than three activity hours per day in your log. If you record more than three hours per day, your instructor will give you a chance to fix your log to fit this criterion.
- The Physical Education department understands that when you play a sport, your competitions and practices may last longer than three hours. That is acceptable and is why we ask that you fill out the Organized or Team Sports Verification Log instead of the Physical Education Log.
- You can find the Organized or Team Sports Verification Log online in your Physical Education course or on page 7 of this workbook.
- The Physical Education Log and the Organized or Team Sports Verification Log are the **only** forms accepted for Physical Education credit. We do not accept handwritten forms.
- Submit your Physical Education Log or Organized or Sports Team Sports Verification log through your Physical Education course.
- It is recommended that you record **50 percent** of your Physical Education activities from this workbook.

You may choose to participate in any of the activities shown in the chart below; be sure to record these in your Physical Education Log or Organized or Team Sports Verification Log. Work is not an acceptable Physical Education activity. Examples of work include occupations, yard work, household chores, etc. Any activity not listed below must be pre-approved by your Physical Education instructor.

Sports	Lifetime/Leisure	Fitness
Archery Baseball Basketball Football Golf Hockey Lacrosse Racket Sports Soccer Swimming Volleyball Water Sports Wrestling	Biking/Scooter/Skateboarding Bowling Canoe/Kayak Dance Frisbee/Bocce/Target Games Horseback Riding Kickball/Four Square Playground Activities Skiing/Skating/Snowboarding Tag/Active Games Walking/Running Wall Climbing	Aerobics Calisthenics Cardio Videos Fitness Videos Gymnastics Jump Rope Martial Arts Stationary Exercise Equipment Yoga Zumba®

PHYSICAL EDUCATION FORMS

PE Log

Grades 6 through 8

The PE Log (Physical Education Log) will track the various activities that you complete as part of the requirements for this course. It is recommended that you complete no more than three activity hours per day.

To complete the PE Log, enter your information in the open fields below. Then, in the table, enter the date you completed the activity, the name of the activity, the amount of time you participated (in hours), and the kit item (if applicable). **Note:** Farm work, part time jobs, and household chores do not count as valid activities.

You must complete all areas of this form in order to receive credit.

Remember to save this document to your computer. You will be instructed to submit the log periodically throughout the course; therefore, you should always be adding your hours to the log. When prompted to submit the log, turn in your completed PE Log to your instructor through your Physical Education course.

Student Name and ID:
_____

Email Address:
_____

Telephone Number:
_____

Parent/Guardian:
_____

Instructor and Course Name:
_____

Total Activity Hours
_____

You may choose to **add** any of the following **unorganized** activities to the Physical Education Log: swimming, basketball, archery, Ultimate Frisbee, walking, running, hiking, biking, wall climbing, golf, bowling, weight lifting, aerobics, cardio, football, snowboarding, volleyball, tumbling/gymnastics, calisthenics, stretching, skiing, canoeing, kayaking, martial arts, horseback riding, Wii Fit, yoga, Zumba, dance, fencing, racket sports, softball, or baseball.

Copyright 2024 © Lincoln Learning Solutions. All rights reserved.

PE Log

Grades 6 through 8

Date	Physical Activity	Participation Time (in hours)	Physical Education Kit Item
09-01	Running	.25	electronic movement band

ORGANIZED OR TEAM SPORTS VERIFICATION LOG

- This form can be submitted in place of or in conjunction with the Physical Education Log.
- The fields on this document should not be altered.
- Remember to save this document to your computer.
- Submit completed electronic sports verification log through your physical education course.
- The sports verification log is for organized or team sports only.
- Please remember to complete the rest of your Physical Education course upon submitting this form.
- Please only list the HOURS, not minutes, of your activities. If you want to list minutes, use decimals such as 0.25 for 15 minutes.

Student Name: _____

Student ID#: _____ Student Grade Level: _____

Physical Education Instructor: _____

Coach's Name: _____ Home School District: _____

Telephone Number: ( ) - _____ Email Address: _____

Total Activity Hours: _____ Parent/Guardian: _____

Students may include organized or team sports from the fall, winter, or spring seasons. Sports may include, but are not limited to: football, golf, soccer, volleyball, tennis, cross country, field hockey, baseball, softball, track, lacrosse, basketball, wrestling, rifling, gymnastics, swimming and diving.

Date	Sport Played	HOURS ONLY	Game or Practice
09-01	Football	1.5 hours	Game

Copyright 2024 © Lincoln Learning Solutions. All rights reserved.

ESSENTIALS
OF FITNESS

HEALTH-RELATED FITNESS COMPONENTS

Health-related fitness components are the areas that make up total fitness. It is important to be balanced in all categories and to stay active in order to ensure good physical health. Staying active has many benefits, such as decreasing the risk of illness and chronic disease; increasing metabolic rate, which allows for food to be converted into energy more easily; building muscular strength and endurance; burning more calories; increasing heart and lung function; and so on. The 5 health-related fitness components provide a guideline on which to base your fitness levels and set goals for your workouts and exercise routines.

BODY COMPOSITION
the ratio of fat to muscle

CARDIOVASCULAR ENDURANCE
the ability of your heart and lungs to supply oxygen to your body

FLEXIBILITY
the ability of your muscles and joints to move through a full range of motion

MUSCULAR ENDURANCE
the ability of your muscles to exert force for an extended period of time

MUSCULAR STRENGTH
the ability of your muscles to exert maximum force in a single effort

SKILL-RELATED COMPONENTS

Skill-related components are the different areas of physical functioning. The 6 skill-related components are not as important for overall health and wellness as the health-related fitness components, but they are vital parts of basic, everyday movements. These components are associated not only with sports and activities, but also with daily function, such as climbing stairs or crossing the street. Being skillful in these areas can also allow you to perform better during athletics.

AGILITY
the ability to change the position of your body quickly but with control

BALANCE
the ability to maintain stabilization while moving and staying still

COORDINATION
the ability to use your senses together with moving body parts

POWER
the ability to use speed and force in movement and actions

REACTION TIME
the ability to move quickly when responding to stimuli

SPEED
the ability to cover a distance within a short period of time

WELLNESS-RELATED COMPONENTS

Wellness-related components are the other aspects of a good quality of life. It takes more than physical fitness to have overall wellness. To live a balanced life, you need to take care of all areas of your mind, body, and spirit. Practicing good habits in the 5 areas of health and wellness can allow you to grow as a person and develop confidence and purpose. This can lead to a joyful, productive life.

EMOTIONAL HEALTH
the ability to control and express your emotions appropriately

ENVIRONMENTAL HEALTH
the ability to maintain a clean and safe area around you

MENTAL HEALTH
the ability to recognize reality and cope with the demands of life

SOCIAL HEALTH
the ability to interact with people and have appropriate relationships

SPIRITUAL HEALTH
the ability to have direction and purpose

Discuss the health-related, skill-related, and wellness-related components with a trusted friend or an adult. List the components that are most important to you and the exercises that you can do to improve and maintain your overall physical and emotional health.

Question	Answer
What components do I want to improve upon or maintain?	
What can I do to reach my goal?	

FITT PRINCIPLE
AND MORE

PRINCIPLES OF FITNESS

The fitness principles below provide structure for creating your own workout plan. Each of the principles has its own classifications, but they all work in coordination with each other to ensure a quality program that will lead to maximum results. After you have a specific goal written, make sure that you review each of the principles thoroughly to create a suitable plan that meets your needs.

THE OVERLOAD PRINCIPLE

The overload principle describes how your body reacts to the workload that is placed upon it. Your body responds to the amount of exercise and training that you make it do and adapts to it. It becomes accustomed to the exercise and the amount of effort that is needed. At this point, you no longer have to work as hard to perform, so change no longer occurs. You consistently want to challenge your body by increasing its workload, therefore increasing your fitness level. You can increase its workload in small stages, but these will lead to big changes over time.

THE SPECIFICITY PRINCIPLE

The specificity principle corresponds to your goals and the types of workouts you do or muscles you use. Your workouts should correspond to the goal at hand. You want to be intentional about the exercises you perform and the muscles you use to focus on reaching your goal. For example, if you wanted to increase your mile time, you would want to concentrate on exercises or workouts that would increase your speed and improve your cardiovascular endurance.

THE FITT PRINCIPLE

The FITT principle is a formula for designing your exercise program. The acronym *FITT* stands for the key components of a good workout.

Frequency: how often you exercise
example: 3 times per week

Intensity: how hard you exercise
example: 80 percent of your maximum heart rate

Time: how long you exercise
example: 60 minutes

Type: what kind of exercise
example: cardiovascular endurance workout, such as running on a treadmill

THE REST AND RECOVERY PRINCIPLE

The rest and recovery principle is very important for reaching your goals and preventing injury. While it is vital to work out consistently to maximize your potential, it is also just as important to rest the muscles that were used to allow growth and development. It is suggested that you push your muscles past the point of exhaustion, as explained in the overload principle, but you do not want to overstrain your muscles and cause injury. For example, when you are strength training, you never want to work the same muscles 2 days in a row because your body needs time to rest and recover.

THE USE OR LOSE PRINCIPLE

The use or lose principle simply stated is the principle that if you do not use it, you will lose it. When you work out or otherwise move your body, you build up your muscles and increase your strength, which is hypertrophy; however, if you do not stay active, you will lose your strength and your muscles will atrophy. Finding a balance of activity and exercise is important to your overall health and wellness. Staying active keeps your body physically healthy and your brain mentally healthy. Possible alternatives are lack of muscle tone, lack of strength, illness, becoming overweight, lower energy levels, and so on.

Activity Recommendations

- **Limit** sitting at computers, playing video games, and watching TV.
- **Every day**, walk or stay active for at least **60 minutes**.
- **3 to 5 times per week**, give your heart and lungs an aerobic workout.
- **3 or more times per week**, strengthen and stretch your muscles.

PLANNING AND PREPARING
FOR EXERCISE

WARM-UP AND COOL-DOWN

Before beginning a workout or exercise program or performing moderate to vigorous activity, you need to be sure that you are physically and mentally prepared. There are steps to take prior to participating in physical activity to ensure safety, success, and results. Having a set plan to follow when you are exercising allows you to maximize your time and allows you to reach your goals more efficiently. Knowing how to properly prepare your body for physical activity helps you prevent injury and keeps you safe. The following warm-up, cool-down, and weather precaution information will provide tools and tips for you to design a workout routine or activity session suited for your needs.

The importance of a warm-up is that it prepares your body for exercise. A good warm-up should increase your heart rate, breathing rate, and body temperature. You can do traditional warm-up activities like jumping jacks or jumping rope, or you can perform other warm-up activities like using cardiovascular endurance equipment, dancing, or walking. Once you have completed your warm-up, you are ready to begin your exercise. Reversely, when you have finished your exercise, you should do a cool-down. Your body needs to return to baseline—your heart rate, breathing rate, and body temperature must all decrease back to a resting level. Some examples of cool-down activities include stretching, walking, and relaxation practices such as deep breathing and guided imagery. Warming up and cooling down are essential to the physical activity process.

WARM-UP SUGGESTIONS:

1. Complete 3 sets of 10 to 15 repetitions of each of the exercises below.

jumping jacks	march in place	monster kicks

2. Use a piece of cardiovascular equipment such as a treadmill, stationary bike, or elliptical for 5 to 10 minutes. Your heart rate, breathing rate, and body temperature should all increase during this time.

COOL-DOWN SUGGESTIONS:

1. Gradually slow your exercise or activity until you are at a walking pace. Continue walking for 5 to 10 minutes or until your heart rate and breathing rate are at a resting rate or slightly above. Finish your cool-down with the static stretches found in the Stretching section of this manual, or create your own stretching routine. This will increase your flexibility and decrease muscle soreness and tightness.

2. Follow the deep breathing sequence of in through your nose and out through your mouth until your breathing is back to normal. While you are breathing, close your eyes and focus on a place that is relaxing to you, such as a beach. Think about the way you feel when you are at this place, physically and mentally. When you are fully relaxed, slowly open your eyes and "awaken" your body.

WEATHER PRECAUTIONS RELATED TO EXERCISE

COLD TEMPERATURES

Cold-weather sports can be fun, but you need to be safe!

Tips for a Safe Workout

- Let someone know where and when you are exercising, or have someone accompany you.
- Layer your clothes. If you get warm, you can take a layer off, but do not take off your coat!
- Wear hats, gloves or mittens, and waterproof boots.
- Go inside if your teeth are chattering or if you are shivering.
- Hydrate! You need water in cold weather as well as in hot weather. Warm drinks and soups can also help warm you up.
- Watch out for slippery surfaces.
- Exercise in safe areas only.

Dangers: Frostbite and Hypothermia

Frostbite: If you are not wearing enough protective clothing, any exposed skin tissue can freeze. This most commonly happens to noses, ears, fingers, and toes.

Hypothermia: This is what occurs when your core body temperature drops. It can result from exposure to cold weather or being in cold water. Symptoms include shivering, a lack of energy, mental confusion, and even more severe symptoms. Do not allow your body to get to this point. When you start shivering, go inside!

HOT TEMPERATURES

Exercising in hot temperatures can be dangerous. Pay attention to your body's signals: Stop exercising and cool down immediately if you are feeling fatigued and are not feeling well.

Tips for a Safe Workout

- Let someone know where and when you are exercising, or have someone accompany you.
- Know the temperature of your exercise environment. Avoid exercising in high temperatures.
- Take it easy in hot temperatures. Take breaks, shorten your workout time, or go indoors to an air-conditioned facility.
- Drink water before you are thirsty, and keep hydrated.
- Wear sunscreen and a sun hat.
- Dress in cool, loose, light-colored clothing.

Dangers: Heat Cramps, Fainting, Heat Exhaustion, and Heatstroke

Heat cramps: Abrupt muscle pain that is caused by heat is heat cramps.

Fainting: You can experience light-headedness or collapsing as a result of exercising, especially in hot conditions.

Heat exhaustion: Heat exhaustion occurs when your core body temperature increases. Sweaty, cold, clammy skin in addition to heat cramps and fainting are symptoms of heat exhaustion. Untreated heat exhaustion leads to heatstroke. Get medical help and cool down your body temperature immediately.

Heatstroke: This occurs when your core body temperature rises above 104 degrees Fahrenheit (40 degrees Celsius). At this stage, the body does not sweat. This is a life-threatening situation that requires medical attention.

Other Precautions to Take

Special note: Pay attention to the humidity level as well as the temperature. Exercising in a high-humidity condition contributes to elevated body temperature and excessive sweating.

For more information, research the signs and symptoms of weather-related health conditions in addition to prevention methods and first aid. Get advice from your doctor about exercising in cold and hot temperatures.

FITNESS TESTS

Fitness tests allow you to assess your current fitness levels. The tests measure the main fitness components: cardiovascular endurance, flexibility, muscular strength, muscular endurance, and the subcomponents speed and agility. The results of the tests will allow you to evaluate your fitness levels and decide which areas you would like to work on in order to increase your overall health and wellness. It is recommended that you take the fitness tests 3 times during the school year (pre, mid, and post).

CARDIOVASCULAR ENDURANCE
ENDURANCE WALK/RUN
The endurance walk/run measures heart and lung endurance. Map out a safe 1-mile route to complete the test. You will need a stopwatch to time your run. It is recommended that you run at a steady pace for the entire mile. Walking may be combined with running, but you are encouraged to complete the test in the shortest amount of time possible.

FLEXIBILITY
V-SIT AND REACH
The V-sit and reach measures the flexibility of your lower back and hamstrings. Mark a straight 2-foot line with a piece of tape, rope, or tape measure on the floor to use as a baseline. Use a tape measure or yardstick to draw a 4-foot measuring line perpendicular to the midpoint of the baseline, extending 2 feet on either side and marked in half inches. The point where the lines intersect is the 0 point. Take off your shoes and sit on the floor with the measuring line between your legs. Place your heels directly behind the baseline, with your feet 8 to 12 inches apart. With your palms facing down, place your hands on top of each other and on the measuring line. Have a partner hold your legs flat while you slowly reach forward as far as possible, keeping your fingers on the line and your feet flexed. You may practice up to 3 times. Then, complete the exercise a final time, holding the distance for 3 seconds. Record your score.
- Keep your legs straight and flex your feet.
- Do not bounce.
- Slowly reach forward. Hold for 3 seconds.

MUSCULAR ENDURANCE
BENT-KNEE SIT-UP
This activity measures your abdominal strength and endurance. Set a stopwatch for 1 minute. Lying down on your back, flex your knees and place your feet flat on the floor about 12 inches from your buttocks. Cross your arms in front of your chest. Keeping your arms in the same position, use your trunk to sit up and touch your elbows to your thighs. Return to the starting position so that your shoulder blades touch the ground. Do not let your head or neck touch the ground. A partner should hold your feet and count how many curl-ups you complete in 1 minute.
- Do not count curl-ups if you are bouncing off the floor, if your arms are not crossed in front of your chest, or if your elbows do not touch your thighs when you are sitting up.

MUSCULAR STRENGTH
FLEXED-ARM HANG, RIGHT-ANGLE PUSH-UPS, AND PULL-UPS
These activities measure upper-body strength and endurance. You only have to complete 1 of these 3 tests.

FLEXED-ARM HANG

Using either an overhand grip (your palms facing away from your body) or an underhand grip (your palms facing toward your body), assume the flexed-arm hang position by bending your elbows and clearing the bar with your chin (place your chin above the bar, but do not rest it on the bar). Keep your chest close to the bar. Try to keep your body as still as possible and to not swing your legs or place your feet on surrounding objects or walls. Time yourself in this position until your chin touches or drops below the bar.

- This is a good skill to practice before attempting pull-ups.
- You may use a chair or have someone lift you to the position.
- When you are finished, let go of the bar slowly and carefully to avoid injury.

RIGHT-ANGLE PUSH-UPS

Situate your body on a mat in a push-up position. Place your hands under your shoulders and point your fingers forward. Keep your legs straight, parallel, and slightly apart, supporting your feet with your toes. Straighten your arms, keeping your back and knees straight. Then, lower your body and bend your elbows 90 degrees. Keep your chest 4 to 5 inches from the floor. Return to the up position. The push-ups should be done to a metronome pace of 1 complete push-up every 3 seconds. Do as many consecutive push-ups as possible until you cannot complete 1 within the set pace.

- Record only the push-ups that you do with proper form.
- Record only the push-ups that you do to the metronome pace.
- Your stomach and legs should not touch the ground. Keep your back straight.

PULL-UPS OR CHIN-UPS

Hang from a horizontal bar at a height where your arms are fully extended and your feet are not touching the ground. You may do a pull-up using an overhand grip (your palms facing away from your body) or a chin-up using an underhand grip (your palms facing toward your body). Pull yourself up until your chin is above the bar; then, return to the full hanging position. Perform as many correct pull-ups or chin-ups as you can.

- Pull-ups should be done slowly and safely by controlling your body back to the starting position.
- Kicking or bending your legs or swinging is prohibited during the test.

SPEED AND AGILITY

SHUTTLE RUN

This sprinting activity measures the subcomponents speed and agility. Mark 2 lines 30 feet apart. Place 2 small items from your Physical Education Kit on 1 of the lines. Start on the opposite line. Use a stopwatch to time yourself in seconds. On a "ready, go" signal, start the stopwatch. Run to pick up 1 item and run back to the starting line, placing the item behind the starting line. Then, run back to pick up the second item and return to the starting line, but hold on to the object and run through the line.

- Do not throw the items.
- It is important that you run through the starting line to achieve a better time.

FITNESS PERFORMANCE SCORECARD

Student Name: _____ Gender: _____

Fitness Challenge	Date: Age: Grade: Height: Weight: Test #1	Date: Age: Grade: Height: Weight: Test #2	Date: Age: Grade: Height: Weight: Test #3
Endurance Walk/Run			
V-Sit and Reach			
Bent-Knee Sit-Up			
Flexed-Arm Hang			
Right-Angle Push-Ups			
Pull-Ups or Chin-Ups			
Shuttle Run			

Copyright 2024 © Lincoln Learning Solutions. All rights reserved.

PHYSICAL EDUCATION PERFORMANCE CHART

Fitness performance charts are tools that you can use to identify your fitness levels based on national averages. The results can show your strengths and weaknesses in relation to your physical fitness and help you set attainable fitness goals.

Compare your scores to the fitness performance chart to see if you have attained your fitness levels. Find your age at the top of the chart and go down the column to see the average and outstanding scores for your fitness levels. Pick an event from the left-hand column and go across the row until you reach your age group. There are 2 groups of scores on the chart: attainment and outstanding achievement. The attainment standard is an average score that represents the 50th percentile based on the current fitness survey. The outstanding achievement is a score at the 85th percentile based on the current fitness survey.

GIRLS' FITNESS PERFORMANCE CHART

EVENTS	LEVEL OF PERFORMANCE	6	7	8	9	10	11	12	13	14	15	16	17	18
ENDURANCE WALK/RUN (Minutes & Seconds)	ATTAINMENT STANDARDS	¼ mile 2:30	¼ mile 2:24	¼ mile 5:02	¼ mile 4:57	¾ mile 7:30	¾ mile 7:25	1 mile 9:54	1 mile 9:50	1 mile 9:50	1 mile 9:50	1 mile 9:52	1 mile 9:54	1 mile 9:50
	OUTSTANDING ACHIEVEMENT	2:05	1:55	3:58	3:53	6:10	6:06	8:15	8:04	8:08	8:00	8:07	8:16	8:16
V-SIT & REACH (inches)	ATTAINMENT STANDARDS	2.5	2	2	2	3	3	3.5	3.5	4.5	5	5.5	4.5	4.5
	OUTSTANDING ACHIEVEMENT	5.5	5	4.5	5.5	6	6.5	7	7	8	8	9	9	8
BENT-KNEE SIT-UPS (One-Minute Time Limit)	ATTAINMENT STANDARDS	22	25	29	31	32	33	35	25	36	35	35	35	36
	OUTSTANDING ACHIEVEMENT	31	34	38	30	40	42	43	45	45	44	44	44	44
FLEXED-ARM HANG* (Seconds & Tenths)	ATTAINMENT STANDARDS	6	7	8	8.5	10	12.4	15	15.9	14	13	12	11	10
	OUTSTANDING ACHIEVEMENT	14.7	19	19.5	22	24	25	32	35	35	29	30	30	28
RIGHT-ANGLE PUSH-UPS (#)	ATTAINMENT STANDARDS	6	8	9	12	13	11	10	11	10	15	12	16	16
	OUTSTANDING ACHIEVEMENT	9	14	17	18	20	20	20	21	20	21	24	25	25
PULL-UPS/CHIN-UPS (#)	ATTAINMENT STANDARDS	1	1	1	1	1	1	1	1	1	1	1	1	1
	OUTSTANDING ACHIEVEMENT	2	2	2	2	2	2	2	2	2	2	2	2	2
SHUTTLE RUN (Seconds)	ATTAINMENT STANDARDS	14.2	13.5	13.1	12.2	12.2	11.8	11.6	11.2	11.2	11.2	11.2	11.2	11.1
	OUTSTANDING ACHIEVEMENT	12.9	12.5	12	11.5	11.3	10.9	10.5	10.3	10.4	10.4	10.4	10.2	10.2

* Modified Fitness Test   ■ Attainment Standards (Represents the 50th percentile)   ■ Outstanding Standards (Represents the 85th percentile)

BOYS' FITNESS PERFORMANCE CHART

EVENTS	LEVEL OF PERFORMANCE	6	7	8	9	10	11	12	13	14	15	16	17	18
ENDURANCE WALK/RUN (Minutes & Seconds)	ATTAINMENT STANDARDS	¼ mile 2:21	¼ mile 2:10	¼ mile 4:22	¼ mile 4:14	¾ mile 6:30	¾ mile 6:30	1 mile 8:34	1 mile 7:54	1 mile 7:33	1 mile 7:27	1 mile 7:21	1 mile 7:08	1 mile 7:08
	OUTSTANDING ACHIEVEMENT	1:55	1:48	3:30	3:30	5:30	5:19	7:10	6:45	6:28	6:18	6:14	6:12	6:12
V-SIT & REACH (inches)	ATTAINMENT STANDARDS	1	1	0.5	1	1	1	1	0.5	1	2	3	3	3
	OUTSTANDING ACHIEVEMENT	3.5	3.5	3	3	4	4	4	3.5	4.5	5	6	7	7
BENT-KNEE SIT-UPS (One-Minute Time Limit)	ATTAINMENT STANDARDS	22	28	31	32	35	37	40	42	45	45	45	45	45
	OUTSTANDING ACHIEVEMENT	31	36	39	43	45	48	49	51	53	53	53	55	55
FLEXED-ARM HANG* (Seconds & Tenths)	ATTAINMENT STANDARDS	8	12	18	22	25	29	35	40	42	45	48	50	55
	OUTSTANDING ACHIEVEMENT	17	22	27	31	35	37	40	45	48	52	60	68	70
RIGHT-ANGLE PUSH-UPS (#)	ATTAINMENT STANDARDS	7	8	9	12	14	15	18	24	24	30	30	37	38
	OUTSTANDING ACHIEVEMENT	9	14	17	18	22	27	31	39	40	42	44	53	55
PULL-UPS/CHIN-UPS (#)	ATTAINMENT STANDARDS	1	1	1	2	2	2	2	3	5	6	7	8	9
	OUTSTANDING ACHIEVEMENT	2	4	5	5	6	6	7	7	10	11	11	13	14
SHUTTLE RUN (Seconds)	ATTAINMENT STANDARDS	13.3	12.8	12.2	11.9	11.5	11.1	10.6	10.2	9.9	9.7	9.4	9.4	9.3
	OUTSTANDING ACHIEVEMENT	12.1	11.5	11.1	10.9	10.3	10	9.8	9.5	9.1	9	8.7	8.7	8.6

* Modified Fitness Test   ■ Attainment Standards (Represents the 50th percentile)   ■ Outstanding Standards (Represents the 85th percentile)

WORKING WITH A PURPOSE: GOAL SETTING

Evaluate and discuss your fitness test results with a trusted adult, and then use the following SMART goal plan to design an exercise program for yourself. Do not compare your results to the results of others. Everyone's body is different.

Have you heard the saying "failing to plan is planning to fail"? This is true of beginning a workout regimen. Starting a workout may be intimidating and confusing, but setting goals and plans for how to achieve those goals will set you up for success and put you on the right track. After performing your fitness tests and reviewing your results, you will have a better understanding of what areas you may need to improve in. Decide which area or areas you would like to work on and why. Knowing why you should be proficient in an area will allow you to have a better understanding of its importance and will keep you working toward improvement. Write a SMART goal and a plan based on the fitness principles and components.

Specific   Measurable   Attainable   Realistic   Timely

Short-Term Goal(s):

_____
_____
_____
_____
_____
_____
_____
_____
_____

Plan(s):

_____
_____
_____
_____
_____
_____
_____
_____
_____
_____

HEALTH-RELATED FITNESS COMPONENTS

5 COMPONENTS OF HEALTH-RELATED PHYSICAL FITNESS

Total fitness is defined by how well your body performs in different categories. There are 5 specific categories that you must focus on in order to allow your body to work the way it was intended to. These health-related fitness components act as a guideline for planning your workout regimen based on your goals.

1. **BODY COMPOSITION:** the ratio of fat to muscle
2. **CARDIOVASCULAR ENDURANCE:** the ability of your heart and lungs to supply oxygen to your body
3. **FLEXIBILITY:** the ability of your muscles and joints to move through a full range of motion
4. **MUSCULAR ENDURANCE:** the ability of your muscles to exert force for an extended period of time
5. **MUSCULAR STRENGTH:** the ability of your muscles to exert maximum force in a single effort

Your goal should be to do a combination of physical and mental activities that allow you to perform tasks and meet the demands of everyday life. Life can be physically and mentally straining; but, if you continually work on your health and wellness daily, you will have a better chance at maintaining an overall good quality of life. Find activities and exercises that you enjoy so that you stay active for a lifetime. Activities in this manual will provide ideas of physical movement and exercises that you can do with or without equipment.

Cardiovascular Endurance
The body's ability to deliver oxygen and nutrients and to remove waste products.
Recommended Exercise: Running

Body Composition
The way in which your body is made up in terms of lean and fat mass.
Recommended Exercise: Swimming

Muscular Strength
The degree to which a muscle can exert force by contracting against resistance.
Recommended Exercise: Weight Training

Flexibility
The ability to move joints and muscles through their full range of movements.
Recommended Exercise: Yoga

Muscular Endurance
The ability of a muscle or group of muscles to continually generate a force over a sustained period of time.
Recommended Exercise: Rowing

BODY COMPOSITION

Body composition describes the percentages of fat, bone, muscle, and water in your body. Your body is made up of fat mass and fat-free mass. Most commonly, body composition refers to the percentage of fat that makes up body mass and how that relates to fitness. Body composition and weight determine leanness, or the amount of fat in your body. Lean muscle burns more calories than fat and helps your body be more efficient.

WHY BODY COMPOSITION MATTERS

A person who has more muscle and less fat has a body that is more efficient at burning calories than the body of a person who has less muscle and more fat. Muscles burn more calories than fat; so, a lean, strong body will burn more calories and have a better metabolism than a less lean, weaker body. A body is also more efficient when it is exercising if it has lean muscle. Lean muscle makes you more capable of completing high-intensity exercises that burn more calories and create greater improvements. Paying attention to and attending to your body composition is important for your overall health.

HOW TO CHANGE BODY COMPOSITION

It is possible to change your body composition; however, this can be difficult. Some people may lack motivation or may just not have a lot of available time, but it is important to try to control your body composition. There are some things that you can do in order to help change your body composition and increase your metabolism.

- Eat healthy meals and snacks.
- Eat small, frequent meals.
- Do not skip breakfast. A healthy breakfast kickstarts your metabolism.
- It takes 20 minutes for your body to feel full, so it should take you about 20 minutes to eat a meal. Do not have a second helping of food until after 20 minutes have passed.
- Exercise often, incorporating the 5 components of fitness.
- Set goals for yourself.

HOW TO MEASURE BODY COMPOSITION

Many people do not often think about measuring body composition or even think that it is important; it is not a common practice to be measured, but there are several methods of measuring body composition, such as hydrostatic weighing, bioelectrical impedance, and skinfold calipers. Using skinfold calipers is the most common method of measuring body composition because skinfold calipers can be found in many health clubs. Skinfold calipers are used to measure folds of fat on your body. A personal trainer will measure from 3 different locations on your body to estimate an overall body fat percentage.

BODY MASS INDEX (BMI)

Body mass index is a weight-to-height ratio. It measures body weight, not body fat. Doctors use your body mass index to determine if your weight is healthy. Below is a BMI chart for you to use.

BODY MASS INDEX CHART FOR YOUNG ADULTS

weight in pounds

height in inches	80	90	100	110	120	130	140	150	160	170	180	190	200	210	220	230	240	250
48	24.4	27.5	30.5	33.6	36.6	39.7	42.7	45.8	48.8	51.9	54.9	58	61	64.1	67.1	70.2	73.2	76.3
50	22.5	25.3	28.1	30.9	33.7	36.6	39.4	42.2	45	47.8	50.6	53.4	56.2	59.1	61.9	64.7	67.5	70.3
52	20.8	23.4	26	28.6	31.2	33.8	36.4	39	41.6	44.2	46.8	49.4	52	54.6	57.2	59.8	62.4	65
54	19.3	21.7	24.1	26.5	28.9	31.3	33.8	36.2	38.6	41	43.4	45.8	48.2	50.6	53	55.4	57.9	60.3
56	17.9	20.2	22.4	24.7	26.9	29.1	31.4	33.6	35.9	38.1	40.4	42.6	44.8	47.1	49.3	51.6	53.8	56
58	16.7	18.8	20.9	23	25.1	27.2	29.3	31.3	33.4	35.5	37.6	39.7	41.8	43.9	46	48.1	50.2	52.2
60	15.6	17.6	19.5	21.5	23.4	25.4	27.3	29.3	31.2	33.2	35.2	37.1	39.1	41	43	44.9	46.9	48.8
62	14.6	16.5	18.3	20.1	21.9	23.8	25.6	27.4	29.3	31.1	32.9	34.7	36.6	38.4	40.2	42.1	43.9	45.7
64	13.7	15.4	17.2	18.9	20.6	22.3	24	25.7	27.5	29.2	30.9	32.6	34.3	36	37.8	39.5	41.2	42.9
66	12.9	14.5	16.1	17.8	19.4	21	22.6	24.2	25.8	27.4	29	30.7	32.3	33.9	35.5	37.1	38.7	40.3
68	12.2	13.7	15.2	16.7	18.2	19.8	21.3	22.8	24.3	25.8	27.4	28.9	30.4	31.9	33.4	35	36.5	38
70	11.5	12.9	14.3	15.8	17.2	18.7	20.1	21.5	23	24.4	25.8	27.3	28.7	30.1	31.6	33	34.4	35.9
72	10.8	12.2	13.6	14.9	16.3	17.6	19	20.3	21.7	23.1	24.4	25.8	27.1	28.5	29.8	31.2	32.5	33.9
74	10.3	11.6	12.8	14.1	15.4	16.7	18	19.3	20.5	21.8	23.1	24.4	25.7	27	28.2	29.5	30.8	32.1
76	9.74	11	12.2	13.4	14.6	15.8	17	18.3	19.5	20.7	21.9	23.1	24.3	25.6	26.8	28	29.2	30.4
78	9.24	10.4	11.6	12.7	13.9	15	16.2	17.3	18.5	19.6	20.8	22	23.1	24.3	25.4	26.6	27.7	28.9
80	8.79	9.89	11	12.1	13.2	14.3	15.4	16.5	17.6	18.7	19.8	20.9	22	23.1	24.2	25.3	26.4	27.5
82	8.36	9.41	10.5	11.5	12.5	13.6	14.6	15.7	16.7	17.8	18.8	19.9	20.9	22	23	24	25.1	26.1
84	7.97	8.97	9.96	11	12	13	13.9	14.9	15.9	16.9	17.9	18.9	19.9	20.9	21.9	22.9	23.9	24.9
86	7.6	8.55	9.51	10.5	11.4	12.4	13.3	14.3	15.2	16.2	17.1	18.1	19	20	20.9	21.9	22.8	23.8

- Optimal: 18.5 - 25
- Overweight: 25.1 - 30
- Obese: 30.1 - 40
- Severely Obese: Greater than 40.1
- Underweight: 17.5 - 18.4
- Severely Underweight: Less than 17.5

A way to determine body fat is to measure with skinfold calipers. This method measures the thicknesses of folds of skin from different locations on your body to calculate a percentage of body fat. A weightlifter may have a higher body weight due to muscles weighing more than fat, which would show a high BMI; however, the same weightlifter measuring with skinfold calipers would get a more accurate measure of body fat.

Being overweight or underweight can be a health risk. Be smart about unrealistic media or social portrayals of idealized body images. Common sense is important to weight control. Eating healthy and exercising moderately are important components of maintaining a healthy body weight.

CARDIOVASCULAR ENDURANCE

Cardiovascular endurance is the ability of your heart to provide oxygen to your muscles during physical activity for a prolonged period of time. This is one of the most important components of physical fitness. Cardiovascular exercise—also called cardio or aerobic exercise—strengthens your heart and lungs and involves large muscle groups such as your leg muscles. Cardiovascular endurance helps your heart transport oxygen in the blood to all your working muscles. It also helps with how well your muscles use that oxygen. To give your heart a proper workout, make sure you do your cardio exercise within your target heart rate zone.

Having a healthy heart is extremely important to your overall wellness. There are different ways to strengthen your heart. In addition to using traditional equipment in a gym, you can exercise at home or in your community. For example, you can do a high-intensity circuit workout. You can also do outdoor activities such as hiking, biking, kayaking, and so on. It is important to find activities that you enjoy so that you are eager to stay active throughout your life.

PULSE

Your pulse is your heart rate, or the number of times your heart beats in a minute. Your pulse is the result of your heart pumping blood through your arteries. When your heart contracts, or pumps, blood moves through blood vessels in your body called arteries. The arteries pulsate as blood rushes through them. You can feel this pulsation in different locations on your body. During exercise, your heart pumps harder to move oxygenated blood to your muscles. Knowing how to check your pulse can help you evaluate your exercise program.

HOW TO CHECK YOUR PULSE

The most common areas to find your pulse are your wrist and your neck.

Wrist (radial artery): Place the tips of your index and middle fingers just below the base of your wrist on the same side as your thumb. Press lightly until you feel a steady pulse.

Neck (carotid artery): Find the center of your neck with your index and middle fingers. Then, place your fingers on either side of your windpipe. Press lightly until you feel a steady pulse.

- Be sure to use your same hand as the side of the neck you are taking your pulse on; for example, you would use your right hand to feel your pulse on the right side of your neck.

- Do not use your thumb. Your thumb has a pulse and could interfere with calculating a proper pulse rate.

Once you have found your pulse, use a watch with a second hand and count your pulse for 15 seconds. Multiply that number by 4 to find your resting heart rate, or how many times your heart beats per minute while your body is at rest. A healthy resting heart rate for someone between the ages of 14 and 21 is between 60 and 100 beats per minute. The better your fitness levels, the lower your heart rate will be.

Use the formula below to calculate your resting heart rate.

pulse after 15 seconds × 4 = resting heart rate

HEART RATE

Being fit means exercising enough to make physical changes to your body. Cardiovascular exercise improves your aerobic capacity and heart rate and helps you maintain your body weight. It is important to keep your heart rate between 60 percent and 80 percent of your maximum heart rate when you are working out. If your exercise is too light, you will not benefit from the workout. If it is too intense, the workout could potentially be hazardous to your body. The table below shows the most favorable pulse rate levels by age and goal.

Use the formula below to calculate your maximum heart rate.

220 - your age = predicted maximum heart rate

TARGET HEART RATE

You experience the most benefits when you exercise in your target heart rate zone. Usually, this is when your exercising heart rate is 60 percent to 80 percent of your maximum heart rate. Do not exercise above 85 percent of your maximum heart rate as this may increase cardiovascular and orthopedic risks. When you are beginning an exercise program, you may need to gradually build up to a level that is within your target heart rate zone. If the exercise feels too hard, slow down. Do not push your body too hard, especially in the beginning.

HOW TO FIND YOUR TARGET HEART RATE ZONE

Maximum Heart Beats per Minute

220 - your age = _____

Multiply the number that you found by 0.6 (60 percent) and 0.8 (80 percent).

Example:

220 - 15 (age) = 205

205 x 0.6 (60% intensity) = 123 (target heart rate)

205 x 0.8 (80% intensity) = 164 (target heart rate)

HEART RATE ZONES FOR CHILDREN AND ADOLESCENTS			
HEART RATE ZONE	FEELS LIKE	EXAMPLE ACTIVITIES	BENEFITS
Performance 100-90%	**VIGOROUS TO VIGOROUS+** • very exhausting • fast breathing • muscles may feel tired	• short sprints • soccer • basketball	Develops maximum performance and speed.
Healthy Heart 90-70%	**MODERATE TO VIGOROUS** • easy to heavy breathing • light muscular strain • average sweating	• games • jogging • cycling • dancing	Improves aerobic fitness and performance capacity.
Active 70-60%	**EASY TO MODERATE** • easy, comfortable breathing • low muscle load • light sweating	• warm-up and cool-down • brisk walking • playing catch • volleyball	Improves basic endurance and muscle tone.

EXERCISE INCREASES BRAIN POWER AND MUSCULAR STRENGTH!

What was your heart rate during your previous workout? _____

Were you in your target heart rate zone? _____

Another way to measure the intensity of your workout is to use the *Borg Rating of Perceived Exertion (RPE) Scale. The RPE scale uses numerical values to determine how hard you are exercising. Number 6 represents no physical exertion. Number 20 represents maximum exertion. The exertion level increases with the value of the number from 6 to 20. Review the chart below.

Scale Range	Level of Exertion
6	No Exertion
7	Extremely Light
8	
9	Very Light
10	
11	Light
12	
13	Somewhat Hard
14	
15	Hard
16	
17	Very Hard
18	
19	Extremely Hard
20	Maximum Exertion

- Numbers 6-11 represent how you should feel using little or no effort, such as when you are lying in bed or sitting in a chair. You can talk in complete sentences and breathing is restful.
- Numbers 12-16 represent how you should feel while you are exercising. This is your target heart rate zone for exercise. Talking while exercising becomes harder, and breathing is deeper.
- Numbers 17-20 represent working too hard. You cannot talk, and breathing is labored or you are breathless. Never push yourself to maximum exertion.

What was your RPE number during your previous workout? _____

Was your intensity level between numbers 12 and 16? _____

BENEFITS OF CARDIOVASCULAR ENDURANCE EXERCISE

CARDIOVASCULAR ENDURANCE ACTIVITIES

AT THE GYM Always have a certified trainer instruct you on the use of an exercise machine.	OUTSIDE THE GYM Always alert someone to where you are going. Never swim alone.
circuit training	aerobics
elliptical trainer	biking
stair-climbing machine	hiking
stationary bike	swimming
treadmill	walking or running

BENEFITS OF CARDIOVASCULAR ENDURANCE

IMPROVE CARDIORESPIRATORY FUNCTION

- Cardio helps strengthen your heart and lungs. If you work out for at least 30 minutes 3 to 5 times per week, you can lower your risk of heart disease, cancer, diabetes, and many other chronic health problems.
- Cardio increases your heart rate, your breathing rate, and your endurance. At a moderately brisk level, your heart rate increases but you can still carry on a conversation.
- You can divide your 30-minute workout into 10-minute increments throughout the day and still receive effective health benefits. Performing a cardio activity at a moderately-brisk pace will decrease your risk of developing diabetes, obesity, high blood pressure, high blood cholesterol, heart disease, and some forms of cancer.

DECREASE RISK OF HEART DISEASE

- According to the Center for Disease Control and Prevention, heart disease causes approximately 1 in 4 deaths in the United States every year. The most common type of heart disease is coronary artery disease which is a buildup of plaque in the arteries.

ACHIEVE WEIGHT-LOSS GOALS

- If you work out at the right intensity, you will burn calories and will move toward your weight-loss goals.

IMPROVE JOINT RANGE OF MOTION

- If you are recovering from back, hip, knee, or ankle injuries, you may have some stiffness in your joints. Doing a gentle walking program can help loosen your joints and help them regain flexibility.

LOWER CHOLESTEROL

- Another major health issue that cardiovascular exercise can prevent is high cholesterol. High cholesterol is a result of eating fatty foods and not exercising. It can cause the arteries within the body to harden, which can limit the blood flow to the heart. Because blood carries oxygen to the heart, any lack of blood can result in chest pain, blockage, and even a heart attack. People who have higher cholesterol levels have an increased risk of heart attack and stroke. By consistently performing cardiovascular exercise, cholesterol levels can often be lowered and controlled, as needed.

PREVENT OSTEOPOROSIS

- Exercises, especially leg exercises, are very beneficial in the prevention of osteoporosis. This condition occurs when bones lose mass, which leads to a decrease in the stability of the bone tissue, thus making the bones more fragile.
- Other than getting the proper amount of calcium, the main methods of prevention of fragile bones are resistance training and cardiovascular exercise, which are achieved simultaneously by performing certain cardiovascular exercises.

MANAGE STRESS

- Working out can be a strategy for stress management that helps to combat depression and insomnia as well as improve brain function.

FLEXIBILITY

FLEXIBILITY

Flexibility is the ability of your joints to move through a full range of motion. You can achieve flexibility by stretching. It is important to include flexibility in your everyday workout. As you get older, you tend to lose your flexibility. Increasing your flexibility improves how well your body can perform during physical activity, reducing your risk of injury. Having good flexibility allows you to do things such as tie your shoes and pick objects up off the ground.

Flexibility increases your performance in cardiovascular endurance, muscular strength, and muscular endurance. Stretching each joint area before exercising helps prepare your body to exercise. Stretching each joint area after exercising helps you maintain overall flexibility. There are 2 types of stretches: static and dynamic. **Static stretches** are positions that you hold for a desired amount of time. These types of stretches focus on your flexibility. **Dynamic stretches** are movements that you do in order to loosen up your joints. These types of stretches are commonly done before completing a vigorous workout or activity.

This manual includes a variety of static and dynamic stretches for each major body part that will help you increase your flexibility.

Below are some guidelines to consider.
- Move your muscles slowly and gently.
- Keep your body in alignment, supporting your limbs and trunk.
- Never force movement. Instead, work with your body and its structure.
- Stretching is okay, but feeling pain is not. If you feel pain, numbness, or tingling, stop immediately.
- Rest between stretches to avoid overexerting your muscles.
- Breathe during your stretches to avoid muscle tension.

Below are some terms to know.

- **extension:** movement of a joint to lengthen the muscle
- **flexion:** movement of a joint to shorten the muscle
- **abduction:** movement of a joint so that the limb is turned away from the middle of the body
- **adduction:** movement of a joint so that the limb is turned toward the middle of the body

STRETCHING EXERCISES

Tips for Proper Static Stretching

- Stretch slowly and steadily. Relax and hold stretches without bouncing.
- Hold each stretch for 20 to 30 seconds.
- Repeat each stretch 2 to 3 times. Remember to do both the right side and the left side.
- Stretch before and after physical activity.

STATIC STRETCHES

NECK STRETCH

muscle focus: sternocleidomastoids and upper trapezii

- Either standing or sitting, look straight ahead so that your head is in a neutral position.
- Tilt your head slowly to the right so that your ear almost touches your shoulder.
- Hold this position for 20 to 30 seconds.
- Bring your head back up to the neutral position.
- Repeat this on the left side.
- Repeat the stretch 2 to 3 times on each side.

SIDE STRETCH

muscle focus: latissimi dorsi and abdominal muscles

- Stand with your feet hip-width apart.
- Place your right hand on your right hip.
- Tilt your body to the right while bringing your left hand and arm up over your head.
- Hold this position for 20 to 30 seconds.
- Stand back up to the starting position.
- Repeat this on the left side.
- Repeat the stretch 2 to 3 times on each side.

SHOULDER AND TRICEP STRETCH

muscle focus: triceps and deltoids

- Raise your right arm to the ceiling.
- Bend your right elbow so that your hand is reaching down your back.
- Bring your left hand up to your right elbow.
- Pull your right elbow with your left hand to stretch your triceps and shoulder.
- Hold this for 20 to 30 seconds.
- Repeat this on the left side.
- Repeat the stretch 2 to 3 times on each side.

LOWER BACK AND HIP STRETCH

muscle focus: glutei maximi, iliotibial tracts (IT bands), sartorii, quadrati lumborum, and sacrospinali

- Start in a seated position with your legs straight out in front of you.
- Bend your right knee and bring it up over your left leg so that your right foot is on the ground next to your left thigh.
- Twist your body to the right, placing your left elbow on the outside of your right thigh.
- Push with your left elbow on your right thigh for a deeper stretch.
- Hold this for 20 to 30 seconds.
- Repeat this on the left side.
- Repeat the stretch 2 to 3 times on each side.

HAMSTRING STRETCH

muscle focus: hamstrings

- Stand with your feet hip-width apart.
- Stepping forward with your right foot, point your toes up and place your heel on the ground.
- Bending forward, bend your left knee and keep your right leg straight.
- Place both hands on your right upper thigh and push down slightly.
- Hold this for 20 to 30 seconds.
- Repeat this on the left side.
- Repeat the stretch 2 to 3 times on each side.

QUADRICEP STRETCH

muscle focus: quadriceps

- Stand with your feet together.
- Focus on a single spot or hold onto something for balance.
- Bending your right knee, bring your right foot up to your buttocks.
- Grab your right ankle with your right hand.

- Pull your foot to your buttocks. Push your hips forward.
- Hold this for 20 to 30 seconds.
- Repeat this with your left foot.
- Repeat the stretch 2 to 3 times on each side.

GROIN STRETCH

muscle focus: adductor muscles

- Sit on the floor with your knees bent to your sides and the bottoms of your feet together.
- Place your elbows on your knees.
- Push down on your knees with your elbows.
- Pull your feet and legs closer to your body to intensify the stretch.
- Hold this for 20 to 30 seconds.
- Repeat the stretch 2 to 3 times on each side.

DYNAMIC STRETCHES:

MONSTER KICKS

muscle focus: hamstrings, glutei maximi, and abdominal muscles

- Start on a solid surface and designate a specific distance to travel.
- Start with your feet together and your arms straight out in front of you.
- Take a step forward and kick with your opposite leg to try to touch your hands. Keep your kicking leg as straight as you can with your foot flexed.
- Continue this kicking pattern, alternating legs for the entire distance. Then, continue this back to the starting position.
- Repeat this cycle 2 to 3 more times.

HIGH KNEES

muscle focus: quadriceps, hamstrings, calves, glutei maximi, and abdominal muscles

- Start on a solid surface and designate a specific distance to travel.
- Take small, quick steps, raising your knees toward your chest. Travel in a straight line to the designated area.
- Move at your own pace. Note that the faster you move your feet and the faster you travel, the more intense the exercise will be.
- Continue this back to the starting position.
- Repeat this cycle 2 to 3 more times.

LUNGE TWISTS

muscle focus: quadriceps, hamstrings, glutei maximi, and abdominal muscles

- Start on a solid surface and designate a specific distance to travel.
- Take a large step forward.
- Bend your front knee and create a 90-degree angle with each of your legs.
- Place your elbows on your stomach and keep your back straight. Turn your torso to the side of your front foot.
- Pick your back leg up to return to the starting position.
- Continue this pattern, alternating legs for the entire distance. Then, continue this back to the starting position.
- Repeat this cycle 2 to 3 more times.

REAR KICKS

muscle focus: quadriceps and hamstrings

- Start on a solid surface and designate a specific distance to travel.
- Stand with your feet together.
- Flexing your foot, bend your right knee to swing your heel toward your buttocks, but do not allow your foot to touch your body.
- Alternate your feet each time.
- Move at your own pace to the designated spot. Then, continue this back to the starting position. Note that the faster you move your feet, the more intense the exercise will be.
- Repeat this cycle 2 to 3 more times.

ARM CIRCLES

muscle focus: deltoids

- Stand with your feet shoulder-width apart and your arms out to your sides so that they are parallel to the ground.
- Keeping your arms straight, move them in a forward circular motion.
- Perform 10 small circles and 10 big circles; then, switch directions and move your arms in a backward circular motion.
- Repeat this cycle 2 to 3 more times.

CARIOCA

muscle focus: abductors, adductors, quadriceps, hamstrings, and abdominal muscles

- Stand with your back straight and your feet together.
- Step to the side with your left foot; then, cross your right foot in front of your left foot.
- Step again to the side with your left foot; then, cross your right foot behind your left foot.
- Repeat this 5 times to the left; then, continue this 5 times to the right.
- Repeat this cycle 2 to 3 more times.

INCHWORMS

muscle focus: hamstrings and abdominal muscles

- Stand with your back straight and your feet slightly apart.
- Try to keep your legs straight while bending at your waist to put your hands on the ground.
- Walk your hands out until your body is in a plank (push-up) position.
- Hold the plank for 1 second; then, walk your feet toward your hands.
- Complete 2 to 3 sets of 10 repetitions.

MUSCULAR STRENGTH

MUSCULAR STRENGTH

Muscular strength refers to the amount of force a muscle can produce. Muscular strength is a vital part of a balanced exercise routine, which includes anaerobic activity and flexibility. Without muscular strength, your body would be weak and unable to perform daily activities.

Having poor muscular strength increases your chance of getting hurt during activities. Some of the benefits of muscular strength training are that it builds muscle, burns fat, and increases your overall health.

Muscular strength training includes resistance methods like using free weights, weight machines, and resistance bands to help you build muscle. Completing some form of muscular strength training 2 or more times per week will help your overall health and wellness and will help maintain your muscle composition. Be sure to review the basic fitness principles before beginning a workout regimen to build muscular strength.

⚠ **CAUTION: Have a certified trainer plan for you and supervise you when you are working with weights.**

Basic Rules for Muscular Strength Training
- Do not lift the same muscle group 2 days in a row.
- Warm up before lifting. **Never begin lifting on cold muscles.**
- Generally, to improve muscular strength, complete 3 to 5 sets of 8 to 12 repetitions.
- Use a spotter for safety when necessary.
- Complete any heavy-resistance exercises with low repetitions. Do not lift weights that are too heavy for you.
- A supervisor or coach should help you set up your program based on your needs.
- Cool down at the end of your workout, stretching the muscles that you used.

DUMBBELL CHEST PRESSES

muscle focus: chest muscles, pectoralis majors, deltoids, and triceps

- Lie with your back flat on a weight bench and your feet flat on the floor.
- Grip a dumbbell firmly with each of your hands.

- Start with the dumbbells level with your chest and your arms bent at 90-degree angles.
- Raise the dumbbells straight up above your chest. Do not lock your elbows.
- Lower the dumbbells back to your chest and press them back up again.
- Complete 3 to 5 sets of 8 to 12 repetitions.

DUMBBELL INCLINE CHEST PRESSES
muscle focus: chest muscles, pectoralis majors, and deltoids

- Adjust a weight bench so that it is at a 45-degree angle with the floor.
- Sit with your back flat on the bench and your feet flat on the floor.
- Grip a dumbbell firmly with each of your hands.
- Start with the dumbbells level with your chest and your arms bent at 90-degree angles.
- Raise the dumbbells straight up above your chest. Do not lock your elbows.
- Lower the dumbbells back to your chest and press them back up again.
- Complete 3 to 5 sets of 8 to 12 repetitions.

SHOULDER PRESSES
muscle focus: deltoids

- Sit straight up either on a weight bench or in a chair.
- Hold a pair of dumbbells by your ears and keep them in line with your shoulders. Bend both elbows to 90-degree angles.
- Lift the dumbbells straight up above your head and straighten your elbows. Do not lock your elbows.
- Lower the dumbbells back to your ears and bend both elbows back to 90 degrees.
- Complete 3 to 5 sets of 8 to 12 repetitions.

OVERHEAD TRICEP EXTENSIONS
muscle focus: triceps

- Stand with your feet hip-width apart.
- Hold a dumbbell behind your head with both hands. Bend both elbows 90 degrees.
- Straighten your elbows while lifting the dumbbell above your head toward the ceiling.
- Bring the dumbbell back to the starting position.
- Complete 3 to 5 sets of 8 to 12 repetitions.

BARBELL BICEP CURLS
muscle focus: biceps and abdominal muscles

- Sitting straight up, place your arms flat on a padded surface.

- Keeping your arms straight, hold the barbell with both hands in front of your stomach. Do not lock your elbows.
- Curl the barbell slowly up to your chin.
- Bring the barbell slowly back to the starting position. Remember to not lock your elbows and to not use your back when you are exerting force.
- Complete 3 to 5 sets of 8 to 12 repetitions.

ALTERNATING BICEP CURLS (DUMBBELL OR MACHINE)

muscle focus: biceps and abdominal muscles

Dumbbells
- Hold a dumbbell in each hand, with your arms down to your sides and your palms facing away from you.
- Keep your arms straight and your elbows close to your sides.
- Bending your right elbow, lift the dumbbell up toward your right shoulder.
- Straightening your elbow, bring the dumbbell slowly back to the starting position. Remember to not lock your elbow or use your back to exert force.
- Repeat this on the left side.
- Complete 3 to 5 sets of 8 to 12 repetitions.

Machine (Not Alternating)
- Sit in the seat on the machine.
- Adjust the weight to a weight that you can handle. Do not attempt a weight that is too heavy for you.
- Grab a handle in each hand. Your arms should be extended at your sides.
- Bending your elbows, lift the handles up toward your shoulders.
- Straightening your elbows, bring the handles slowly back to the starting position. Remember to not lock your elbows.
- Complete 3 to 5 sets of 8 to 12 repetitions.

1-ARM DUMBBELL ROW

muscle focus: latissimi dorsi, rhomboids, lower trapezii, and erector spinae

- Hold a dumbbell with your right hand.
- Place your left knee and left hand on a sturdy bench.
- Extend your right arm toward the floor.
- Bending your right elbow, pull the dumbbell up toward your right side. Your elbow should be pointing up toward the ceiling.
- Lower the dumbbell slowly back to the starting position.
- Repeat this on the left side.
- Complete 3 to 5 sets of 8 to 12 repetitions.

LUNGES

muscle focus: glutei maximi, hamstrings, and quadriceps

- Hold a dumbbell in each hand.
- Stand with your feet hip-width apart.
- Step forward with a foot and bend your knee at a 90-degree angle. Make sure that your knee does not go over your toes. Your back leg should almost be straight behind you.
- Bend your back knee to lower yourself to almost touching the ground.
- Come back up slowly, bringing your front leg back to the starting position.
- Switch legs.
- Complete 4 to 6 sets of 10 to 20 repetitions.

SQUATS

muscle focus: glutei maximi, hamstrings, and erector spinae

- Stand with your feet shoulder-width apart.
- Hold a dumbbell up near your shoulders with each hand.
- Bending your knees, lower your buttocks toward the ground. Keep your back straight.
- Do not let your knees go past your toes. If they do, you are going down too low or your legs are too close together.
- Straightening your knees, bring yourself back to the starting position.
- Complete 4 to 6 sets of 10 to 20 repetitions.

BACK EXTENSIONS

muscle focus: erector spinae

Machine

- Using a back-extension machine if you are at a gym, sit so that the padded bar is just below your shoulder blades.
- Adjust the weight rack to a weight that you can handle. Do not attempt a weight that is too heavy for you.
- Place your arms at your sides or on your thighs. Push the padded bar with your back so that your back is extended.
- Bring yourself slowly back to the starting position.
- Complete 4 to 6 sets of 10 to 20 repetitions.

Fitness Ball

- If you are at home and do not have a back-extension machine, you can use a fitness ball. Lie flat with your abdomen on the ball. Place your hands behind your head. Lift your upper body off the ball so that only your lower abdomen is on the ball.
- Complete 4 to 6 sets of 10 to 20 repetitions.

MUSCULAR ENDURANCE

MUSCULAR ENDURANCE

Muscular endurance is the ability of your muscles to exert force for an extended period of time, such as by sustaining repeated movements against resistance. As a main component of fitness, muscular endurance is important for everyone, not just people who play sports.

Some examples of muscular endurance include lifting weight for more repetitions or running for an extended period of time. Muscular endurance helps you do everyday activities such as carrying a small child through a store or walking up several flights of stairs.

Muscular strength and muscular endurance go hand in hand in that your strength can affect the measure of your endurance. It is vital to maintain good muscular endurance to be able to perform activities of daily living and more.

Muscular Endurance Tips
- Muscular endurance relies on muscular strength.
- Muscular endurance exercises are characterized by lower resistance with more repetitions or sets.
- Generally, to improve muscular endurance, complete 4 to 6 sets of 10 to 20 repetitions.
- Change up your resistance; it is okay to lift a little heavier on some days and lighter on others.
- Keep yourself hydrated.
- Warm up before beginning an endurance workout and cool down after.

PUSH-UPS

muscle focus: pectoralis majors, pectoralis minors, deltoids, triceps, biceps, and abdominal muscles

- Lie face down on a mat or the floor.
- Bending your elbows, place your hands next to your shoulders.
- Push with your hands to lift your body up off the mat or floor. Straighten your elbows when you come up.
- Keep your feet on the floor.
- Lower yourself slowly back to the floor, keeping your elbows close to your body.
- Complete 4 to 6 sets of 10 to 20 repetitions.

INCLINE PUSH-UPS

muscle focus: lower pectoralis muscles, deltoids, triceps, biceps, and abdominal muscles

- Face a weight bench with your hands on the bench and your feet on the floor.
- Your hands should be just outside your shoulders and your elbows should be bent.
- Push with your hands so that your elbows are straight but not locked.
- Lower yourself slowly back to the starting position.
- Complete 4 to 6 sets of 10 to 20 repetitions.

DECLINE PUSH-UPS

muscle focus: pectoralis majors, deltoids, triceps, biceps, and abdominal muscles

- Place your feet on a weight bench and your hands on the ground.
- Place your hands just outside of your shoulders.
- Push with your hands so that your elbows are straight but not locked.
- Lower yourself back to the starting position.
- Complete 4 to 6 sets of 10 to 20 repetitions.

TRICEP DIPS

muscle focus: triceps

- Place your hands behind you on a weight bench or other safe elevated surface with your fingers pointing forward.
- Place your feet out in front of you so that you are in an inclined position.
- Bending your elbows, lower yourself slowly to the ground.
- Straightening your elbows, lift yourself slowly back up to the starting position.
- Complete 4 to 6 sets of 10 to 20 repetitions.

CRUNCHES

muscle focus: abdominal muscles

- Lie flat on your back either on a yoga mat or the floor with your knees bent.
- Place your hands behind your head.
- Lift your torso straight up until your shoulder blades are off the mat or floor. Tighten your abdominal muscles.
- Lower your torso back onto the mat or floor.
- Complete 4 to 6 sets of 10 to 20 repetitions.

SIDE CRUNCHES

muscle focus: abdominal muscles and oblique muscles

- Lie flat on your back either on a yoga mat or the floor with your knees bent.
- Place your arms and hands at your sides.
- Lift your shoulders slightly off the mat or floor.
- Bend to the right side so that your fingertips touch the heel of your right foot.
- Keep your lower back on the mat or floor.
- Complete 4 to 6 sets of 10 to 20 repetitions.
- Repeat this on the left side.

PLANKS

muscle focus: abdominal muscles

- Lie face down on either a mat or the floor.
- Bend your elbows and place them just under your shoulders. Your back should be in an extension position.
- Place your feet straight out behind you hip-width apart.
- Lift your body so that all of your weight is in your elbows, forearms, and feet.
- Keep your back flat and your abdomen tight.
- Hold this for 30 seconds.
- Lower yourself slowly back to the ground.
- Once 30 seconds starts to get easy, increase your time gradually.

BACK EXTENSIONS

muscle focus: erector spinae (iliocostales, longissimi, and spinales)

- Place the fitness ball on the floor.
- Place your abdomen on the ball. Your legs should be extended behind you and about shoulder-width apart for balance.
- Place your hands behind your head on your neck (like when doing a crunch).
- Lift your upper body so that you are hyperextending your back.
- Come back down to the starting position.

PULL-UPS

muscle focus: latissimi dorsi and biceps

- Find a bar that is secure enough to hold your body weight.
- Hold onto the bar with both hands. Your hands should be placed wider than your shoulders, or outside of your shoulders. Your palms should be facing **away** from you.
- Pull your body up high enough so that your chin is slightly above the bar.
- Lower yourself slowly back to the starting position.
- Complete 3 to 5 sets of 8 to 12 repetitions.

CHIN-UPS

muscle focus: latissimi dorsi and biceps

- Find a bar that is secure enough to hold your body weight.
- Hold onto the bar with your hands shoulder-width apart. Your palms should be facing toward you.
- Pull your body up high enough so that your chin is slightly above the bar.
- Lower yourself slowly back to the starting position.
- Complete 3 to 5 sets of 8 to 12 repetitions.

PHYSICAL EDUCATION KITS

PHYSICAL EDUCATION KITS

Physical Education is critical to developing the whole child. The National Association of Sport and Physical Education (NASPE) recommends that children have 60 minutes per day of physical activity. The Physical Education Kit has been designed to help create activities for each age. The kit includes various equipment that is designed to enhance your physical skills and fitness based on your age group. Equipment instructions are provided in the PE manual, online course and USB.

GRADE 6 EQUIPMENT KIT

- Electronic Band
- Playground Ball
- 28.5" Basketball
- Soccer Ball Size 5
- Volleyball Lite
- Flying Disc
- Agility Ladder
- 8 Disc-Cones
- 8' Jump Rope
- 2 Stretch Bands
- Whiffle Ball Set
- Pickle Ball Set
- Backpack
- Pump

GRADE 7 EQUIPMENT KIT

- Backpack
- Badminton Set
- Playground Ball
- Basketball
- Disc Cones
- Golf Iron/ Golf Balls
- 9' Jump Rope
- Movement Band
- Pump
- 22" Tennis Racket
- 3 Foam Tennis Balls
- Soccer Ball
- 2 Stretch Bands
- Wiffle Ball Bat/Balls

GRADE 8 EQUIPMENT KIT

- Backpack
- 30" Fitness Ball
- Playground Ball
- Disc Cones
- Juggle Pack
- 9' Jump Rope
- Movement Band
- Pickleball Paddles/ Balls
- Pump
- Tennis Racket
- 3 Tennis Balls
- Volleyball
- Hockey Stick/Puck/ Ball

ELECTRONIC MOVEMENT BAND

Welcome! However you may choose to move, you will have fun watching your moves add up as your electronic movement band records all of your physical activity—not just steps. The electronic movement band keeps you aware of your daily physical activity so that you can make healthy decisions to keep moving. So, what are you waiting for? It is time to get started!

The instructions to set up your electronic movement band are included with the device.

DID YOU KNOW?

Learning and using all this information is great; but, if you do not understand why it is important to take care of yourself both physically and mentally, the odds of you staying active as an adult will decrease. Lack of activity as an adult can result in many problems and illnesses. You might not think about it now, but the habits that you create as a child and young adult will affect you as an adult. Consider the information below.

- Lack of physical activity can lead to a greater risk of developing high blood pressure, cardiovascular disease, and other conditions.
- As you transition into adulthood and start a career, activity can help you manage stress and anxiety and can limit work burnouts.
   - Depending on your career choice, your opportunity to be active during the day can be significantly limited by your schedule, so finding exercise or activity that you thoroughly enjoy is imperative to your health and wellness.
   - On the other hand, if you have a career that is physically demanding, you want to make sure that you can perform at that job to the best of your ability.
- On a less obvious but more important scale, maintaining your physical and mental health is vital to being able to complete activities of daily living. Such activities include getting in and out of bed, getting yourself dressed and ready, climbing stairs, stepping onto a ladder or stepstool, walking through an amusement park, and so on.
   - These activities may seem minor and you might take for granted that you can do these things with ease now; but, if you are in poor health, these activities can be very difficult, if not impossible.

GRADE 6
PE EQUIPMENT KIT

SAFETY ALERT!

Before you exercise, make sure that you are properly warmed up and have enough room to perform each activity. Wear proper equipment and follow activity-specific safety rules. Stay hydrated and take breaks as needed. Exercise only if you are healthy, and always exercise at your own pace. If an exercise starts to hurt, if you feel dizzy, or if you feel light-headed, stop the exercise completely and get help. Upon completion of any workout, cool down and stretch.

WARM-UP AND COOL-DOWN

⚠️ **CAUTION: Stretching should not be painful; ease up if stretching hurts. See the Flexibility section of your PE Manual for more information.**

WARM-UP

The purpose of a warm-up is to gradually increase heart rate, breathing rate, body temperature, and muscle temperature. Warming up prior to exercising increases circulation and blood flow to your muscles. When your muscles are warmed up, their performance—such as in the areas of strength and speed—is enhanced and risk of injury is decreased.

Before you begin any workout, you should always warm up. Getting your heart and muscles prepared for exercise is important. There are numerous ways to get your body ready to participate in physical activity. **The Flexibility section of your PE Manual includes a variety of dynamic and static stretches for each major body part that will help you increase your flexibility.**

Elements of a Warm-Up

1. **Low-intensity cardio**: Walk, slow jog, or slow swim for 5 to 10 minutes to increase your heart rate, breathing rate, and body temperature before your workout.
2. **Dynamic stretch**: Perform a repeated motion—such as kicks, high knees, lunges, or arm circles—that will loosen up your joints and prepare your muscles for the exercise that you are about to do. Perform each dynamic stretch for at least 30 seconds.
3. **Static stretch**: Stretch your muscles slowly and hold each stretch for 20 to 30 seconds without bouncing in order to lengthen your muscles and increase your flexibility. Some important areas to stretch as a part of your warm-up are your neck, sides, shoulders, triceps, back, hamstrings, quadriceps, and groin.

Example ▢ + ▢ + ▢ = **EFFECTIVE WARM-UP**

PERSONAL WARM-UP ACTIVITY

1. Select an exercise activity to participate in.
2. Design your personal warm-up plan for the activity that you selected. Any dynamic and static stretches that you choose to complete should be specific to the exercise activity that you chose.
3. Have a trusted adult or friend assess your stretches to make sure that you are using proper form.
4. Explain how the warm-up will decrease your risk of injury for this activity. _____

Copyright 2024 © Lincoln Learning Solutions. All rights reserved.

Procedure	Enter your personal warm-up regimen below.
1. **Low-intensity cardiovascular exercise:** Exercise for 5 to 10 minutes.	
2. **Dynamic stretches:** Perform dynamic stretches specifically for the selected activity.	
3. **Static stretches:** Perform static stretches specifically for the selected activity.	

COOL-DOWN

After you have finished your workout, exercise, or activity, it is imperative that your body returns to its normal state. You want to avoid stopping immediately and sitting down **unless you are in pain, dizzy, or injured**. Be sure to slow your heart rate and breathing rate back to or slightly above their resting rates. There are several ways to do this. You can simply walk or slow down your exercise for a few minutes, or you can find your own way to slow your body back down. You also may want to incorporate static stretches to increase flexibility and to avoid your muscles tightening. **The Flexibility section of your PE Manual includes a variety of static stretches for each major body part.** Always keep hydrated by drinking water before, during, and after exercise.

Elements of a Cool-Down

1. **Slow down**: Walk or gradually slow down your exercise—such as returning to a slow swim if you are swimming—until your heart rate, breathing rate, and body temperature are back to normal.
2. **Static stretch**: Stretch your muscles slowly and hold each stretch for 20 to 30 seconds without bouncing in order to lengthen your muscles and increase flexibility. Some important areas to stretch as part of your cool-down are your neck, sides, shoulders, triceps, back, hamstrings, quadriceps, and groin.

WALK + STATIC STRETCHES = EFFECTIVE COOL-DOWN

Design your personal cool-down plan. You can perform the same cool-down each time you finish a physical activity or you can change each time in order to reflect the exercise activity, such as by slowing your pedaling if you are biking.

Procedure	Enter your personal cool-down regimen below.
1. **Slow down:** Perform this slowed activity for 5 to 10 minutes.	
2. **Static stretches:** Perform several lower-body and upper-body stretches.	

AEROBIC EXERCISE

Aerobic exercise—also referred to as cardio or cardiovascular exercise—is any exercise that is done in your target heart rate zone and is performed for an extended period. Aerobic exercise is important for strengthening your heart muscle. The stronger your heart muscle, the longer you can perform physical activity before getting tired. Being able to perform physical activity without tiring is often referred to as being in shape.

The purpose of this lesson is to encourage you to do an aerobic workout for at least 30 minutes 3 to 5 days per week in order to experience health benefits.

⚠ **CAUTION: Wear proper equipment and follow activity-specific safety rules.**

AEROBIC EXERCISE

BENEFITS OF AEROBIC EXERCISE

- strengthens your heart and lung functions
- lowers blood pressure
- controls sugar in your blood
- burns calories and fat
- increases your energy
- reduces stress
- decreases your risk of cardiovascular diseases
- increases mental ability

After reviewing the benefits of aerobic exercise, discuss them with a trusted adult. Ask for help setting up an aerobic exercise program that works for you.

There are a variety of exercises to choose from. Choose aerobic exercises that will fit into your lifestyle and that you enjoy. Limit excuses and make a commitment to exercise!

Write down an excuse that you have used to avoid aerobic exercise and how you overcame or will overcome that obstacle.

My Excuse for Not Exercising	What I Did to Overcome That Excuse

TYPES OF AEROBIC EXERCISE

Sports: Examples include soccer, basketball, volleyball, swimming, hockey, lacrosse, tennis, badminton, pickleball, handball, gymnastics, dance, martial arts, wrestling, track and field, and so on.

Outdoor pursuits: Examples include walking, jogging, biking, canoeing, kayaking, golfing, fly fishing, hiking, rock climbing, horseback riding, skiing, and so on.

Fitness gyms: Find a gym that is convenient for you to attend where you can complete circuit exercises, use aerobic machines, take classes, and more.

Stationary exercise equipment: Examples include using a jump rope, treadmill, elliptical trainer, bike, mini trampoline, and so on.

Exercise apps or videos: Use a workout tutorial on an app, website, video, or other digital source.

Your own sequence workouts: You can also design your own workout sequences by following the steps below.

- Create your personal aerobic workout routines by blending activities that involve basic locomotor skills such as jogging in place, jumping jacks, high knees, and so on.
- Design the intensity and duration of the exercise according to your level of fitness.
- Perform your personal routine for some or all your aerobic workouts.

SAMPLE WORKOUT

The following is a sample workout that you can complete on your own and that does not require equipment. When you are beginning any exercise program, begin with workouts that match your fitness level and then build accordingly. You want to feel refreshed after each exercise session, not exhausted. Use your pulse rate to monitor aerobic workouts.

Each exercise is performed for 30 seconds: 10 seconds using a light force and slow pace, 10 seconds using a moderate force and moderate pace, and 10 seconds using a strong force and fast pace.

Practice each of the following exercises, concentrating on proper form, prior to engaging in a workout.

JUMPING JACKS:

Jump out so that your feet are apart and your arms are in a V above your head; then, jump in so that your feet are together and your arms are down by your sides. Continue this movement pattern.

MARCH:

Walk, lifting your knees to waist height and swinging your arms.

HIGH KNEES:

Alternate lifting your knees to waist height.

VERTICAL JUMPS:

Bend your knees and jump up. Swing your arms behind you at the start of the jump. Swing your arms forward and up while you are jumping.

BURPEES:

Stand with your feet shoulder-width apart. Bend your knees and place your hands on the floor. Extend your legs back so that you are in a push-up position. Return to the bent-knee position. Return to standing. Repeat this movement pattern.

FLOOR RUNS:

From a push-up position, run your legs in toward your chest and then back out.

Jumping jacks

March

High knees

Vertical jumps

Burpees

Floor runs

JOGGING IN PLACE:

Run slowly in place.

SIDE SLIDES:

Step to the side with your right foot. Bring your left foot to your right foot in a step-together motion. Repeat this to the left.

REAR KICKS:

Alternate lifting the heels of your feet toward your upper thighs. Do not let your feet make contact with your body.

KNEE TUCKS:

While standing, jump up and tuck your knees. Try to touch your knees with your extended hands. Gently land with your knees slightly bent.

¼-SQUAT JUMPS:

With your legs apart, lower your body by bending your knees and hips until your hips are even with your knees. Jump to the right, making a quarter turn and landing gently in a squat position. Continue until you are back to the starting position. Repeat the exercise to the left. For a challenge, try half turns and full turns.

CARIOCAS (GRAPEVINE):

Step to the side with your right foot and then cross your left foot in front of your right foot. Uncross your right foot and step to the right and then cross your left foot behind your right foot. Repeat this step-cross-step-cross movement.

Rest by walking slowly for 30 seconds. Hydrate as necessary.

Repeat all of the exercises 3 more times for a 24-minute aerobic workout.

EXTENSION: Use the above information to create a workout that you would enjoy.

Jogging in place

Side slides

Rear kicks

Knee tucks

¼-squat jumps

Cariocas (grapevine)

Record at least 3 aerobic exercise sessions that you participated in outside of PE class for 1 week. Record the time of each session.

An exercise can be any of the following.

1. a sport-related game
2. an outdoor pursuit
3. a self-created workout routine set to music

	Monday	Tuesday	Wednesday	Thursday	Friday	Saturday	Sunday
Exercise							
Time							
Exercise Heartrate							

List at least 1 response to each the following questions about aerobic exercise.

Question	Response
What positive emotional response did you experience by participating in aerobic exercise?	
What aerobic exercise activity did you enjoy the most?	
Why would the enjoyment of your favorite aerobic exercise activity lead to a lifetime of fitness for you?	

♥ HEALTH INTEGRATION

Use available technology to monitor your pulse rate and workout intensity. Apply the results to your overall fitness plan.

AGILITY LADDER

The purpose of these activities is to promote balance, speed, strength, and coordination through a variety of movement patterns. You may apply these movement patterns to many sports and activities. Practicing balance, speed, strength, and coordination skills help improve your agility. Agility is the ability to efficiently change the direction of your body.

⚠ **CAUTION: Find a safe environment, a safe surface, and adequate personal space to exercise. Do not step on the rungs of the ladder. Exercise at your own pace and only if you are healthy.**

TIPS: Place the agility ladder on the floor. If you are training for a specific sport, you may place the ladder on the playing surface. For example, a soccer player may want to train in the grass, while a basketball player may want to train on a floor surface. When moving from a standing position, push off and land on the balls of your feet. Keep your knees relaxed and your arms bent at a 90-degree angle. Stand tall and keep your head as steady as you can.

JUMP THE LADDER
- Stand tall and face the ladder. Point your toes toward the beginning of the ladder.
- Bend your knees and jump in and out of each square until you reach the end of the ladder.
- Bend your knees in order to land softly in each square. Land on the balls of your feet.

SIDEWAY JUMPS
- Stand sideways at the beginning of the ladder. Point the right side of your body toward the end of the ladder.
- Bend your knees and jump in and out of each square until you reach the end of the ladder.
- Bend your knees in order to land softly in each square. Land on the balls of your feet.
- Return with the left side of your body facing the ladder.

HOP THE LADDER
- Stand tall and face the ladder. Point your toes toward the beginning of the ladder. (7803-k-6)
- Bend your left knee and lift it off the ground. Hop and land softly on the ball of your right foot.
- Hop in and out of each square until you reach the end of the ladder.
- Return to the starting position and switch feet.

SIDEWAY HOPS
- Stand sideways at the beginning of the ladder. Point the right side of your body toward the end of the ladder.
- Bend your left knee and lift it off the ground. Hop and land softly on the ball of your right foot.
- Hop in and out of each square until you reach the end of the ladder.
- Return to the starting position and switch feet.

Copyright 2024 © Lincoln Learning Solutions. All rights reserved.

MARCH THE LADDER

- Stand tall with your toes facing the beginning of the ladder.
- March down the ladder, placing one foot in each square.

RUN THE LADDER

- Stand tall with your toes facing the beginning of the ladder.
- Run down the ladder, placing one foot in each square.

HIGH KNEES

- Stand tall with your toes facing the beginning of the ladder.
- Lift your knees high, near waist level, while moving down the ladder.
- Place one foot in each square.
-

AGILITY SIDE STEP

- Stand tall at the left side of the first square of the ladder, pointing your toes toward the end of the ladder. Align your right foot next to the ladder.
- Step sideways into the first square with your right foot.
- As you bring your left foot into the same square, step out with your right foot and then out with your left foot.
- You should now be standing on the right side of the ladder. Align your left foot next to the ladder.
- Step with your left foot into the second square.
- As you bring your right foot into the same square, step out with your left foot and then out with your right foot.
- Continue this in-out-in-out pattern to the end of the ladder.

AGILITY SIDE JUMPS

- Stand tall at the left side of the first square of the ladder, pointing your toes toward the end of the ladder. Align your right foot next to the ladder.
- Jump sideways into the first square with both feet.
- Jump sideways out of the first square with both feet.
- You should now be standing on the right side of the ladder. Align your left foot next to the ladder.
- Jump sideways into the second square with both feet.
- Continue this in-out-in-out pattern to the end of the ladder.

HOPSCOTCH LADDER

- Stand tall with your toes facing the beginning of the ladder.
- Jump with both feet and land on your right foot in the first square.
- Hop quickly on your right foot and land on both feet in the second square.
- Jump with both feet and land on your left foot in the third square.

- Hop quickly on your left foot and land on both feet in the fourth square.
- Continue this hopscotch pattern to the end of the ladder.

INSIDE-OUTSIDE THE LADDER

- Stand tall with your toes facing the beginning of the ladder.
- Step **into** the first square with your right foot and then your left foot.
- Step to the **outside** of the second square with your right foot to the right side of the square and your left foot to the left side of the square.
- Repeat this pattern to the end of the ladder: Step inside the odd-numbered squares and outside of the even-numbered squares.
- Return to the beginning of the ladder, stepping with your left foot first each time. Keep the same pattern.

EXTENSIONS

- Try your own movements while working with the ladder.
- Try a variety of footwork patterns at different speeds.
- Ladder push-up: Face the side of the ladder at the first square. Placing both hands in the first square, get into a push-up position. Do a push-up. Staying in that position, walk your hands and feet to the next square and do another push-up. Continue this down the ladder. You may also place a hand in each square for wide push-ups.

DANCE

Dancing is an exercise option for aerobic workout, for competition, or just for fun. You can dance on your own or with others. Dancing is expressing yourself through repeated patterns of movement which are usually set to music. Some forms of dance include creative, tap, ballet, hip-hop, modern, folk, square, jazz, line, Latin, ballroom, and social.

The purpose of this lesson is for you to perform basic locomotor movements using common dance concepts in rhythmic patterns to create your own dance for aerobic exercise.

PERSONAL DANCE ROUTINE

COMMON CONCEPTS OF DANCE TO USE FOR YOUR PERSONAL DANCE

- The concept of space includes the following.
  - high, medium, or low **levels**
  - forward, backward, right, or left **directions**
  - curved, zigzag, straight, circle, or square **pathways**
- The concept of time includes the following.
  - slow, medium, or fast **speeds**
  - a pattern for **rhythm**
- The concept of force includes the following.
  - applying light, moderate, or strong **weights**

CREATE A DANCE

Start with the 3 dance steps below. Then, complete the routine by adding your own dance steps. Set your dance to music.

1. Learn a sidestep.
   - Step to the right with your right foot.
   - Bring your left foot in to meet your right foot.
   - Touch your left toes to the floor with a light force, but do not put weight on them.
   - Repeat this to the left.
2. Learn a step-hop.
   - Step out to the right side with your right foot.
   - Bring your left foot in and simultaneously jump with a medium force.
   - Land with both feet together.
   - As you land, clap your hands.
   - Repeat this to the left.
3. Combine the sidestep and step-hop for a double step (step together, step-hop, clap).
   - Step to the right with your right foot.
   - Bring your left foot in to meet your right foot.
   - Step out to the right side with your right foot.
   - Bring your left foot in and simultaneously jump, land, and clap.
   - Repeat this to the left.

Sidestep

Step-hop

4. Perform the double step 4 times.
5. Next, add your dance steps to complete the dance.
   - Choose locomotor skills to blend (slides, cariocas, turns, and so on).
   - Use your arms to accompany the footwork, for example: step, cross, step, clap.
   - Perform the skills at different levels.
   - Move in different directions.
   - Move in different pathways.
   - Move at slow, medium, and fast speeds.
   - Use light, moderate, and strong force to move your body.
   - Create a pattern.
   - Use an 8 count for each move.

Option: Dance with a partner or small group for a social experience.

RATE YOUR ENJOYMENT OF DANCE

On a scale from 1 to 4, where 1 is not enjoyable and 4 is very enjoyable, rate this activity.

1	It was not enjoyable, and I will not participate again.
2	It was not enjoyable, but I will participate again for exercise.
3	It was enjoyable, and I will dance again.
4	It was very enjoyable, and I will create more dances.

RESEARCH INTEGRATION

1. Join a dance class or dance to a dance video.

HEALTH INTEGRATION

Count your pulse to determine if you are exercising in your personal target heart rate zone. Apply the results to your overall fitness plan. Many people choose to complete aerobic workouts through dance.

JUMP ROPE

Jumping rope is an exercise activity that you can enjoy individually or with friends. It helps you develop coordination, balance, rhythm, agility, and timing. Jumping rope is an efficient way to perform aerobic exercise and build muscular strength and endurance in your legs. It can be done daily and in a small space almost anywhere there is a safe, stable surface.

The purpose of this lesson is to provide you with the skills that you need to establish and implement your goal: to improve sport-related skills, to improve cardiovascular endurance, or both.

JUMP ROPE BASICS

FITTING THE JUMP ROPE TO YOUR HEIGHT

- Place a jump rope handle in each hand.
- Stand on the middle of the rope with 1 foot.
- Move the handles straight up, making sure that the rope is straight and pulled tight.
- The tops of the handles should reach close to your shoulders.

Fitting The Jump Rope To Your Height

ELEMENTS OF JUMP ROPE

- Keep your eyes forward.
- When you are turning the rope, keep your elbows near your sides, maintaining a 45-degree angle and making 2-inch circles with your wrists.
- Leave just enough space for the rope to pass under your feet when you jump.
- Stay on the balls of your feet.
- Land softly, keeping your knees slightly bent.

BASIC SKILLS

Practice each of the following exercises, concentrating on proper form, prior to engaging in a workout.

BASIC JUMP

- Pick up the rope. Holding a handle in each hand, rest the rope behind your feet. Stand on the balls of your feet. This is the ready position.
- Your hands should be just above the height of your waist.
- Swing the rope up and over your head.
- Jump over the rope when it approaches your toes.
- Continue as long as you can without stopping.

Basic jump

BACKWARD JUMP

- Begin with the rope in front of your feet.
- Swing the rope up and over your head.
- Jump over the rope when it approaches your feet.

Backward jump

SAMPLE OF A CARDIOVASCULAR CONDITIONING WORKOUT	SAMPLE OF A WORKOUT TO IMPROVE FOOTWORK SPEED
• basic jump 1 minute • march or jog in place 30 seconds • basic jump 1 minute • march or jog in place 30 seconds • backward jump 1 minute • march or jog in place 30 seconds • backward jump 1 minute • march or jog in place 30 seconds • repeat for a 12-minute workout	• basic jump 1 minute at a medium pace • basic jump 30 seconds at a fast pace • rest 30 seconds • back jump 1 minute at a medium pace • back jump 30 seconds at a fast pace • rest 30 seconds • basic jump 30 seconds at a medium pace • basic jump 1 minute at a fast pace • rest 30 seconds • back jump 30 seconds at a medium pace • back jump 1 minute at a fast pace • rest 30 seconds • repeat as needed
DESIGN YOUR PERSONAL CARDIOVASCULAR JUMP ROPE ROUTINE	**DESIGN YOUR PERSONAL FOOTWORK SPEED ROUTINE**

CHALLENGE SKILLS

The following challenges are for students who have mastered the basic jump rope skills. The challenge level is recommended for you if you want to improve agility and further explore jump rope activities.

JUMP ROPE CHALLENGE SKILLS

Practice each of the following exercises, concentrating on proper form, prior to engaging in a workout.

HOP ON 1 FOOT (SWITCH)

- Perform the basic jump on 1 foot instead of 2 feet.

Hop on 1 foot (switch)

SKIER

- With both feet together, hop from side to side while turning the rope.

Skier

CROSSOVERS

- After the rope moves over your head, cross the rope in front of you, jump, and uncross the rope.

Crossovers

FRONT KICKS

- Kick 1 foot forward as the rope passes under your feet with a skip-step between.
- Alternate kicks.

Front kicks

Design your personal jump rope routine by blending the basic skills and the challenge skills.

BLENDING: Perform a jump rope skill and transition smoothly to another jump rope skill without stopping between moves.

Check off the blended challenge skills that you have successfully completed at least 3 consecutive times.

_____ Blend forward consecutive jumps, crossovers, and skiers.

_____ Blend backward consecutive jumps, right-foot hops, and left-foot hops, all while backward turning.

_____ Blend forward consecutive jumps, front kicks, and skiers.

_____ Create your personal blend.

PARTNER SKILLS

Jump rope can have a social component. Individual jumping with a friend may motivate you and may make your workout more fun. Partner or long jump rope requires 2 or more participants.

PARTNER JUMP ROPE SKILLS

Practice each of the following exercises, concentrating on proper form, prior to engaging in a workout.

PARTNER CHAIN JUMP

- Make sure that each person has their own rope.
- Standing side by side, face forward in the ready position.
- Exchange inside handles with your partner; hold your handle with your outside hand and your partner's handle with your inside hand.
- Turn the rope over your head and jump together.
- Establish a rhythm with your partner. Jump rope together to that rhythm.

Partner chain jump

FACING YOUR PARTNER JUMP

- You will need 1 rope.
- Stand face-to-face with your partner.
- Have 1 person hold the rope.
- If you are holding the rope, stand facing your partner and turn the rope.
- If you are not holding the rope, stand facing your partner and jump rope with your partner as they turn the rope.
- No matter who is holding and turning the rope, establish a rhythm with your partner and jump rope together.

Facing your partner jump

SIDE BY SIDE JUMP

- You will need 1 rope.
- Stand beside your partner.
- Hold a handle of the rope with your outside hand. Your partner should hold the other handle in their outside hand.
- Jump rope together as you work together to turn the rope.

Side by side jump

List at least 1 response to each of the following questions about jumping rope.

Question	Response
What jump rope activity do you enjoy the most?	
Why did you enjoy the above-mentioned activity the most?	

RESEARCH INTEGRATION
Research Double Dutch Jump Rope basic skills.

HEALTH INTEGRATION
Count your pulse to determine if you are exercising in your personal target heart rate zone.

STRENGTH BUILDING

Muscles that are not used and not exercised become weak. Strength training, or resistance training, builds muscular strength and endurance.

The purpose of this lesson is to encourage you to perform strength-training exercises 2 or more days per week in order to experience health benefits. A certified trainer should help you set up a balanced, effective strength program.

⚠ **CAUTION: Have a certified trainer plan for you and supervise you when you are working with weights.**

STRENGTH TRAINING

BENEFITS OF STRENGTH TRAINING

- strengthens your skeletal muscles
- strengthens your heart muscle
- strengthens your bones
- improves your posture
- lowers your risk of exercise-related injury
- burns calories and fat
- reduces stress

After reviewing the benefits of strength training, discuss them with a trusted adult. Ask for help setting up a program that works for you and for help staying committed to that program.

There are a variety of exercises from which to choose. Do strength exercises for the muscles of your upper body, lower body, and core. Choose the intensity of each exercise to fit your fitness level. For example, if you are struggling to do a right-angle push-up, switch to a knee push-up. Limit excuses and make a commitment to exercise!

STRENGTH-TRAINING EXERCISE IDEAS

Weightlifting machines: You can use large stationary machines like those typically found in gyms.

Free weights: You can use free-weight equipment such as dumbbells, barbells, medicine balls, kettlebells, resistance bands, and weighted ropes to perform strength-training exercises.

Pilates or yoga: Pilates and yoga sessions are excellent workouts for muscle lengthening and muscle strengthening.

Personal workouts: You can use your own body weight as a source of resistance and create your own strength-training workouts. Create a personal workout by blending basic strength-building exercises such as sit-ups, push-ups, pull-ups, planks, and so on, and design the intensity and duration of each exercise according to your level of fitness. Include upper-body, lower-body, and core exercises in your workout. Perform your personal routine for some or all your strength-training workouts.

SAMPLE

The following is a sample personal strength-training workout that uses personal body weight as resistance. Practice each of the following exercises, concentrating on proper form, prior to engaging in a workout.

IN-OUT ABS

muscle focus: abdominal muscles

Intensity Level 1

Sit on a cushioned surface with your elbows flat on the ground slightly behind your hips. Keeping your knees bent, lift both legs until they are parallel to the ground. Extend your legs straight out in front of you and then return to the bent-knee position.

In-out abs: Intensity Level 1

Intensity Level 2

Sit on a cushioned surface with your hands flat on the ground slightly behind your hips. Keeping your knees bent, lift both legs until they are parallel to the ground. Extend your legs straight out in front of you and then return to the bent-knee position.

In-out abs: Intensity Level 2

Intensity Level 3

Sit on a cushioned surface with your arms held straight above your head. Keeping your knees bent, lift both legs until they are parallel to the ground. Extend your legs straight out in front of you and then return to the bent-knee position.

In-out abs: Intensity Level 3

FORWARD LUNGES

muscle focus: glutei maximi, hamstrings, and quadriceps

Intensity Level 1

Perform alternate forward lunges. Start with your feet together. Step 1 foot forward and bend your knee as low as you comfortably can. Do not exceed a 90-degree angle. Return to the starting position and then repeat the exercise with your other leg.

Forward lunges: Intensity Level 1

Intensity Level 2

Perform alternate forward lunges. Start with your feet together. Step 1 foot forward and bend your knee to a 90-degree angle. Return to the starting position and repeat the exercise with your other leg.

Forward lunges: Intensity Level 2

Intensity Level 3

Start with your feet together. Step your right foot forward and bend your knee to a 90-degree angle. Go back to the starting position. Continue lunging with your right foot until you have completed the repetitions. Next, lunge by stepping forward with your left foot until you complete the repetitions.

Forward lunges: Intensity Level 3

RIGHT-ANGLE PUSH-UPS

muscle focus: pectoralis majors, deltoids, triceps, biceps, and abdominal muscles

Intensity Level 1

Perform knee push-ups. Kneel on a cushioned surface with your back straight and your hands on the ground under your shoulders. Bend your elbows 90 degrees and then return to the straight-arm position, or plank position.

Intensity Level 2

Lie on your stomach. Place your hands under your shoulders. Straighten your arms to lift up your body. Make sure that your back and legs are straight from head to toe. Lower your body by bending your elbows as far as you can without exceeding 90. Straighten your arms to lift your body back up to the plank position, keeping your back and legs straight.

Intensity Level 3

Lie on your stomach. Place your hands under your shoulders. Straighten your arms to lift up your body. Make sure that your back and legs are straight from head to toe. Lower your body by bending your elbows 90 degrees. Straighten your arms to lift your body back up to the plank position, keeping your back and legs straight.

Right-Angle Push-ups: Intensity Level 1

Right-Angle Push-ups: Intensity Level 2

Right-Angle Push-ups: Intensity Level 3

ALTERNATE 6 INCHES

muscle focus: abdominal muscles

Intensity Level 1

Lie on your back on a cushioned surface. Pull 1 knee toward your chest. Extend your other leg straight out in front of you and parallel to the floor. Hold your extended leg 6 to 10 inches above the ground for 3 seconds. Switch legs.

Intensity Level 2

Lie on your back on a cushioned surface. Extend 1 leg up toward the ceiling with your knee bent. Extend your other leg straight out in front of you and parallel to the floor. Hold your extended leg 6 to 10 inches above the ground for 6 seconds. Switch legs.

Intensity Level 3

Lie on your back on a cushioned surface. Extend 1 leg straight up toward the ceiling. Extend your other leg straight out in front of you and parallel to the floor. Hold your extended leg 6 inches above the ground for 6 seconds. Switch legs.

Alternate 6 inches: Intensity Level 1

Alternate 6 inches: Intensity Level 2

Alternate 6 inches: Intensity Level 3

SQUATS

muscle focus: glutei maximi, hamstrings, and quadriceps

Intensity Level 1

Stand with your legs shoulder-width apart and your hands on your hips. Lower your body by bending your knees and hips as low as you comfortably can. Do not lower your hips below knee level.

Squats: Intensity Level 1

Intensity Level 2

Stand with your legs shoulder-width apart and your arms extended out in front of you at shoulder height. With your legs apart, lower your body by bending your knees and hips until your hips are even with your knees.

Intensity Level 3

Perform ¼-squat jumps. Standing with your legs shoulder-width apart, lower your body by bending your knees and hips until your hips are even with your knees. Jump to the right, making a quarter turn and landing gently in a squat position. Continue until you are back to the starting position. Repeat the exercise to the left.

Squats: Intensity Level 2

Squats: Intensity Level 3

TRICEPS PUSH-UPS (NARROW PUSH-UPS)

muscle focus: pectoralis majors, pectoralis minors, deltoids, triceps, biceps, and abdominal muscles

Intensity Level 1

Perform knee push-ups. Kneel on a cushioned surface with your back straight and your hands on the ground inside your shoulders. Bend your elbows 90 degrees and return to straight arms.

Intensity Level 2

Lie on your stomach. Place your hands on the floor close to your body at chest level. Lift your body up with your triceps until you return to the straight-arm position. Make sure that your back and legs are straight from head to toe. Lower your body by bending your elbows as far as you can without exceeding 90 degrees. Return to the straight-arm position.

Intensity Level 3

Lie on your stomach. Place your hands on the floor close to your body at chest level. Lift your body up with your triceps until you return to the straight-arm position. Make sure that your back and legs are straight from head to toe. Lower your body by bending your elbows 90 degrees. Return to the straight-arm position.

Triceps push-ups

Triceps push-ups: Intensity Level 1

Right-Angle Push-ups: Intensity Level 2

Right-Angle Push-ups: Intensity Level 3

SIT-UPS

muscle focus: abdominal muscles

Intensity Level 1

Perform fitness curl-ups. Lie on a cushioned surface with your knees flexed and your feet about 12 inches from your buttocks. With your arms at your sides, slide your fingertips 3 to 4 inches forward along the ground, simultaneously lifting your head and shoulders off the ground. Slowly lower your head and shoulders back to the ground.

Intensity Level 2

Perform sit-ups. Lie on a cushioned surface with your knees flexed and your feet about 12 inches from your buttocks. A partner may hold your feet. Cross your arms, placing your hands on opposite shoulders and holding your elbows close to your chest. Raise your body until your elbows touch your thighs; then, lower your body until your shoulder blades touch the ground.

Intensity Level 3

Perform sit-ups. Lie on a cushioned surface with your knees flexed and your feet about 12 inches from your buttocks. Cross your arms, placing your hands on opposite shoulders and holding your elbows close to your chest. Raise your body until your elbows touch your thighs; then, lower your body until your shoulder blades touch the ground.

Sit-ups: Intensity Level 1

Sit-ups: Intensity Level 2

Sit-ups: Intensity Level 3

STEP-BACK LUNGES

muscle focus: glutei maximi, hamstrings, and quadriceps

Intensity Level 1

Perform alternate step-back lunges. Start by standing with your feet together and your hands on your hips. Step back with 1 foot and lower your knee as low as you comfortably can. Go back to the starting position and repeat this with your other leg.

Intensity Level 2

Perform alternate step-back lunges with high arms. Start by standing with your feet together and your arms extended straight above your head. Step back with 1 foot and lower your knee as far as you comfortably can. Return to the starting position and repeat this with your other leg.

Intensity Level 3

Start by standing with your feet together. Step back with your right foot and lower your knee as far as you comfortably can. Return to the starting position and continue lunging back with your right foot until you have completed the repetitions. Next, step back with your left foot until you complete the repetitions. Your hands may remain on your hips or remain extended.

Step-back lunges: Intensity Level 1

Step-back lunges: Intensity Level 2

Step-back lunges: Intensity Level 3

WIDE PUSH-UPS

muscle focus: pectoralis majors, deltoids, triceps, biceps, and abdominal muscles

Intensity Level 1

Kneel on a cushioned surface with your back straight and your hands on the ground outside your shoulders. Bend your elbows 90 degrees. Return to the straight-arm position.

Wide push-ups

Intensity Level 2

Lie on your stomach. Place your hands outside your shoulders. Lift your body up to a straight-arm position. Make sure that your back and legs are straight from head to toe. Lower your body by bending your elbows as far as you can without exceeding 90 degrees. Return to the straight-arm position.

Wide push-ups: Intensity Level 1

Intensity Level 3

Lie on your stomach. Place your hands outside your shoulders. Lift your body up to a straight-arm position. Make sure that your back and legs are straight from head to toe. Lower your body by bending your elbows 90 degrees. Return to the straight-arm position.

Wide push-ups: Intensity Level 2

HOW TO USE YOUR BODY WEIGHT IN A STRENGTH-TRAINING WORKOUT

- Warm up before your workout. Cool down after your workout.
- Choose the appropriate level of intensity for you.
- Perform each exercise 2 to 3 days per week.
- Begin with 1 set of 10 repetitions of each exercise. Increase sets and repetitions when the exercise becomes easy for you.
- Your goal should be to reach 3 sets of 15 repetitions of each exercise.

Wide push-ups: Intensity Level 3

List at least 1 response to each of the following questions about strength training.

Question	Response
What positive emotional response did you experience by participating in strength training?	
Why would the enjoyment of strength training lead you to a lifetime of fitness?	

RESEARCH INTEGRATION

Research this Strength Building section to explain why each exercise includes 3 levels of intensity.

RESISTANCE BANDS

Resistance bands are elastic bands that are used to improve flexibility, muscular strength, muscular endurance, and body composition. When you first use resistance bands, start with the lightest resistance and then gradually increase to a higher resistance as you get stronger.

The purpose of this lesson is to encourage you to use resistance bands for strength training.

FITNESS TIP: Secure the resistance band in a way that the length is appropriate to give resistance for the entire exercise. Wrap the band around your hands if you need to increase your resistance level.

CAUTION: Check the resistance band for damage or wear before exercising. When you are exercising, secure the band before adding any resistance.

BENEFITS OF STRENGTH TRAINING WITH RESISTANCE BANDS

- is an effective overall strength workout that does not require weights
- offers a variety of resistance adjustments for beginner through advanced levels
- requires inexpensive pieces of equipment
- requires equipment that is easy to carry with you when you are traveling

Practice each of the following exercises, concentrating on proper form, prior to engaging in a workout.

SQUATS

muscle focus: quadriceps, hamstrings, and glutei maximi

- Stand on the middle of the band with your feet shoulder-width apart.
- Hold an end of the band in each hand. Bend your elbows and place your hands by your ears.
- Bend your legs as if you were sitting in a chair. Bend until your legs are at 90-degree angles. Do not let your knees go past your toes.
- Stand back up to the starting position. Do not lock your knees.

Squats

LEG EXTENSIONS

muscle focus: quadriceps, hamstrings, and glutei maximi

- Lay with your back flat on the ground and with your right knee bent to your chest.
- Wrap your band around the bottom of your right foot, holding an end in each hand.
- Keep your left leg flat on the ground.
- Hold the band firmly in your hands and push your right leg straight out without fully straightening your knee.
- Bring your leg slowly back to the starting position.
- After completing the set, switch to your left leg.

Leg extensions

OVERHEAD PRESSES

muscle focus: pectoralis majors, anterior deltoids, and triceps

- Sit in a chair on the middle of the resistance band so that you have an even amount of space on either side.
- Sit up straight and place an end of the band in each hand.
- Bend your elbows, bringing your hands up to your ears. The band should run parallel to your triceps.
- Extend both hands straight up and above your head.
- Bend your elbows, lowering your hands slowly back to the starting position.

Overhead presses

LATERAL RAISES

muscle focus: pectoralis majors, pectoralis minors, biceps, triceps, and front fibers of deltoids

- Place an end of the band under your right foot and the other end in your right hand.
- Keeping your right arm straight at your side, make sure that the tension of the band is at a good level. If the resistance is not enough, wrap the band around your hand until it feels comfortable.
- Keeping your right arm straight, raise it out to your side so that it is parallel to the ground.
- Bring your right arm slowly back to your side. Keep your arm straight during the entire exercise.
- After completing the repetitions, repeat the exercise with your left arm.

Lateral raises

TRICEPS EXTENSIONS

muscle focus: biceps and triceps

- Stand with your feet shoulder-width apart.
- Hold the band with an end in each hand.
- Bring the band behind your back so that your left hand is resting on your lower back and your right hand is just above your head with your elbow bent. The band should be parallel to your spine.
- Holding your left arm in place, extend your right arm straight above your right shoulder.
- Bend your right arm back to the starting position.
- After completing the repetitions, repeat the exercise with your left arm.
- If you need more resistance, wrap the band around your hands until it feels comfortable.

Tricep extensions

BICEPS HAMMER CURLS

muscle focus: biceps and triceps

- Stand on the middle of the exercise band with your feet shoulder-width apart.
- Hold both ends of the exercise band with your palms facing in toward your body.
- Bend at your elbows and slowly bring both hands toward the respective shoulder while keeping your elbows by your sides and your palms turned in toward your body.
- Return your arms slowly back to the starting position without fully straightening your elbows.

Biceps hammer curls

Copyright 2024 © Lincoln Learning Solutions. All rights reserved.

Have a trusted adult or friend evaluate you for correct form for the previous exercises. Did you respond positively to the feedback?

Reciprocate and evaluate your friend. Were you able to provide feedback in a positive manner?

How to Use Resistance Bands in a Strength-Training Workout

- Warm up before your workout. Cool down after your workout.
- Perform each resistance band exercise 2 to 3 days per week. Do not exercise the same muscle group on consecutive days.
- Begin with 1 set of 10 repetitions for each exercise. Increase sets and repetitions when the exercise becomes easy for you.
- Your goal should be to reach 3 sets of 10 to 15 repetitions.
- Wrap the band to increase resistance as necessary.

EXERCISE STATIONS

Bring Movement Together with Exercise Stations

READY
Get the equipment you will need.

SET
Set up the four stations in a safe area and set the time you will be at each station.

GO!
Choose your starting station and complete all four stations.

Tips for Exercising through the Stations:
- Refer to the corresponding lesson for skills, procedures, and safety.
- Warm up and cool down.
- Find a safe space to exercise.
- Work well with others.

EXERCISE STATIONS

STATION 1
AGILITY LADDER

(agility ladder per student)

Practice your favorite agility ladder skills.

STATION 2
STRENGTH EXERCISES

Choose one or more strength exercises to perform.

(Examples: sit-ups, push-ups, and planks)

STATION 4
RESISTANCE BAND EXERCISES

(resistance band per student)

Choose one or more resistance band exercises to perform.

(Examples: bicep curls, tricep extensions, standing chest presses)

STATION 3
JUMP ROPE

(jump rope per student)

Practice your favorite jump rope skills.

Suggested time: one minute per station; repeat four or five times.

SPORTS-RELATED AND SKILL-RELATED ACTIVITIES

FITNESS TIP: Prior to beginning your physical education activities, read the following safety information that applies to every lesson, review the timeline, and review the assessment rubric.

SAFETY ALERT: Before you exercise, make sure that you are properly warmed up and have enough room to perform each activity. Wear proper equipment and follow activity-specific safety rules. Stay hydrated and take breaks as needed. Exercise only if you are healthy, and always exercise at your own pace. If an exercise starts to hurt, if you feel dizzy, or if you feel light-headed, stop the exercise completely and get help. Upon completion of any workout, cool down and stretch.

TIMELINE

Review all of the activity information before beginning. Use the scoring rubrics as assessment tools. You may ask a trusted adult or friend to observe your performance and provide feedback. Progress according to your skill level. The time that it takes you to complete a module will depend on your personal progress.

Practice and assess the first skill until competent.

Continue to progress until you have practiced and assessed each skill until competent.

Apply skills in a game situation.

ASSESSMENT RUBRIC

You will find a rubric assessment tool following some of the basic skills. Use this tool to evaluate and score your progress in learning the elements of a new skill.

SKILL	PROGRESSING	COMPETENT	PROFICIENT
skill 1	1 or 2 of the elements	3 or 4 out of 5 elements	all elements met

Copyright 2024 © Lincoln Learning Solutions. All rights reserved.

BASKETBALL

Learning and practicing basketball helps you develop the skills necessary for playing games outside of PE class. Basketball enhances health-related and skill-related components of fitness. Learning basketball skills will not only help improve your basketball game but may also enhance your skills in other sports and activities. Playing basketball is a great aerobic workout.

The official game of basketball is played by 2 opposing teams that are each made up of 5 players. The players play on a basketball court. Points are scored when the ball goes through a basketball hoop. There are also other basketball games and activities that you can enjoy, such as independent shooting and dribbling challenges, shooting games, and half-court games of 1-on-1, 2-on-2, and 3-on-3 versions of the official game.

The purpose of this lesson is for you to participate in aerobic exercise and in skill-building activities. Game participation will depend upon the availability of a facility and players. Any time you play a game of basketball, be sure to follow game rules, communicate with teammates in a positive and effective manner, and exhibit appropriate behavior with your team and the opposing team.

⚠ **CAUTION: Do not overinflate the basketball.**

DRIBBLING SKILLS

Learning to dribble efficiently with both your right hand and left hand is necessary for playing basketball.

BASIC STATIONARY DRIBBLING

- Using your dominant hand, spread your fingers and push the ball down gently toward the ground with your finger pads. Do not slap the ball.
- Let the ball bounce on the ground and come back to your hand. Do not let the ball bounce higher than your waist.
- Flex your wrist and push the ball back to the ground with your finger pads. This is a continuous movement; do not catch the ball after every bounce.
- Dribble with your head up.
- Keep your eyes looking forward, not watching the ball.
- Repeat dribbling the ball with your non-dominant hand.

Basic stationary dribbling

SKILL	PROGRESSING	COMPETENT	PROFICIENT
right-handed dribble	1 or 2 of the elements	3 or 4 out of 5 elements	all elements met
left-handed dribble	1 or 2 of the elements	3 or 4 out of 5 elements	all elements met

STATIONARY DRIBBLING

- See how many times you can dribble the ball with your dominant hand without losing control of the ball.
- Push the ball down with different amounts of force to make it bounce at different levels.
- Try pushing the ball with a soft force so that it bounces at a low level.
- Try pushing the ball with a hard force so that it bounces at a high level.
- Dribble with your dominant hand.
- Dribble with your non-dominant hand.
- Dribble the ball from 1 hand to the other.

DRIBBLING WHILE MOVING

- Dribble from 1 hand to the other while moving.
- Dribble while moving, increasing and decreasing speed.
- Dribble while moving and change directions.

CROSSOVER DRIBBLING

- Set up disc cones about 2 feet apart in a zigzag pattern.
- Start at the first cone and dribble the basketball to the next cone using the hand with which you are most comfortable.
- Reach the second cone and do a crossover (switch hands) in order to move on to the next cone.
- Complete a crossover at each cone until you have reached the last cone.
- Turn around and do the same thing back to the first cone.
- Continue this until you feel comfortable with dribbling and crossing over.

Crossover dribbling

CHALLENGE SKILLS

The following challenge skills are for those who are proficient in basic stationary dribbling. The challenge drills reinforce dribbling effectively with both the right hand and left hand. Practice as appropriate to your needs.

FIGURE-8 DRIBBLE

- Stand with your legs wide and your knees bent.
- Dribble the ball through your legs and around your ankles in a figure-8 pattern.
- Alternate hands while dribbling.
- Reverse directions for an advanced challenge.

Figure-8 dribble

FRONT 2, BACK 2 DRIBBLE

- Stand with your legs shoulder-width apart and your knees bent.
- Dribble twice in front of your body. Alternate hands while dribbling, but do not put both hands on the ball at the same time.
- Switch hands behind you, and dribble twice behind your body. This is a 1, 2, 3, 4 count.
- Move while making quarter turns for an advanced challenge.

Front, back 2 dribble

2-BALL DRIBBLE

- Dribble 2 balls at the same time.
- Keep the balls at the same height.

2-ball dribble

Copyright 2024 © Lincoln Learning Solutions. All rights reserved.

2-BALL HIGH-LOW DRIBBLE

- Dribble a ball with each hand.
- Dribble the ball on the right high while simultaneously dribbling the ball on the left low.
- Dribble the ball on the right low while simultaneously dribbling the ball on the left high.

2-ball high-low dribble

2-BALL FIGURE-8 DRIBBLE

- Dribble 1 ball between your legs while circling the other ball around 1 of your legs.
- When the ball that is circling your leg reaches the middle point between your legs, switch it with the ball between your legs.

2-ball figure-8 dribble

Check off the challenge skills that you have mastered.

_____FIGURE-8 DRIBBLE

_____FRONT 2, BACK 2 DRIBBLE

_____2-BALL DRIBBLE

_____2-BALL HIGH-LOW DRIBBLE

_____2-BALL FIGURE-8 DRIBBLE

PASSING SKILLS

There are 2 common passes that are used in the game of basketball. The bounce pass and chest pass are used to move the ball to your teammates. You can practice these passes with a partner or against a wall.

BOUNCE PASS AND CATCH

BOUNCE PASS

- Stand facing the target.
- Hold the ball with both hands at chest level and your elbows out.
- Step toward the target.
- Extend both arms toward the target. The ball should bounce on the floor between you and the target before it reaches the target.

Bounce Pass

CATCH

- When you are catching, watch the ball all the way until it reaches your hands.
- Move your hands toward the ball.
- Give with the ball (pull the ball slightly toward you) as it hits your hands to make a soft catch.

Catch

SKILL	PROGRESSING	COMPETENT	PROFICIENT
bounce pass	1 or 2 of the elements	3 out of 4 elements	all elements met
bounce-pass catch	1 of the elements	2 out of 3 elements	all elements met

CHEST PASS AND CATCH

CHEST PASS

- Stand facing the target.
- Hold the ball with both hands at chest level and your elbows out.
- Step toward the target.
- Extend both arms toward the target. The ball should not bounce on the floor.

CATCH

- When you are catching, watch the ball all the way until it reaches your hands.
- Move your hands toward the ball.
- Give with the ball (pull the ball slightly toward you) as it hits your hands to make a soft catch.

Chest pass

Catch

SKILL	PROGRESSING	COMPETENT	PROFICIENT
chest pass	1 or 2 of the elements	3 out of 4 elements	all elements met
chest-pass catch	1 of the elements	2 out of 3 elements	all elements met

PRACTICE PASSING WITH A PARTNER

- How many bounce passes can you and your partner do in a row?
- How many chest passes can you and your partner do in a row?
- Bounce pass to your partner. Your partner will send a chest pass back. Switch roles.
- Bounce pass as you and your partner move down the court.
- Chest pass as you and your partner move down the court.

BASIC SHOOTING SKILLS

BASIC SHOOTING

- Stand facing the hoop with your feet shoulder-width apart and your knees slightly bent.
- Place your dominant hand on the back of the basketball and bend your wrist. Place your non-dominant hand on the side of the ball.
- Place the ball on the finger pads of your dominant hand.
- Use your non-dominant hand as your guide.
- Position your elbow so that it is behind the ball, not out to the side.
- Look at the target—the front of the rim.
- Push your dominant hand toward the target while straightening your legs to give you more power to shoot.
- Shoot the ball toward the target and follow through with your arm and wrist. Snap your wrist as the ball leaves your hand.

Basic shooting skills

- Remember BEEF.
  - **Balance** the ball in your dominant hand.
  - Place your **elbow** behind the ball, not out to the side.
  - Keep your **eyes** on the target.
  - **Follow** through with a snap of your wrist.

SKILL	PROGRESSING	COMPETENT	PROFICIENT
BEEF elements	1 or 2 of the elements	3 out of 4 elements	all elements

SHOOTING DRILLS
PRACTICE SHOOTING
- Practice some shooting drills after you become comfortable shooting the basketball.
- Pick different spots on the court, both closer and farther away from the hoop.
- Map out a pattern in your mind as to what spots you will go to first, second, third, and so on.
- Practice shooting from each spot.
- Start on 1 side of the hoop and move around to the other side.
- Work back around to the starting position.

FOUL LINE SPELLING GAME
- You will need 2 or more players.
- Line up behind the foul line.
- The goal of the game is to be the first player to spell A-E-R-O-B-I-C.
- The first person takes a shot from behind the foul line.
- If the player makes the basket, the player gets a letter and goes to the back of the line to wait for their next turn.
- If the player misses, the player does not get a letter and goes to the back of the line.
- The next player in line repeats the above procedure.
- Continue to play until a player spells A-E-R-O-B-I-C.

OFFENSIVE AND DEFENSIVE SKILLS
Agile footwork is an essential component of basketball. Practice footwork skills to improve your offensive and defensive play.

OFFENSIVE SKILLS
Practice each of the following skills, concentrating on proper form, prior to using them in a game or other competition.

OFFENSIVE READY POSITION
The ready position allows a player to move quickly in any direction. It is used for both offense and defense.

- With your elbows out, hold the ball with both hands to the dominant side of your chest.
- Bend your knees to keep your body low.
- Stand with your feet shoulder-width apart.
- Keep your head up and your weight on the balls of your feet.

SKILL	PROGRESSING	COMPETENT	PROFICIENT
offensive ready position	1 or 2 of the elements	3 out of 4 elements	all elements met

PIVOT

The purpose of the pivot in a basketball game is for you to look around and decide to dribble, pass, or shoot.

- Plant 1 foot, which will be your pivot foot, in place on the ground.
- Place your weight on the balls of your feet.
- Slide your non-pivot foot and rotate your body 180 degrees.
- Repeat this exercise with your other foot.

SKILL	PROGRESSING	COMPETENT	PROFICIENT
pivot	1 of the elements	2 out of 3 elements	all elements

FAKE

- Look in 1 direction, and then pass or move in another direction.
- Stay on the balls of your feet.
- Move quickly.

SKILL	PROGRESSING	COMPETENT	PROFICIENT
fake	1 of the elements	2 out of 3 elements	all elements

GIVE AND GO

The purpose of the give and go in a basketball game is to for you to pass the ball to a teammate and to quickly relocate so that you can receive a pass.

- Pass the ball to a teammate.
- Move quickly to relocate and support your offense.
- Indicate (call out) that you are ready and open to receive the ball.
- Catch the ball.

SKILL	PROGRESSING	COMPETENT	PROFICIENT
give and go	1 or 2 of the elements	3 out of 4 elements	all elements

DEFENSIVE SKILLS

Practice each of the following skills, concentrating on proper form, prior to using them in a game or other competition.

DEFENSIVE SLIDES

The purpose of defensive slides in basketball is to keep up with your opponent and to legally take the ball or legally disrupt the opponent's pass or shot.

- Place your weight on the balls of your feet.
- Slide to the side with quick steps.
- Do not cross your feet.
- Keep your knees bent.
- Face your hips toward your opponent.
- Hold your hands up at chest level.
- Keep your eyes on your opponent's waistline.
- Stay with your opponent.
- Anticipate and react quickly to your opponent's movements.

SKILL	PROGRESSING	COMPETENT	PROFICIENT
defensive slides	1, 2, 3, 4, or 5 of the elements	6, 7, or 8 out of 9 elements	all elements met

PRACTICE OFFENSIVE AND DEFENSIVE SKILLS

- Practice the **pivot** by planting your right foot and rotating your left foot until you feel comfortable with the movement.
- Practice the **pivot** by planting your left foot and rotating your right foot until you feel comfortable with the movement.
- Practice the **give and go** with a partner and a defender. Pass the ball, quickly relocate, and then receive the pass, avoiding the defender.
- Practice the **fake** independently. Set up a cone as a decoy. Fake the pass toward the cone and then pass to your partner until you feel comfortable with the movement.
- Practice the **fake** with a partner defending you. Dribble, fake, and move in another direction to get around the defensive player. Do this until you feel comfortable with the fake.
- Practice the **defensive slide** with a partner. As your partner dribbles, defensive slide to try to prevent them from making a successful pass or shot. Do this until you feel comfortable with the defensive slide.

BASKETBALL GAME

- The game is played by 2 opposing teams of 5 players each. Each team has a point guard, a shooting guard, a small forward, a power forward, and a center.
- The game is played on a basketball court 92 feet long and 50 feet wide.
- A 10-foot-high basketball hoop with a net is at each end of the court.
- The object of the game is to move the ball down the court by passing or dribbling and to score by shooting the ball through the opposing team's hoop.

- A high school game is divided into 8-minute quarters of play time with a rest period after 2 quarters of play.
- The team with the most points is the winning team.
- The game begins with a jump ball at mid-court. A referee tosses the ball between 2 opposing players.
- The team that possesses the ball is on offense, and the other team is on defense.
- The player with the ball must dribble, pass, or shoot.
- When they are moving with the ball, the player must dribble. When the player stops dribbling, they cannot take any more steps.
- If a player walks without dribbling, the ball is turned over to the opposing team.
- The players on defense try to intercept, or take away, the ball.

DEMONSTRATE POSITIVE GAME BEHAVIOR

- Follow the rules of the game.
- Do not commit a foul or make illegal physical contact against an opposing player.
    - A foul against a non-shooting player results in a turnover, which is a change in possession of the ball between teams.
    - A foul against a shooting player results in the team getting free shots—2 shots for a foul on a player shooting a 2-point shot and 3 shots for a player shooting a 3-point shot.
    - A player who commits 5 fouls is removed from the game.
- Be supportive and encouraging to your teammates.
- Treat your opponents with respect.

SKILL	PROGRESSING	COMPETENT	PROFICIENT
game behavior	1 or 2 of the elements	3 out of 4 elements	all elements met

HOW TO SCORE

- An arc line, referred to as a 3-point line, is marked on the basketball court.
    - A player who makes a basket from behind the 3-point line is awarded 3 points.
    - A player who makes a basket from inside the 3-point line is awarded 2 points.
- Foul shots are worth 1 point each.

OPTIONAL 1-ON-1 GAME

Playing 1-on-1 allows you to play basketball and complete an aerobic workout when you only have 2 players. This is an example of how to break down the barrier of not having enough players for an official game and create a solution.

- You can play a 1-on-1 half-court game with 2 players.
- Determine the boundaries.
- Determine who starts with the ball.
- Begin behind the half-court line of your established boundary.
- After a score, the opposing player takes the ball out to the half-court line and tries to score.
- Scoring is the same as in the official rules.
- You will have to call your own fouls or have another person referee.
- Treat your opponent with respect.
- If there are more players, you can play 2-on-2 or 3-on-3 games.

Copyright 2024 © Lincoln Learning Solutions. All rights reserved.

Prior to playing 1-on-1, establish and review the game rules so that you and your opponent understand them. If problems arise, work to solve them in a positive and effective manner. Appreciate different players' abilities. An example of a rule that you may want to decide upon is the boundaries.

Below are our game rules for safety and fairness.
1.
2.
3.
4.
5.

RATE YOUR ENJOYMENT OF THE BASKETBALL ACTIVITY THAT YOU ENJOYED MOST

On a scale from 1 to 4, where 1 is not enjoyable and 4 is very enjoyable, rate this activity.

1	It was not enjoyable, and I will not participate again.
2	It was not enjoyable, but I will participate again for exercise.
3	It was enjoyable, and I will play again.
4	It was very enjoyable, and I will initiate future games.

RESEARCH INTEGRATION

1. Attend a basketball game or watch a basketball game on television. It can be men's, women's, or co-ed basketball at any level—youth, high school, college, or professional. Identify the basketball skills you have learned that are used by the players throughout the game.

HEALTH INTEGRATION

Count your pulse during and after playing basketball to determine if you are exercising in your personal target heart rate zone. Apply the results to your overall fitness plan. Many people choose to complete aerobic workouts by playing in fast-paced games like basketball.

FLYING DISC

The purpose of these activities is to develop the skills necessary for tracking an object and hand-eye coordination. You may do this activity individually or with friends.

⚠️ **CAUTION: Practice throwing and catching the flying disc in a safe environment. You should master the following skills with a ball prior to using a disc. Do not throw if someone is between you and the target, and do not walk into the path of another person throwing.**

BACKHAND GRIP

- Hold the disc in your dominant hand.
- Hold the disc parallel to the ground with your thumb on top.
- Rest your index finger on the edge of the disc, and curl your remaining fingers under the disc.

SKILL	PROGRESSING	COMPETENT	PROFICIENT
grip	1 of the elements	2 out of 3 elements	all elements met

BACKHAND THROW

- Hold the disc in your dominant hand.
- Bend your elbow and keep the disc close to your body so it is touching your forearm. The back of your hand should be facing the target.
- Step toward the target with your dominant foot.
- Snap your wrist and release the disc while extending your arm.

SKILL	PROGRESSING	COMPETENT	PROFICIENT
throw	1 or 2 of the elements	3 out of 4 elements	all elements met

CATCH

- Stay in front of the disc as it comes toward you.
- Keep your hands up and your eyes on the disc.
- Place a hand on each side of the disc, clamp down, and squeeze it to catch.

SKILL	PROGRESSING	COMPETENT	PROFICIENT
catching	1 of the elements	2 out of 3 elements	all elements met

PRACTICE THE SKILLS

- Using the backhand grip, practice throwing toward the target.
- Increase your distance as you improve.
- Pass and catch with a partner.

PICKLEBALL

Pickleball is a sport that combines badminton, tennis, and table tennis. These skills may help you develop concentration and hand-eye-object coordination. Playing a game of pickleball also gives you a cardiovascular workout.

⚠ **CAUTION: Make sure that nobody is close to you before you swing the paddle. Do not walk into the path of another person who is swinging a paddle.**

PICKLEBALL SKILLS

STROKES

READY POSITION

- Wait for the ball, keeping your paddle in front of the middle of your chest. This way, you are ready to return the ball from wherever it goes.
- Bend your knees and stand with your feet shoulder-width apart.
- Keep your head up and your weight on the balls of your feet.
- Hold the paddle in your dominant hand.

HANDSHAKE GRIP

- Hold the paddle in your dominant hand away from your body and at waist height.
- Placing the head of the paddle vertical to the ground, point the handle toward your belly button.

UNDERHAND STROKE

- Hold the paddle so that the head is facing the ground and is positioned under the ball.
- Flick your wrist to hit the ball with the center of the paddle.
- Rotate your forearm so that it faces upward on contact.
- Follow through to your target.

SKILL	PROGRESSING	COMPETENT	PROFICIENT
underhand stroke	1 or 2 of the elements	3 out of 4 elements	all elements met

OVERHAND STROKE

- Bend your elbow slightly and position the paddle under the ball.
- Flick your wrist to hit the ball with the center of the paddle.
- Extend your arm when you make contact.
- Follow through to your target.

SKILL	PROGRESSING	COMPETENT	PROFICIENT
overhand stroke	1 or 2 of the elements	3 out of 4 elements	all elements met

FOREHAND STROKE

- The paddle should be on the same side of your body as your dominant hand.
- Face the palm of your hand forward.
- Extend your arm and flick your wrist to hit the ball.
- Point the face of the paddle up to get the ball over the net.
- Follow through to your target.

SKILL	PROGRESSING	COMPETENT	PROFICIENT
forehand stroke	1 or 2 of the elements	3 or 4 out of 5 elements	all elements met

BACKHAND STROKE

- Rotate the paddle and extend it across your body.
- Rotate your feet and shoulders in the same direction as the paddle.
- Face the back of your hand (your knuckles) forward.
- Flick your wrist as you hit the ball with the center of the paddle.
- Follow through to your target.

OPTION: 2-HANDED BACKHAND STROKE

- Place your non-dominant hand below your dominant hand.
- Rotate the paddle.
- Rotate your feet and shoulders in the same direction as the paddle.
- Flick your wrists as you hit the ball with the center of the paddle.
- Follow through to your target.

SKILL	PROGRESSING	COMPETENT	PROFICIENT
backhand stroke	1 or 2 of the elements	3 or 4 out of 5 elements	all elements met

UNDERHAND SERVE

- Hold the paddle in your dominant hand. Hold the ball in your non-dominant hand.
- Hold the head of the paddle down toward the ground.
- Step forward with your non-dominant foot.
- Drop the ball slightly below your waist.
- Hit the ball with the center of the paddle. Flick your wrist as you make contact.
- Follow through to your target.
- Serve successfully 70 percent of the time.

SKILL	PROGRESSING	COMPETENT	PROFICIENT
underhand serve	1, 2, 3, or 4 of the elements	5 or 6 out of 7 elements	all elements met

PRACTICE THE STROKES

- Practice each stroke by hitting the ball against a wall with the paddle.
    - Allow the ball to bounce before striking it.
    - Volley the ball against the wall. This means that you should not allow the ball to bounce off the ground.
- Strike the ball toward the wall using various levels of force.
- Aim and strike the ball to the left of the target.
- Aim and strike the ball to the right of the target.
- Hit the ball back and forth with a partner. How many times can you hit it back and forth?

SHOTS

DINK SHOT

The most effective short-hand shots, or dinks, are those that bounce in front of the no-volley line (the area 7 feet from the net, where volleying is not allowed). Dinks should be short and low.

LOB

A lob is high and pushes your opponent to the rear of the court. This slows down the game to give you a chance to get ready for your opponent's shot.

DRIVE

A drive is a hard, fast hit that is difficult to return.

PRACTICE THE SHOTS

Practice the shots independently by bouncing or tossing the ball at the appropriate height for each shot. Practice with a net set up.

- Practice the dink shot forward and crosscourt.
- Practice the lob shot.
- Practice the drive shot.
- Describe a shot and then execute it. Do this for the 3 shots.
- Have a partner toss the ball for you. Practice each shot and then switch roles. Be supportive and encouraging to your partner.

PLAYING A GAME

- Pickleball is a singles game with 2 players or a doubles game with 4 players.
- Start by serving the ball underhand from the right side of the court. Serve diagonally to your opponent on the left. Stand behind the serving line when you start your serve.
    - If a point is scored, the server then serves from the left side of the court. Continue this side-to-side pattern until the serve is lost. In a doubles game, the other teammate then serves. Once the second teammate loses the serve, the opposing team serves.
- The ball must land in the opponent's section of the court.
- Your opponent must let the ball bounce once before returning the serve.

- After each team hits the ball once, you may either let the ball bounce once or hit it. This starts the game.
- Points are only scored when a player is serving.
- Games are played to 11 points. A team must win by 2 points.
- Faults include the following.
    - hitting the ball out of bounds
    - serving faults
    - allowing the ball to bounce more than once
    - hitting the ball on the fly in the non-volley zone
    - hitting the ball to the wrong service court

PICKLEBALL OPTIONS

- Play at picnics and group outings.
- Make a net by tying jump ropes together and then tying the jump ropes to the tops of chairs. If there are 2 trees in your playing area, tie the jump ropes to the trees. You may also go to a park with a tennis court and set smaller boundaries on the tennis court.

DEMONSTRATE POSITIVE GAME BEHAVIOR

- Follow the rules.
- Call for a shot, when appropriate, to identify that you are going to hit it. This is for safety and game efficiency.
- Be supportive and encouraging to your teammate.
- Treat your opponents with respect.

SKILL	PROGRESSING	COMPETENT	PROFICIENT
game behavior	1 or 2 of the elements	3 out of 4 elements	all elements met

RATE YOUR ENJOYMENT OF PICKLEBALL

On a scale from 1 to 4, where 1 is not enjoyable and 4 is very enjoyable, rate this activity.

1	It was not enjoyable, and I will not participate again.
2	It was not enjoyable, but I will participate again for exercise.
3	It was enjoyable, and I will play again.
4	It was very enjoyable, and I will initiate future games.

♥ HEALTH INTEGRATION

Count your pulse during and after playing pickleball to determine if you are exercising in your personal target heart rate zone. Apply the results to your overall fitness plan. Many people choose to complete aerobic workouts by playing in casual games with friends.

PLAYGROUND BALL GAMES

You can use a playground ball for many fun activities to improve your skills and cardiovascular conditioning.

⚠️ **CAUTION:** Find a safe environment, a safe surface, and adequate personal space to exercise. Exercise at your own pace and only if you are healthy. Do not overinflate the ball.

FOUR SQUARE AND TWO SQUARE GAMES

FOUR SQUARE

Using chalk or ropes, divide a 10-foot by 10-foot space into four squares. You will need four players for this game. Number the squares 1, 2, 3, and 4. The goal of the game is to reach the fourth spot and be the server. Players move in numerical order.

RULES

- Each player stands in a square. Extra players stand in the wait line near square 1.
- The player in square 4 is the server.
- If you are the server, serve underhand to the square of your choice. Note: You must bounce the ball before you serve and strike it.
- Serve again if the ball lands on a line.
- A miss results in a player moving to square 1 or to the wait line.
- Misses include double bounces, out of bounds, and catches.

TWO SQUARE

Using chalk or ropes, divide a 10-foot by five-foot space into two squares. You will need two players for this game.

RULES

- Player 1 serves underhand.
- The ball must bounce in square 2 before returning to square 1.
- Players alternate serves and earn a point when the receiving player misses.
- Serve again if the ball lands on a line.
- Misses include double bounces, out of bounds, and catches.

KICKBALL GAMES

You will need a safe playing area, bases, and a playground ball.

ONE PLAYER

- Kick a stationary playground ball with the inside of your foot.
- Mark the distance it traveled.
- Try again.

TWO PLAYERS

- Set up a playing field with first base, second base, third base, home base, and a pitching mound.
- If you are the pitcher, roll the ball toward the kicker positioned at home base. Try to make it to home base before the kicker returns.
- If you are the kicker, kick the ball and run the bases. Try to make it to home base before the pitcher.
- Take turns at the different positions.

THREE OR MORE PLAYERS

- Set up the playing field the same as the two players' game.
- There is one pitcher and one kicker, and the remaining players are outfielders.
- If you are the pitcher, roll the ball toward the kicker positioned at home base. Try to make it to home base before the kicker returns.
- If you are the kicker, kick the ball and run the bases. Try to make it to home base before the pitcher.
- If you are an outfielder, try to get the ball to the pitcher before the kicker returns to home base.
- Take turns at the different positions.

Prior to playing the game, establish and review the game rules so that all participants understand them. If problems arise, work as a group to solve them in a positive and effective manner. Appreciate different players' abilities.

Below are our game rules for safety and fairness.
1.
2.
3.
4.
5.

SOCCER

Soccer is a sport that is popular around the globe. The object of the game is to use your feet to dribble, pass, and kick a ball in order to score goals by getting the ball into your opponent's net.

People of all skill levels enjoy playing casual or competitive games of soccer. In most communities, there are soccer leagues for everyone from preschoolers to adults. Playing soccer is a great way to improve footwork, interact with others, have fun, and complete an aerobic workout.

The purpose of this lesson is for you to participate in soccer activities. Students who practice soccer skills are more likely to join a game and exercise outside of PE class. You will practice skills, learn game rules, be encouraged to communicate with teammates in a positive and effective manner, and be reminded to exhibit appropriate behavior with your team and the opposing team.

⚠️ **CAUTION: Wear appropriate safety equipment. Do not overinflate the ball.**

SOCCER SKILLS

DRIBBLING

Use your peripheral vision, or your side vision, to watch the ball as you dribble it. Dribbling is a series of small, controlled touches that you complete in order to move with the ball in your possession. Dribble the ball with the insides and outsides of your feet as well as with the tops of your feet, where your shoelaces lay. Do not dribble the ball with your toes, otherwise, you risk losing control of the ball.

- Start with the ball positioned in front of you on the ground.
- Dribble forward, keeping the ball close—no more than 3 to 5 feet in front of you.
- Move the ball with the insides, outsides, and/or tops of both of your feet.
- Keep your head up.
- Match your speed to your skill.
- Change directions.

SKILL	PROGRESSING	COMPETENT	PROFICIENT
dribbling	1, 2, or 3 of the elements	4 or 5 out of 6 elements	all elements

PASSING

Passing the ball is an important part of soccer. Players pass the ball to each other in order to keep the other team from gaining control of the ball and to progress the ball up the field toward the other team's goal.

- Start with the soccer ball on the ground, next to the inside of your dominant foot.
- Position the inside of your kicking foot behind the middle of the soccer ball.
- Establish your non-kicking foot slightly behind you.
- Swing your kicking leg back, keeping it straight throughout your entire kick.
- Contact the middle of the ball with the inside of your foot. Follow through your kick with your foot and leg.
- Use appropriate force and direction to keep your pass on target.

SKILL	PROGRESSING	COMPETENT	PROFICIENT
passing	1, 2, or 3 of the elements	4 or 5 out of 6 elements	all elements

TRAPPING: OPTION 1

Trapping is a way of stopping the ball, receiving a pass, or gaining control of the ball.

- Start with the ball positioned in front of you on the ground.
- Place your dominant foot on top of the ball. To do this, lift your foot slightly off the ground, keeping your ankle locked and your toes up.
- Repeat this with your non-dominant foot.

SKILL	PROGRESSING	COMPETENT	PROFICIENT
trapping: option 1	1 of the elements	2 out of 3 elements	all elements

TRAPPING: OPTION 2

Trapping is also a way to stop the ball in order to quickly gain control and transition to your next move.

- When the soccer ball comes toward you, turn the ankle of whichever foot you are trapping with so that your instep, or the inside of your foot, is facing forward.
- Cushion the ball with your foot as you stop it lightly, as if you were catching an egg.
- Repeat this with your other foot.

SKILL	PROGRESSING	COMPETENT	PROFICIENT
trapping: option 2	1 of the elements	2 out of 3 elements	all elements

SHOOTING

The purpose of shooting is to get the soccer ball into your opponent's goal by striking it with your foot.

- Place 2 discs about 4 feet apart and 5 feet in front of you. Place the soccer ball on the ground in front of you.
- Stand so that your dominant leg, or kicking leg, is pulled back behind you.
- Place your non-kicking foot alongside the soccer ball, with your toes pointing at the goal that you made.
- Bend the knee of your kicking leg by pulling your foot back. Then, in a single motion, swing your leg forward, straightening your leg and pointing your toes to kick the soccer ball with the top of your foot. Kick the center of the soccer ball with the laces of your shoe, pointing your toes down. You do not want to kick the soccer ball with your toes.
- Follow through your kick, making sure that you finish with your toes pointing toward the goal.

SKILL	PROGRESSING	COMPETENT	PROFICIENT
shooting	1 or 2 of the elements	3 or 4 out of 5 elements	all elements

PRACTICE THE SKILLS

After mastering the basic soccer skills, put them all together in practice activities.

DRIBBLE

- Practice dribbling by placing discs in various locations around your practice area. As you are dribbling, weave in and out of the discs.

TRAP

- Place 2 discs about 4 feet apart to create a goal. Make your goal 10 to 20 feet away from you.
- Toss the ball up in the air, trapping it with your foot and guiding it to the ground just in front of you.
  - After mastering trapping the soccer ball with your feet, try trapping it using your thigh. Throw the soccer ball up in the air and bend your knee so that your thigh is just under the soccer ball. As the soccer ball comes back down, cushion it with your thigh. Allow the ball to hit your thigh and then guide it with your thigh as it falls to the ground.
- Dribble the soccer ball toward the goal.
- When you get about 5 feet away from the goal, shoot the ball through the discs.

Trap

PASS

- Set up 2 discs about 3 feet apart. Aim to kick the soccer ball between the discs.
- If you kick the soccer ball in the middle, the soccer ball will go straight.
- Move to the left of the discs. Try passing the soccer ball between the discs from the left. Kick the right side of the ball with the instep of your right foot to make the soccer ball go to the left.
- Move to the right of the discs. Try passing the soccer ball between the discs from the right. Kick the left side of the ball with the instep of your left foot to make the ball go to the left.

Pass

SHOOT ON GOAL

- Place 2 discs about 4 feet apart to use as your goal.
- Shoot the soccer ball between the discs that you set up as a goal.
- Dribble the soccer ball toward the goal and shoot. You can add extra discs between you and the goal to act as pathways that you can dribble through or points where you can change directions before shooting on goal.

STRATEGIES TO REMEMBER

- When you are dribbling the soccer ball, keep it close to you.
- When you are passing the ball, kick with the instep of your foot.
- When you are trapping the ball, cushion it as if you were catching an egg.
- When you are shooting the soccer ball, point your toes down and kick the middle of the ball with the top of your foot. Your non-kicking foot should be next to the ball, pointing toward the target. When you follow through, make sure that your kicking toes end up pointing toward the target as well.

CHALLENGE SKILLS

The following advanced skills are for those who have mastered the basic skills. The challenge skills are recommended for those who want to improve their footwork.

TOE TAPS

With the ball stationary on the ground, hop onto your right foot and tap the top of the ball with the toes of your left foot. Then, hop onto your left foot and tap the top of the ball with the toes of your right foot. Continue this pattern. How fast can you go?

Toe taps

SIDE TO SIDE

With the ball between your feet, move the ball from side to side with the insteps of your feet while taking small hops.

Side to side

PULL BACK/REVERSE DIRECTION

Place your foot on top of the ball. Pull your foot back so that the ball rolls along the bottom of your foot from back to front. This will pull the ball back so that you can make a quick turn to dribble or pass in the opposite direction.

Pull back/Reverse direction

BACKSPIN/CATCH

Position your toes on the top of the ball to start. In a single motion, roll your toes backward and down along the ball to roll the ball back onto your toes.

Backspin/Catch

SCISSORS

Swing 1 foot around the ball. Then, swing your other foot around the ball in the opposite direction. Try again, switching the directions that you swing your feet.

Scissors

KNEE JUGGLE

Drop the ball onto your knee, softly bouncing it back up. Use the same knee or your other knee to bounce the ball. See how many times you can bounce the ball on your knees to keep it from hitting the ground.

Knee juggle

INSIDE FOOT JUGGLE

Hold up 1 of your feet, bending at the knee to angle the instep of your foot up. Drop the ball and bounce it back up with the instep of your foot. Use the same foot or the instep of your other foot to bounce the ball back up again before it hits the ground. How many times can you juggle the ball with the insides of your feet before it touches the ground?

Inside foot juggle

OUTSIDE FOOT JUGGLE

Drop the ball softly. Use the outside of 1 of your feet, angling your ankle down, to kick the ball back up. Repeat this with 1 or both of your feet. How long can you juggle the ball without it hitting the ground?

Outside foot juggle

TOE JUGGLE

Drop the ball slightly in front of you. Gently kick the ball back up with the top part of your foot. Continue this with 1 or both of your feet to juggle the ball without letting it hit the ground for as long as you can.

COMBINATION JUGGLE

Use a combination of your knees and the insides, outsides, and tops of your feet to keep the ball up for as long as you can.

Toe juggle

OFFENSIVE AND DEFENSIVE SKILLS

Quick, fast, agile footwork is an essential component of a soccer game. Practice footwork skills to improve offensive and defensive play.

OFFENSIVE SKILLS

FAKE

- Look 1 direction, but pass or move the ball in another direction.
- Stay on the balls of your feet.
- Move quickly.

SKILL	PROGRESSING	COMPETENT	PROFICIENT
fake	1 of the elements	2 out of 3 elements	all elements

GIVE AND GO

The purpose of the give and go in a soccer game is for you to pass the ball to a teammate and quickly relocate so that you can receive a pass.

- Pass the ball to a teammate.
- Move quickly to relocate and support your offense.
- Indicate (call out) that you are ready and open to receive the ball.
- Receive the ball.

SKILL	PROGRESSING	COMPETENT	PROFICIENT
give and go	1 or 2 of the elements	3 out of 4 elements	all elements

THROW-IN

The only time that a player other than a goalie can use their hands to touch the ball in a game is to perform a throw-in. A throw-in occurs when the ball goes out of bounds on either of the long sides of the field. The team that sends the ball out of bounds loses possession of the ball. The other team gains control of the ball and throws it in from the point where it went out of bounds.

- Hold the ball in front of your body with both hands.
- Lift the ball over and behind your head.
- Step forward and throw the ball to a teammate. You cannot be the first person to touch the ball after you throw it in; or, you cannot throw-in to yourself.
- Follow through toward your target.
- Both of your feet must remain on the ground when you complete a throw-in. You can drag your back foot, but you cannot hop.

SKILL	PROGRESSING	COMPETENT	PROFICIENT
throw-in	1 or 2 of the elements	3 or 4 out of 5 elements	all elements

DEFENSIVE SKILLS

DEFENSIVE READY POSITION

The ready position allows a player to move quickly in any direction. It is used for both offense and defense.

- Bend your knees to keep your body low.
- Stand with your feet shoulder-width apart.
- Keep your head up and your weight on the balls of your feet.
- Hold your arms extended out above waist height.
- Be ready to move and react quickly.
- Anticipate direction.

SKILL	PROGRESSING	COMPETENT	PROFICIENT
defensive ready position	1, 2, or 3 of the elements	4 or 5 out of 6 elements	all elements met

DEFENSIVE SLIDES

The purpose of the defensive slides in soccer is to keep up with your opponent and to legally take the ball or legally disrupt the opponent's pass or shot.

- Place your weight on the balls of your feet.
- Slide to the side with quick steps.
- Do not cross your feet.
- Keep your knees bent.
- Square your hips so that they face your opponent.
- Hold your hands up at chest level.
- Keep your eyes on your opponent's waistline.
- Stay with your opponent.
- Anticipate and react quickly to your opponent's movements.

SKILL	PROGRESSING	COMPETENT	PROFICIENT
defensive slides	1, 2, 3, 4, or 5 of the elements	6, 7, or 8 out of 9 elements	all elements met

PRACTICING OFFENSIVE AND DEFENSIVE SKILLS

- Practice the **give and go** with a partner and a defender. Pass the ball, quickly relocate, and then receive the pass, avoiding the defender.
- Practice the **fake** independently. Set up a cone as a decoy. Fake the pass toward the cone, and then pass to your partner. Practice until you feel comfortable with the movement.
- Practice the **fake** with a partner defending you. Dribble, fake, and then move in another direction to get around the defensive player. Practice until you feel comfortable with the fake.
- Practice the **defensive slides** with a partner. As your partner dribbles, defensive slide to try to prevent the player from making a successful pass or shot. Practice until you feel comfortable with the defensive slide.

SOCCER GAME

ABOUT THE GAME
- To begin, 2 opposing teams of 11 players each including a goalie are established.
- All players must wear shin guards, socks that cover their shin guards, and appropriate cleats.
- The game is played on a rectangular grass or turf field.
- A goal is located at each end of the field.
- The object of the game is to move the ball down the field by passing or dribbling with your feet and to score by getting the ball into your opponent's goal.
- A game is divided into 45-minute halves.
- A goal is worth 1 point.
- The team with the most points at the end of the second half wins.

PLAYING THE GAME
- The game begins with a coin toss made by a referee at midfield.
- The team that possesses the ball is on offense and the other team is on defense.
- The first player to touch the ball at kickoff can only touch the ball once. They must kick the ball or pass it to another player who can dribble, pass, or kick the ball.
- No players except for the goalies or a player who is performing a throw-in can touch the ball with their hands. The entire arm counts as a hand in soccer, which means that a player cannot touch the ball anywhere from their fingertips to their upper arm.
- It is legal to use any body part other than a hand to contact the ball.
- If a player illegally uses their hands, which is referred to as a handball, the ball is turned over to the opposing team.
- The players on defense try to intercept, or take away, the ball from the offensive team to gain possession of the ball.

GAME APPLICATION FOR A 5 AGAINST 5 MODIFIED SOCCER GAME

Tips for Game Time Activity:
- Refer to the corresponding lesson for skills, procedures, and safety.
- Warm up and cool down.
- Find a safe space to exercise.
- Play well with others.

You will need ten players, a playing field, and an adult to supervise the game, and chart.

5 AGAINST 5 MODIFIED SOCCER GAME

MATERIALS	ORGANIZATION	SAFETY AND MORE

One soccer ball per game
 	
Two goals per game
 	
Soccer disc cones can be used for goals and dividing the playing field.
	2 teams:
	  1. one goalie
	  2. one defense player
	  3. two frontline players (offense)
	
	Example:
	^^^^^^^^^^^^^^^^^^^^
	^ 2 4 | 4 2 ^
	1 1
	^ 3 5 | 5 3 ^
	^^^^^^^^^^^^^^^^^^^^
	
	At the signal, switch positions. Goalie and defense players move to the front line.
	Frontline players move to either goalie or defense positions.
	Rotate until all players experience playing goalie.
		Establish boundaries.
		Establish the perimeters the five players adhere to:
		The goalie remains in goalie area.
		The defenders are allowed to midfield.
		Frontline players are allowed from ¾ of the way back on their side to the opposing goal.
		(Establishing perimeters for the positions encourages teamwork and passing.)
		Suggested rules:
		No kicking-dribble, pass, and trap only.
		For out-of-bounds balls, a player from the opposing team throws the ball back into play.
		Goalies throw in after a score.
		Goalie and players throwing the ball back in-bounds may use their hands.

DEMONSTRATE POSITIVE GAME BEHAVIOR

- Follow all game rules.
- Do not conduct any fouls against another player (do not make illegal physical contact) and do not exhibit any unsportsmanlike behavior.
    - Fouls and unsportsmanlike behavior can result in a free kick, a yellow card warning, or a red card ejection from the game for the offending player.
- Be supportive and encouraging to your teammates.
- Treat your opponents with respect.

SKILL	PROGRESSING	COMPETENT	PROFICIENT
game behavior	1 or 2 of the elements	3 out of 4 elements	all elements met

RATE YOUR ENJOYMENT OF THE SOCCER ACTIVITY THAT YOU ENJOYED MOST

On a scale from 1 to 4, where 1 is not enjoyable and 4 is very enjoyable, rate this activity.

1	It was not enjoyable, and I will not participate again.
2	It was not enjoyable, but I will participate again for exercise.
3	It was enjoyable, and I will play again.
4	It was very enjoyable, and I will initiate future games.

RESEARCH INTEGRATION

1. Attend a soccer game or watch a soccer game on television. It can be men's, women's, or co-ed soccer at any level—youth, high school, college, or professional. Identify the soccer skills you have learned that are used by the players throughout the game.

HEALTH INTEGRATION

1. Count your pulse after practicing skills and after playing in a game to determine if you are exercising in your personal target heart rate zone. Predict and then compare the difference between your heart rate after playing in the goalie position and your heart rate after playing in a running, or field, position. Apply the results to your overall fitness plan. Many people choose to complete aerobic workouts by playing in fast-paced games like soccer.

2. Have a discussion about the protective gear that is worn by a soccer player and why they wear this gear.

VOLLEYBALL

The official game of volleyball is played by 2 teams of 6 players on an indoor volleyball court. Another popular version of volleyball is beach volleyball, which is played by 2 teams of 2 to 6 players on a sand surface. The object of the game is to strike a ball over a net onto the ground so that the opposing team cannot return it.

You may play volleyball as a competitive sport or as an opportunity for social play. Casual games of volleyball can be played by as few as 2 players and set up in a yard, park, beach, or gym.

The purpose of this lesson is for you to participate in aerobic exercise and in skill-building activities. When you play volleyball, be sure to follow the rules, communicate with teammates in a positive and effective manner, and exhibit appropriate behavior with your team and the opposing team.

⚠️ **CAUTION: Do not overinflate the ball.**

VOLLEYBALL SKILLS

The following striking skills will not only help to improve your volleyball game, but they may also enhance skills used in other sports and activities.

READY POSITION

The ready position will enable you to react quickly.

- Stand with your legs shoulder-width apart.
- Balance on the balls of your feet.
- Bend your knees slightly.
- Hold your shoulders rounded and slightly forward.
- Hold your arms in front of you and ready to react.

SKILL	PROGRESSING	COMPETENT	PROFICIENT
ready position	1 or 2 of the elements	3 or 4 out of 5 elements	all elements met

FOREARM GRIP

Try both of the following grips to decide which works better for you.

1. Right-handed players: Make a fist with your left hand, wrap the fingers of your right hand around your left hand, and line up your thumbs side by side on top. Left-handed players: Make a fist with your right hand, wrap the fingers of your left hand around your right hand, and line up your thumbs side by side on top.

2. Place 1 hand out flat with your palm up. Place the other hand underneath with the palm up. Curl your thumbs until they are next to each other, centered, and pointing down.

FOREARM PASS (BUMP)

- Stand in the ready position.
- Use the correct grip.
- Contact the ball with your forearm platform.
- Follow through toward your target.

SKILL	PROGRESSING	COMPETENT	PROFICIENT
forearm pass	1 or 2 of the elements	3 out of 4 elements	all elements met

FOREARM PASS (BUMP) PRACTICE

- Forearm pass and catch: Toss the ball to yourself to begin. Pass it back up with your forearm platform, reaching toward your target and catching it. Do not allow your swing to be out of control.
- Forearm pass: Toss the ball to yourself to begin, then continue to pass it. How many times can you pass in a row?
- Wall forearm passes: Toss the ball to yourself to begin, then pass it against a wall. How many times can you pass in a row?
- Partner wall forearm passes: Take turns passing against a wall with a partner.
- Partner toss, forearm pass, and catch: Toss the ball to your partner. Your partner passes it back to you. You catch it. Switch roles.
- Partner forearm passes: How many times can you pass back and forth with a partner?

OVERHAND PASS (SET)

- Stand in the ready position.
- Hold your hands level with your forehead with your elbows bent. Form the size and shape of the ball with your fingers and thumbs.
- Contact the ball with your finger pads, not tips.
- Use a soft touch near your forehead and extend your elbows to push the ball up into the air.

SKILL	PROGRESSING	COMPETENT	PROFICIENT
overhand pass	1 or 2 of the elements	3 out of 4 elements	all elements met

OVERHAND PASS (SET) PRACTICE

- Set and catch: Toss the ball to yourself to begin, set it back up with your finger pads, and catch it.
- Set: Toss the ball to yourself to begin, then continue to set it. How many times can you set in a row?
- Wall sets: Toss the ball to yourself to begin, then set it against a wall. How many times can you set in a row?
- Partner wall sets: Take turns setting against a wall with a partner.
- Partner toss, set, and catch: Toss the ball to your partner. Your partner sets it back to you. You catch it. Switch roles.
- Partner sets: How many times can you set back and forth with a partner?

UNDERHAND SERVE

- Put your non-dominant foot forward.
- Hold the ball on the palm of your non-dominant hand. Position that arm across your body at waist height.
- Make a fist with your striking hand.
- Bring your striking arm back and then forward, striking the ball with the heel of your hand.
- Shift your weight to your front foot.
- Serve successfully 70 percent of the time.

SKILL	PROGRESSING	COMPETENT	PROFICIENT
underhand serve	1 or 2 of the elements	4 or 5 out of 6 elements	all elements met

UNDERHAND SERVE PRACTICE

- Wall serves: Practice serving toward a wall.
- Partner serves: Serve to a partner and volley back and forth using the set and bump skills.

CHALLENGING VOLLEYBALL SKILLS

The following advanced skills are for students who have mastered the basic skills. The challenge level is recommended if you want to further explore the volleyball activity.

OVERHAND SERVE

- Put your non-dominant foot forward.
- Turn the non-dominant side of your body slightly toward the net or target.
- Hold the ball in your non-dominant hand.
- Bend your striking arm with your hand cupped near your ear.
- Contact: Toss the ball 2 to 3 feet in the air, placing your weight on your back foot. Shift your weight to your front foot as you strike the ball approximately 12 inches above your head.
- Follow through in the direction of the ball.

SKILL	PROGRESSING	COMPETENT	PROFICIENT
overhand serve	1 or 2 of the elements	3, 4, or 5 out of 6 elements	all elements met

OVERHAND SERVE PRACTICE

- Wall serves: Practice serving toward a wall.
- Partner serves: Serve to a partner and volley back and forth using the set and bump skills.

OVERHAND HITTING (SPIKE)

1 player: Follow the overhand serve techniques.

2 players: A teammate hits the ball up high near the net.

- As a hitter, approach from behind using a 4-step approach.
- Place your dominant foot forward.
- Step forward with your non-dominant foot, then quick step with your dominant then non-dominant foot. For example, if you are right-handed, you would start with your right foot forward, step left, then right, then left.
- Begin with your arms at waist height in front of your body. Swing them backward then forward until both of your arms are reaching high with your dominant arm slightly forward.
- Strike the ball with the fleshy part of your dominant hand.
- Follow through, facing the direction in which you want the ball to go.

SKILL	PROGRESSING	COMPETENT	PROFICIENT
overhand hit (spike)	1 or 2 of the elements	3, 4, or 5 out of 6 elements	all elements met

EXTENSION

If you have an available outdoor wall or garage door and permission from your parent or guardian, you can place a horizontal line of tape or chalk mark 7 feet 4½ inches from the ground to represent the height of a net. Begin approximately 10 feet back and practice the underhand and overhand serves. When you are successful, move back farther. Continue this until you are able to serve from 30 feet back, which is the official serving distance.

VOLLEYBALL GAMES

REGULATION VOLLEYBALL GAME

- There are 6 people on a team: 3 front row players and 3 back row players.
- Players rotate in order to reach the serving position.
- The players from the same team all rotate 1 position clockwise when it is their team's turn to serve.
- The serving position is behind the end line. Most players will serve from the right end line; however, for left-handed servers, you may serve from anywhere behind the end line.
- The objective is to serve the ball across the net into the opponent's court within the boundaries. The ball can hit the net on the way over and still be playable.
- Each team is allowed 3 hits, but no player can hit the ball twice in a row.
- A player may not make contact with any part of the net.
- A ball contacting the net is considered playable.

SCORING

- The serve starts the game.
- When the serving team wins the rally, a point is scored.
- If the rally is won by the non-serving team, that team gets a point and a chance to serve.
- The first team to score 25 points and be ahead by at least 2 points wins the game.
- A match consists of either winning 2 out of 3 games or 3 out of 5 games.

GAME APPLICATION FOR A MODIFIED VOLLEYBALL GAME

Tips for Game Time Activity:
- Refer to the corresponding lesson for skills, procedures, and safety.
- Warm up and cool down.
- Find a safe space to exercise.
- Play well with others.

You will need twelve or more players and an adult to supervise this game.

MODIFIED VOLLEYBALL GAME

MATERIALS	ORGANIZATION	SAFETY AND MORE
| One volleyball. A net, jump rope, or disc cones can be used to divide the playing area. | Divide players into two teams. Arrange students so that three players are in the front row and three players are in the back row.<br><br>```
        X   X | X   X (Server)
        X   X | X   X
(Server) X   X | X   X
```<br><br>The player in serve position underhand serves 10 feet in front of the end line.<br>The server has two chances to get the serve in-bounds and over the net.<br>Return the ball by forearm passing or setting.<br>Rotate clockwise on a side-out. | Players should "call out" if they are attempting to hit the ball to avoid collisions.<br>3 players may strike the ball before it goes over the net.<br>A player cannot strike the ball two times in a row.<br>A side-out is when the serving team misses a point. |

DEMONSTRATE POSITIVE GAME BEHAVIOR

- Follow the rules.
- Call out when you are attempting to strike the ball to avoid collisions.
- Be supportive and encouraging to your teammates.
- Treat your opponents with respect.

SKILL	PROGRESSING	COMPETENT	PROFICIENT
game behavior	1 or 2 of the elements	3 out of 4 elements	all elements met
```

RATE YOUR ENJOYMENT OF VOLLEYBALL

On a scale from 1 to 4, where 1 is not enjoyable and 4 is very enjoyable, rate this activity.

1	It was not enjoyable, and I will not participate again.
2	It was not enjoyable, but I will participate again for exercise.
3	It was enjoyable, and I will play again.
4	It was very enjoyable, and I will initiate future games.

RESEARCH INTEGRATION

1. Attend a volleyball game or watch a volleyball game on television and compare the skills you have practiced for the game of volleyball with the skills the players use.

HEALTH INTEGRATION

Count your pulse to determine if you are exercising in your personal target heart rate zone. Count your pulse after practicing skills and after playing in a game. Apply the results to your overall fitness plan.

WIFFLE® BALL

Similar to baseball, Wiffle® ball is a game that uses a lightweight ball and a plastic bat. Playing Wiffle® ball helps you improve hand-eye-object coordination, tracking, and timing.

⚠ **CAUTION:** Make sure that nobody is close to you before you swing the bat. Do not walk into the path of another person who is swinging a bat. Do not throw the bat.

WIFFLE® BALL SKILLS
STRIKING AND BASE-RUNNING SKILLS
GRIP AND STANCE
GRIP

- If you are right-handed, wrap your left hand below your right hand at the bottom of the bat. If you are left-handed, wrap your right hand below your left hand at the bottom of the bat.
  - Smaller batters may benefit from choking up on the bat, or holding the bat a little higher up from the base of the handle.
- Your hands should be touching each other.

STANCE

- Position your body perpendicular to the plate.
- Bending your knees slightly, place your feet so that they are shoulder-width apart. Your hips, knees, and shoulders should be squared. This stance should be comfortable.
- Once your feet are inside the batter's box, face your shoulder toward the pitcher and point the tip of the bat up toward the sky. If you are right-handed, face your left shoulder toward the pitcher. If you are left-handed, face your right shoulder toward the pitcher.

SKILL	PROGRESSING	COMPETENT	PROFICIENT
grip and stance	1 or 2 of the elements	3 or 4 out of 5 elements	all elements met

STRIKING A BALL FROM A PITCH

- Check your position to see if your swing will cross over the plate. Stand in the batter's box and touch the opposite side of the plate with the bat. Adjust your stance if necessary.
- While in the correct position, practice swinging all the way through, keeping the bat level with the ground and twisting your body as you hit the ball.

- The whole swing should be in your hips. Try to get in the habit of twisting your whole body rather than just swinging your arms.
- Take a small step toward the pitcher as they throw the ball. Rotate your hips toward the pitcher, moving your hands through the strike zone and over the plate. Watch the ball as it comes toward you and over the plate before you hit it into the outfield.
- After swinging the bat, face your hips toward the pitcher. Pivot your back foot, but do not let it come off the ground.
- During a game, after you hit the ball, drop the bat to the ground and run to first base.

SKILL	PROGRESSING	COMPETENT	PROFICIENT
striking	1 or 2 of the elements	3 or 4 out of 5 elements	all elements met

BASE RUNNING

- Drop the bat to the ground after you hit the ball.
- Immediately sprint as fast as you can to first base.
- Run on and through the base.

SKILL	PROGRESSING	COMPETENT	PROFICIENT
base running	1 of the elements	2 out of 3 elements	all elements met

THROWING, CATCHING, AND FIELDING SKILLS

OVERHAND THROW

An overhand throw can be used by the field players and the pitcher.

- Take a first step, such as a hop or shuffle step, toward your target.
- Bring your throwing arm back, up, and around.
- Step with your opposite foot.
- Rotate your hips as you twist with your throw.
- Release the ball high in your throw, when your throwing arm is in an L shape near your ear.
- Follow through your throw to make it accurate.

SKILL	PROGRESSING	COMPETENT	PROFICIENT
overhand throw	1, 2, or 3 of the elements	4 or 5 out of 6 elements	all elements met

CATCHING

- Track the ball with your eyes.
- Step toward your target.
- Extend your hands to the level of the ball.
- Give with the ball (pull it slightly toward you) as it hits your hands for a soft catch.

SKILL	PROGRESSING	COMPETENT	PROFICIENT
catching	1 or 2 of the elements	3 out of 4 elements	all elements met

FIELDING GROUND BALLS

- Keep your body low and ready.
- Scoop up the ball as it rolls.
- Look to your target.
- Throw accurately to your target.

SKILL	PROGRESSING	COMPETENT	PROFICIENT
fielding	1 or 2 of the elements	3 out of 4 elements	all elements met

SKILL PRACTICE

THROW AND CATCH

- Throw and catch a ball against a wall.
- Throw and catch a ball with a partner.
- Throw and catch a ball with a partner while moving.

BATTING FOR DISTANCE

- As a batter, hit a pitch that is thrown to you by a partner.
- The pitcher will place a disc cone where the ball landed, marking the distance it traveled.
- Hit another pitch, trying to increase the distance you hit the ball from your last hit.
- Take turns batting and pitching with your partner.

BATTING FOR DIRECTION

- Place disc cones in the right, left, and center field.
- Before you bat, call out the direction in which your hit will go: right field, left field, or center field.
- Hit a pitch from your partner in the determined direction.
- Take turns batting and pitching with your partner.

BATTING FOR FORCE

- Before you bat, call out what the force of your hit will be—soft, medium, or hard.
- Hit a pitch from your partner with the force that you called out.
- Take turns batting and pitching with your partner.

3 PLAYERS PRACTICE GAME: STRIKING, FIELDING, AND BASE RUNNING

- Set up a playing field with first base, second base, third base, home base, and a pitching mound.
- Choose 1 player to be the pitcher, 1 player to be the batter, and the remaining players to be outfielders.
- If you are the pitcher, pitch the ball to the batter until the batter gets a hit. Retrieve the ball and run to home base before the batter gets there.
- If you are the batter, run the bases after you hit the ball. If the pitcher gets to home base before you, you are out.
- If you are an outfielder, retrieve the ball and give it back to the pitcher before the batter gets to home base.
- Take turns in the different positions.

WIFFLE® BALL GAME

- Wiffle® ball teams can range from being made up of 1 to 10 players.
- The pitcher throws 3 balls to each batter, and the batter must attempt to hit them.
- If you fail to hit the ball within 3 pitches, you strike out.
- Do not run to the next base until the batter hits the ball.
- If you hit the ball into the single zone, you advance 1 base. If you hit the ball into the double zone, you advance 2 bases. If you hit the ball past the triple zone, you get a home run.
- Every player who makes it around the bases scores a run for their team.
- You are out if the batted ball is caught in the air, a fielder tags you when you are running to a base, or the ball is fielded and thrown to a base before you get there.
- An inning is over when all the batters have had their turns or if 3 batters strike out.
- At the end of the game, the team with the most runs is the winner. Games may last a set time or last a set number of innings.

GAME NOTES

1. A **foul ball** is a ball that the batter hits outside of the baseline. The batter gets another pitch if this happens. There are unlimited foul balls unless a defensive player catches a fly ball.
2. The field is split up into different **zones**. The suggested sizes of these zones are given below, but the zones can be adjusted according to your play area.
   - The single zone is 24 feet from home base.
   - The double zone is 20 feet from the single zone.
   - The triple zone is 20 feet from the double zone.
   - The home run zone is 20 feet from the triple zone.

3. A **strike** occurs when the batter swings and misses the ball. The batter is out after 3 strikes.
4. A **fly ball** is a ball that is hit up in the air. Fly balls are often caught to strike a player out.
5. The **pitcher** is the defensive player who stands on the pitching mound and pitches (throws) the ball to the batter.

6. The **catcher** is the defensive player who plays behind home base. The catcher returns the ball to the pitcher and tags players out at home base.

7. An **outfielder** is a defensive player who plays behind the baseline to retrieve the ball when it is hit far.

8. A **baseman** is a defensive player who plays on first, second, or third base. The 3 basemen should stand near their bases. To prevent colliding with a runner, the basemen should not stand on their bases; however, the basemen can touch their bases to strike a runner out.

RATE YOUR ENJOYMENT OF WIFFLE® BALL

On a scale from 1 to 4, where 1 is not enjoyable and 4 is very enjoyable, rate this activity.

1	It was not enjoyable, and I will not participate again.
2	It was not enjoyable, but I will participate again for exercise.
3	It was enjoyable, and I will play again.
4	It was very enjoyable, and I will initiate future games.

RESEARCH INTEGRATION

1. Attend a baseball game or watch a baseball game on television and compare the skills that you have practiced for the game of Wiffle® ball with the skills that the baseball players use.

HEALTH INTEGRATION

Count your pulse after practicing Wiffle® ball skills and after playing in a Wiffle® ball game to determine if you are exercising in your personal target heart rate zone. Apply the results to your overall fitness plan. Often, when you are playing in games that require you to take turns, you may find that your pulse rate is not in your aerobic target zone. If that is the case for you, remember that you still need to get your aerobic exercise in for the week. Enjoy the game and count it toward your 60 minutes per day of being active.

GRADE 7
PE EQUIPMENT KIT

SAFETY ALERT!

Before you exercise, make sure that you are properly warmed up and have enough room to perform each activity. Wear proper equipment and follow activity-specific safety rules. Stay hydrated and take breaks as needed. Exercise only if you are healthy, and always exercise at your own pace. If an exercise starts to hurt, if you feel dizzy, or if you feel light-headed, stop the exercise completely and get help. Upon completion of any workout, cool down and stretch.

WARM-UP AND COOL-DOWN

⚠ **CAUTION: Stretching should not be painful; ease up if stretching hurts. See the Flexibility section of your PE Manual for more information.**

WARM-UP

The purpose of a warm-up is to gradually increase heart rate, breathing rate, body temperature, and muscle temperature. Warming up prior to exercising increases circulation and blood flow to your muscles. When your muscles are warmed up, their performance—such as in the areas of strength and speed—is enhanced and risk of injury is decreased.

Before you begin any workout, you should always warm up. Getting your heart and muscles prepared for exercise is important. There are numerous ways to get your body ready to participate in physical activity. **The Flexibility section of your PE Manual includes a variety of dynamic and static stretches for each major body part that will help you increase your flexibility.**

Elements of a Warm-Up

1. **Low-intensity cardio**: Walk, slow jog, or slow swim for 5 to 10 minutes to increase your heart rate, breathing rate, and body temperature before your workout.
2. **Dynamic stretch**: Perform a repeated motion—such as kicks, high knees, lunges, or arm circles—that will loosen up your joints and prepare your muscles for the exercise that you are about to do. Perform each dynamic stretch for at least 30 seconds.
3. **Static stretch**: Stretch your muscles slowly and hold each stretch for 20 to 30 seconds without bouncing in order to lengthen your muscles and increase your flexibility. Some important areas to stretch as a part of your warm-up are your neck, sides, shoulders, triceps, back, hamstrings, quadriceps, and groin.

Example + + = EFFECTIVE WARM-UP

PERSONAL WARM-UP ACTIVITY

1. Select an exercise activity to participate in.
2. Design your personal warm-up plan for the activity that you selected. Any dynamic and static stretches that you choose to complete should be specific to the exercise activity that you chose.
3. Have a trusted adult or friend assess your stretches to make sure that you are using proper form.
4. Explain how the warm-up will decrease your risk of injury for this activity. _____

Procedure	Enter your personal warm-up regimen below.
1. **Low-intensity cardiovascular exercise:** Exercise for 5 to 10 minutes.	
2. **Dynamic stretches:** Perform dynamic stretches specifically for the selected activity.	
3. **Static stretches:** Perform static stretches specifically for the selected activity.	

COOL-DOWN

After you have finished your workout, exercise, or activity, it is imperative that your body returns to its normal state. You want to avoid stopping immediately and sitting down **unless you are in pain, dizzy, or injured**. Be sure to slow your heart rate and breathing rate back to or slightly above their resting rates. There are several ways to do this. You can simply walk or slow down your exercise for a few minutes, or you can find your own way to slow your body back down. You also may want to incorporate static stretches to increase flexibility and to avoid your muscles tightening. **The Flexibility section of your PE Manual includes a variety of static stretches for each major body part.** Always keep hydrated by drinking water before, during, and after exercise.

Elements of a Cool-Down

1. **Slow down**: Walk or gradually slow down your exercise—such as returning to a slow swim if you are swimming—until your heart rate, breathing rate, and body temperature are back to normal.
2. **Static stretch**: Stretch your muscles slowly and hold each stretch for 20 to 30 seconds without bouncing in order to lengthen your muscles and increase flexibility. Some important areas to stretch as part of your cool-down are your neck, sides, shoulders, triceps, back, hamstrings, quadriceps, and groin.

WALK + STATIC STRETCHES = EFFECTIVE COOL-DOWN

Design your personal cool-down plan. You can perform the same cool-down each time you finish a physical activity or you can change each time in order to reflect the exercise activity, such as by slowing your pedaling if you are biking.

Procedure	Enter your personal cool-down regimen below.
1. **Slow down:** Perform this slowed activity for 5 to 10 minutes.	
2. **Static stretches:** Perform several lower-body and upper-body stretches.	

AEROBIC EXERCISE

Aerobic exercise—also referred to as cardio or cardiovascular exercise—is any exercise that is done in your target heart rate zone and is performed for an extended period. Aerobic exercise is important for strengthening your heart muscle. The stronger your heart muscle, the longer you can perform physical activity before getting tired. Being able to perform physical activity without tiring is often referred to as being in shape.

The purpose of this lesson is to encourage you to do an aerobic workout for at least 30 minutes 3 to 5 days per week in order to experience health benefits.

⚠ **CAUTION: Wear proper equipment and follow activity-specific safety rules.**

AEROBIC EXERCISE

BENEFITS OF AEROBIC EXERCISE

- strengthens your heart and lung functions
- lowers blood pressure
- controls sugar in your blood
- burns calories and fat
- increases your energy
- reduces stress
- decreases your risk of cardiovascular diseases
- increases mental ability

After reviewing the benefits of aerobic exercise, discuss them with a trusted adult. Ask for help setting up an aerobic exercise program that works for you.

There are a variety of exercises to choose from. Choose aerobic exercises that will fit into your lifestyle and that you enjoy. Limit excuses and make a commitment to exercise!

Write down an excuse that you have used to avoid aerobic exercise and how you overcame or will overcome that obstacle.

My Excuse for Not Exercising	What I Did to Overcome That Excuse

TYPES OF AEROBIC EXERCISE

Sports: Examples include soccer, basketball, volleyball, swimming, hockey, lacrosse, tennis, badminton, pickleball, handball, gymnastics, dance, martial arts, wrestling, track and field, and so on.

Outdoor pursuits: Examples include walking, jogging, biking, canoeing, kayaking, golfing, fly fishing, hiking, rock climbing, horseback riding, skiing, and so on.

Fitness gyms: Find a gym that is convenient for you to attend where you can complete circuit exercises, use aerobic machines, take classes, and more.

Stationary exercise equipment: Examples include using a jump rope, treadmill, elliptical trainer, bike, mini trampoline, and so on.

Exercise apps or videos: Use a workout tutorial on an app, website, video, or other digital source.

Your own sequence workouts: You can also design your own workout sequences by following the steps below.

- Create your personal aerobic workout routines by blending activities that involve basic locomotor skills such as jogging in place, jumping jacks, high knees, and so on.
- Design the intensity and duration of the exercise according to your level of fitness.
- Perform your personal routine for some or all your aerobic workouts.

SAMPLE WORKOUT

The following is a sample workout that you can complete on your own and that does not require equipment. When you are beginning any exercise program, begin with workouts that match your fitness level and then build accordingly. You want to feel refreshed after each exercise session, not exhausted. Use your pulse rate to monitor aerobic workouts.

Each exercise is performed for 30 seconds: 10 seconds using a light force and slow pace, 10 seconds using a moderate force and moderate pace, and 10 seconds using a strong force and fast pace.

Practice each of the following exercises, concentrating on proper form, prior to engaging in a workout.

JUMPING JACKS:

Jump out so that your feet are apart and your arms are in a V above your head; then, jump in so that your feet are together and your arms are down by your sides. Continue this movement pattern.

MARCH:

Walk, lifting your knees to waist height and swinging your arms.

HIGH KNEES:

Alternate lifting your knees to waist height.

VERTICAL JUMPS:

Bend your knees and jump up. Swing your arms behind you at the start of the jump. Swing your arms forward and up while you are jumping.

BURPEES:

Stand with your feet shoulder-width apart. Bend your knees and place your hands on the floor. Extend your legs back so that you are in a push-up position. Return to the bent-knee position. Return to standing. Repeat this movement pattern.

FLOOR RUNS:

From a push-up position, run your legs in toward your chest and then back out.

Jumping jacks

March

High knees

Vertical jumps

Burpees

Floor runs

JOGGING IN PLACE:

Run slowly in place.

SIDE SLIDES:

Step to the side with your right foot. Bring your left foot to your right foot in a step-together motion. Repeat this to the left.

REAR KICKS:

Alternate lifting the heels of your feet toward your upper thighs. Do not let your feet make contact with your body.

KNEE TUCKS:

While standing, jump up and tuck your knees. Try to touch your knees with your extended hands. Gently land with your knees slightly bent.

¼-SQUAT JUMPS:

With your legs apart, lower your body by bending your knees and hips until your hips are even with your knees. Jump to the right, making a quarter turn and landing gently in a squat position. Continue until you are back to the starting position. Repeat the exercise to the left. For a challenge, try half turns and full turns.

CARIOCAS (GRAPEVINE):

Step to the side with your right foot and then cross your left foot in front of your right foot. Uncross your right foot and step to the right and then cross your left foot behind your right foot. Repeat this step-cross-step-cross movement.

Rest by walking slowly for 30 seconds. Hydrate as necessary.

Repeat all of the exercises 3 more times for a 24-minute aerobic workout.

EXTENSION: Use the above information to create a workout that you would enjoy.

Jogging in place

Side slides

Rear kicks

Knee tucks

¼-squat jumps

Cariocas (grapevine)

Copyright 2024 © Lincoln Learning Solutions. All rights reserved.

Record at least 3 aerobic exercise sessions that you participated in outside of PE class for 1 week. Record the time of each session.

An exercise can be any of the following.

1. a sport-related game
2. an outdoor pursuit
3. a self-created workout routine set to music

	Monday	Tuesday	Wednesday	Thursday	Friday	Saturday	Sunday
Exercise							
Time							
Exercise Heartrate							

List at least 1 response to each the following questions about aerobic exercise.

Question	Response
What positive emotional response did you experience by participating in aerobic exercise?	
What aerobic exercise activity did you enjoy the most?	
Why would the enjoyment of your favorite aerobic exercise activity lead to a lifetime of fitness for you?	

RESEARCH INTEGRATION

Research Newton's laws of motion and their connection to movement. How does the sample workout apply Newton's second law of motion?

HEALTH INTEGRATION

Use available technology to monitor your pulse rate and workout intensity. Apply the results to your overall fitness plan.

DANCE

Dancing is an exercise option for aerobic workout, for competition, or just for fun. You can dance on your own or with others. Dancing is expressing yourself through repeated patterns of movement which are usually set to music. Some forms of dance include creative, tap, ballet, hip-hop, modern, folk, square, jazz, line, Latin, ballroom, and social.

The purpose of this lesson is for you to perform basic locomotor movements using common dance concepts in rhythmic patterns to create your own dance for aerobic exercise.

PERSONAL DANCE ROUTINE

COMMON CONCEPTS OF DANCE TO USE FOR YOUR PERSONAL DANCE

- The concept of space includes the following.
    - high, medium, or low **levels**
    - forward, backward, right, or left **directions**
    - curved, zigzag, straight, circle, or square **pathways**
- The concept of time includes the following.
    - slow, medium, or fast **speeds**
    - a pattern for **rhythm**
- The concept of force includes the following.
    - applying light, moderate, or strong **weights**

CREATE A DANCE

Start with the 3 dance steps below. Then, complete the routine by adding your own dance steps. Set your dance to music.

1. Learn a sidestep.
    - Step to the right with your right foot.
    - Bring your left foot in to meet your right foot.
    - Touch your left toes to the floor with a light force, but do not put weight on them.
    - Repeat this to the left.

    Sidestep

2. Learn a step-hop.
    - Step out to the right side with your right foot.
    - Bring your left foot in and simultaneously jump with a medium force.
    - Land with both feet together.
    - As you land, clap your hands.
    - Repeat this to the left.

    Step-hop

3. Combine the sidestep and step-hop for a double step (step together, step-hop, clap).
    - Step to the right with your right foot.
    - Bring your left foot in to meet your right foot.
    - Step out to the right side with your right foot.
    - Bring your left foot in and simultaneously jump, land, and clap.
    - Repeat this to the left.

Copyright 2024 © Lincoln Learning Solutions. All rights reserved.

4. Perform the double step 4 times.
5. Next, add your dance steps to complete the dance.
    - Choose locomotor skills to blend (slides, cariocas, turns, and so on).
    - Use your arms to accompany the footwork, for example: step, cross, step, clap.
    - Perform the skills at different levels.
    - Move in different directions.
    - Move in different pathways.
    - Move at slow, medium, and fast speeds.
    - Use light, moderate, and strong force to move your body.
    - Create a pattern.
    - Use an 8 count for each move.

Option: Dance with a partner or small group for a social experience.

RATE YOUR ENJOYMENT OF DANCE

On a scale from 1 to 4, where 1 is not enjoyable and 4 is very enjoyable, rate this activity.

1	It was not enjoyable, and I will not participate again.
2	It was not enjoyable, but I will participate again for exercise.
3	It was enjoyable, and I will dance again.
4	It was very enjoyable, and I will create more dances.

RESEARCH INTEGRATION

1. Research creative dance.
2. Join a dance class or dance to a dance video.
3. Join a dance from the USB if provided in your PE program.

HEALTH INTEGRATION

Count your pulse to determine if you are exercising in your personal target heart rate zone. Apply the results to your overall fitness plan. Many people choose to complete aerobic workouts through dance.

JUMP ROPE

Jumping rope is an exercise that meets components of both skill-related fitness and health-related fitness. It helps you develop coordination, balance, rhythm, agility, and timing. Jumping rope is an efficient way to perform aerobic exercise and build muscular strength and endurance in your legs. It can be done daily and in a small space almost anywhere there is a safe, stable surface.

The purpose of this lesson is to provide you with the skills that you need to establish and implement your goal: to improve sport-related skills, to improve cardiovascular endurance, or both.

JUMP ROPE BASICS

FITTING THE JUMP ROPE TO YOUR HEIGHT

- Place a jump rope handle in each hand.
- Stand on the middle of the rope with 1 foot.
- Move the handles straight up, making sure that the rope is straight and pulled tight.
- The tops of the handles should reach close to your shoulders.

Fitting The Jump Rope To Your Height

ELEMENTS OF JUMP ROPE

- Keep your eyes forward.
- When you are turning the rope, keep your elbows near your sides, maintaining a 45-degree angle and making 2-inch circles with your wrists.
- Leave just enough space for the rope to pass under your feet when you jump.
- Stay on the balls of your feet.
- Land softly, keeping your knees slightly bent.

BASIC SKILLS

Practice each of the following exercises, concentrating on proper form, prior to engaging in a workout.

BASIC JUMP

- Pick up the rope. Holding a handle in each hand, rest the rope behind your feet. Stand on the balls of your feet. This is the ready position.
- Your hands should be just above the height of your waist.
- Swing the rope up and over your head.
- Jump over the rope when it approaches your toes.
- Continue as long as you can without stopping.

Basic jump

BACKWARD JUMP

- Begin with the rope in front of your feet.
- Swing the rope up and over your head.
- Jump over the rope when it approaches your feet.

Backward jump

SAMPLE OF A CARDIOVASCULAR CONDITIONING WORKOUT	SAMPLE OF A WORKOUT TO IMPROVE FOOTWORK SPEED
• basic jump 2 minutes • march or jog in place 30 seconds • basic jump 2 minutes • march or jog in place 30 seconds • backward jump 2 minutes • march or jog in place 30 seconds • backward jump 2 minutes • march or jog in place 30 seconds • repeat for a 20-minute workout	• basic jump 1 minute at a medium pace • basic jump 30 seconds at a fast pace • rest 30 seconds • back jump 1 minute at a medium pace • back jump 30 seconds at a fast pace • rest 30 seconds • basic jump 30 seconds at a medium pace • basic jump 1 minute at a fast pace • rest 30 seconds • back jump 30 seconds at a medium pace • back jump 1 minute at a fast pace • rest 30 seconds • repeat as needed
DESIGN YOUR PERSONAL CARDIOVASCULAR JUMP ROPE ROUTINE	**DESIGN YOUR PERSONAL FOOTWORK SPEED ROUTINE**

CHALLENGE SKILLS

The following challenges are for students who have mastered the basic jump rope skills. The challenge level is recommended for you if you want to improve agility and further explore jump rope activities.

JUMP ROPE CHALLENGE SKILLS

Practice each of the following exercises, concentrating on proper form, prior to engaging in a workout.

HOP ON 1 FOOT (SWITCH)

- Perform the basic jump on 1 foot instead of 2 feet.

Hop on 1 foot (switch)

SKIER

- With both feet together, hop from side to side while turning the rope.

Skier

CROSSOVERS

- After the rope moves over your head, cross the rope in front of you, jump, and uncross the rope.

Crossovers

FRONT KICKS

- Kick 1 foot forward as the rope passes under your feet with a skip-step between.
- Alternate kicks.

Front kicks

Design your personal jump rope routine by blending the basic skills and the challenge skills.

BLENDING: Perform a jump rope skill and transition smoothly to another jump rope skill without stopping between moves.

Check off the blended challenge skills that you have successfully completed at least 3 consecutive times.

_____ Blend forward consecutive jumps, crossovers, and skiers.

_____ Blend backward consecutive jumps, right-foot hops, and left-foot hops, all while backward turning.

_____ Blend forward consecutive jumps, front kicks, and skiers.

_____ Create your personal blend.

PARTNER SKILLS

Jump rope can have a social component. Individual jumping with a friend may motivate you and may make your workout more fun. Partner or long jump rope requires 2 or more participants.

PARTNER JUMP ROPE SKILLS

Practice each of the following exercises, concentrating on proper form, prior to engaging in a workout.

PARTNER CHAIN JUMP

- Make sure that each person has their own rope.
- Standing side by side, face forward in the ready position.
- Exchange inside handles with your partner; hold your handle with your outside hand and your partner's handle with your inside hand.
- Turn the rope over your head and jump together.
- Establish a rhythm with your partner. Jump rope together to that rhythm.

Partner chain jump

FACING YOUR PARTNER JUMP

- You will need 1 rope.
- Stand face-to-face with your partner.
- Have 1 person hold the rope.
- If you are holding the rope, stand facing your partner and turn the rope.
- If you are not holding the rope, stand facing your partner and jump rope with your partner as they turn the rope.
- No matter who is holding and turning the rope, establish a rhythm with your partner and jump rope together.

Facing your partner jump

SIDE BY SIDE JUMP

- You will need 1 rope.
- Stand beside your partner.
- Hold a handle of the rope with your outside hand. Your partner should hold the other handle in their outside hand.
- Jump rope together as you work together to turn the rope.

Side by side jump

List at least 1 response to each of the following questions about jumping rope.

Question	Response
What jump rope activity do you enjoy the most?	
Why did you enjoy the above-mentioned activity the most?	

RESEARCH INTEGRATION
Research competitive jump rope.

HEALTH INTEGRATION
Count your pulse to determine if you are exercising in your personal target heart rate zone.

STRENGTH BUILDING

Skeletal muscles are soft tissues that are attached to bones and are responsible for moving the body. Your body is made up of over 600 muscles. Muscles work in pairs to pull on bones to create movement. Opposing muscles, or antagonistic muscles, should be equally trained because they work together. For example, when you bend your elbow, your triceps relaxes while your biceps contracts.

Muscles that are not used and not exercised become weak. Strength training, or resistance training, builds muscular strength and endurance.

The purpose of this lesson is to encourage you to perform strength-training exercises 2 or more days per week in order to experience health benefits. A certified trainer should help you set up a balanced, effective strength program.

⚠️ **CAUTION: Have a certified trainer plan for you and supervise you when you are working with weights.**

STRENGTH TRAINING

BENEFITS OF STRENGTH TRAINING

- strengthens your skeletal muscles
- strengthens your heart muscle
- strengthens your bones
- improves your posture
- lowers your risk of exercise-related injury
- burns calories and fat
- reduces stress

After reviewing the benefits of strength training, discuss them with a trusted adult. Ask for help setting up a program that works for you and for help staying committed to that program.

There are a variety of exercises from which to choose. Do strength exercises for the muscles of your upper body, lower body, and core. Choose the intensity of each exercise to fit your fitness level. For example, if you are struggling to do a right-angle push-up, switch to a knee push-up. Limit excuses and make a commitment to exercise!

STRENGTH-TRAINING EXERCISE IDEAS

Weightlifting machines: You can use large stationary machines like those typically found in gyms.

Free weights: You can use free-weight equipment such as dumbbells, barbells, medicine balls, kettlebells, resistance bands, and weighted ropes to perform strength-training exercises.

Pilates or yoga: Pilates and yoga sessions are excellent workouts for muscle lengthening and muscle strengthening.

Personal workouts: You can use your own body weight as a source of resistance and create your own strength-training workouts. Create a personal workout by blending basic strength-building exercises such as sit-ups, push-ups, pull-ups, planks, and so on, and design the intensity and duration of each exercise according to your level of fitness. Include upper-body, lower-body, and core exercises in your workout. Perform your personal routine for some or all your strength-training workouts.

SAMPLE

The following is a sample personal strength-training workout that uses personal body weight as resistance. Practice each of the following exercises, concentrating on proper form, prior to engaging in a workout.

IN-OUT ABS

muscle focus: abdominal muscles

Intensity Level 1

Sit on a cushioned surface with your elbows flat on the ground slightly behind your hips. Keeping your knees bent, lift both legs until they are parallel to the ground. Extend your legs straight out in front of you and then return to the bent-knee position.

In-out abs: Intensity Level 1

Intensity Level 2

Sit on a cushioned surface with your hands flat on the ground slightly behind your hips. Keeping your knees bent, lift both legs until they are parallel to the ground. Extend your legs straight out in front of you and then return to the bent-knee position.

In-out abs: Intensity Level 2

Intensity Level 3

Sit on a cushioned surface with your arms held straight above your head. Keeping your knees bent, lift both legs until they are parallel to the ground. Extend your legs straight out in front of you and then return to the bent-knee position.

In-out abs: Intensity Level 3

FORWARD LUNGES

muscle focus: glutei maximi, hamstrings, and quadriceps

Intensity Level 1

Perform alternate forward lunges. Start with your feet together. Step 1 foot forward and bend your knee as low as you comfortably can. Do not exceed a 90-degree angle. Return to the starting position and then repeat the exercise with your other leg.

Forward lunges: Intensity Level 1

Intensity Level 2

Perform alternate forward lunges. Start with your feet together. Step 1 foot forward and bend your knee to a 90-degree angle. Return to the starting position and repeat the exercise with your other leg.

Forward lunges: Intensity Level 2

Intensity Level 3

Start with your feet together. Step your right foot forward and bend your knee to a 90-degree angle. Go back to the starting position. Continue lunging with your right foot until you have completed the repetitions. Next, lunge by stepping forward with your left foot until you complete the repetitions.

Forward lunges: Intensity Level 3

RIGHT-ANGLE PUSH-UPS

muscle focus: pectoralis majors, deltoids, triceps, biceps, and abdominal muscles

Intensity Level 1

Perform knee push-ups. Kneel on a cushioned surface with your back straight and your hands on the ground under your shoulders. Bend your elbows 90 degrees and then return to the straight-arm position, or plank position.

Intensity Level 2

Lie on your stomach. Place your hands under your shoulders. Straighten your arms to lift up your body. Make sure that your back and legs are straight from head to toe. Lower your body by bending your elbows as far as you can without exceeding 90. Straighten your arms to lift your body back up to the plank position, keeping your back and legs straight.

Intensity Level 3

Lie on your stomach. Place your hands under your shoulders. Straighten your arms to lift up your body. Make sure that your back and legs are straight from head to toe. Lower your body by bending your elbows 90 degrees. Straighten your arms to lift your body back up to the plank position, keeping your back and legs straight.

Right-Angle Push-ups: Intensity Level 1

Right-Angle Push-ups: Intensity Level 2

Right-Angle Push-ups: Intensity Level 3

ALTERNATE 6 INCHES

muscle focus: abdominal muscles

Intensity Level 1

Lie on your back on a cushioned surface. Pull 1 knee toward your chest. Extend your other leg straight out in front of you and parallel to the floor. Hold your extended leg 6 to 10 inches above the ground for 3 seconds. Switch legs.

Intensity Level 2

Lie on your back on a cushioned surface. Extend 1 leg up toward the ceiling with your knee bent. Extend your other leg straight out in front of you and parallel to the floor. Hold your extended leg 6 to 10 inches above the ground for 6 seconds. Switch legs.

Intensity Level 3

Lie on your back on a cushioned surface. Extend 1 leg straight up toward the ceiling. Extend your other leg straight out in front of you and parallel to the floor. Hold your extended leg 6 inches above the ground for 6 seconds. Switch legs.

Alternate 6 inches: Intensity Level 1

Alternate 6 inches: Intensity Level 2

Alternate 6 inches: Intensity Level 3

SQUATS

muscle focus: glutei maximi, hamstrings, and quadriceps

Intensity Level 1

Stand with your legs shoulder-width apart and your hands on your hips. Lower your body by bending your knees and hips as low as you comfortably can. Do not lower your hips below knee level.

Squats: Intensity Level 1

Copyright 2024 © Lincoln Learning Solutions. All rights reserved.

Intensity Level 2

Stand with your legs shoulder-width apart and your arms extended out in front of you at shoulder height. With your legs apart, lower your body by bending your knees and hips until your hips are even with your knees.

Intensity Level 3

Perform ¼-squat jumps. Standing with your legs shoulder-width apart, lower your body by bending your knees and hips until your hips are even with your knees. Jump to the right, making a quarter turn and landing gently in a squat position. Continue until you are back to the starting position. Repeat the exercise to the left.

Squats: Intensity Level 2

Squats: Intensity Level 3

TRICEPS PUSH-UPS (NARROW PUSH-UPS)

muscle focus: pectoralis majors, pectoralis minors, deltoids, triceps, biceps, and abdominal muscles

Intensity Level 1

Perform knee push-ups. Kneel on a cushioned surface with your back straight and your hands on the ground inside your shoulders. Bend your elbows 90 degrees and return to straight arms.

Intensity Level 2

Lie on your stomach. Place your hands on the floor close to your body at chest level. Lift your body up with your triceps until you return to the straight-arm position. Make sure that your back and legs are straight from head to toe. Lower your body by bending your elbows as far as you can without exceeding 90 degrees. Return to the straight-arm position.

Intensity Level 3

Lie on your stomach. Place your hands on the floor close to your body at chest level. Lift your body up with your triceps until you return to the straight-arm position. Make sure that your back and legs are straight from head to toe. Lower your body by bending your elbows 90 degrees. Return to the straight-arm position.

Triceps push-ups

Triceps push-ups: Intensity Level 1

Right-Angle Push-ups: Intensity Level 2

Right-Angle Push-ups: Intensity Level 3

SIT-UPS

muscle focus: abdominal muscles

Intensity Level 1

Perform fitness curl-ups. Lie on a cushioned surface with your knees flexed and your feet about 12 inches from your buttocks. With your arms at your sides, slide your fingertips 3 to 4 inches forward along the ground, simultaneously lifting your head and shoulders off the ground. Slowly lower your head and shoulders back to the ground.

Sit-ups: Intensity Level 1

Intensity Level 2

Perform sit-ups. Lie on a cushioned surface with your knees flexed and your feet about 12 inches from your buttocks. A partner may hold your feet. Cross your arms, placing your hands on opposite shoulders and holding your elbows close to your chest. Raise your body until your elbows touch your thighs; then, lower your body until your shoulder blades touch the ground.

Sit-ups: Intensity Level 2

Intensity Level 3

Perform sit-ups. Lie on a cushioned surface with your knees flexed and your feet about 12 inches from your buttocks. Cross your arms, placing your hands on opposite shoulders and holding your elbows close to your chest. Raise your body until your elbows touch your thighs; then, lower your body until your shoulder blades touch the ground.

Sit-ups: Intensity Level 3

STEP-BACK LUNGES

muscle focus: glutei maximi, hamstrings, and quadriceps

Intensity Level 1

Perform alternate step-back lunges. Start by standing with your feet together and your hands on your hips. Step back with 1 foot and lower your knee as low as you comfortably can. Go back to the starting position and repeat this with your other leg.

Step-back lunges: Intensity Level 1

Intensity Level 2

Perform alternate step-back lunges with high arms. Start by standing with your feet together and your arms extended straight above your head. Step back with 1 foot and lower your knee as far as you comfortably can. Return to the starting position and repeat this with your other leg.

Step-back lunges: Intensity Level 2

Intensity Level 3

Start by standing with your feet together. Step back with your right foot and lower your knee as far as you comfortably can. Return to the starting position and continue lunging back with your right foot until you have completed the repetitions. Next, step back with your left foot until you complete the repetitions. Your hands may remain on your hips or remain extended.

Step-back lunges: Intensity Level 3

WIDE PUSH-UPS

muscle focus: pectoralis majors, deltoids, triceps, biceps, and abdominal muscles

Intensity Level 1

Kneel on a cushioned surface with your back straight and your hands on the ground outside your shoulders. Bend your elbows 90 degrees. Return to the straight-arm position.

Wide push-ups

Intensity Level 2

Lie on your stomach. Place your hands outside your shoulders. Lift your body up to a straight-arm position. Make sure that your back and legs are straight from head to toe. Lower your body by bending your elbows as far as you can without exceeding 90 degrees. Return to the straight-arm position.

Wide push-ups: Intensity Level 1

Intensity Level 3

Lie on your stomach. Place your hands outside your shoulders. Lift your body up to a straight-arm position. Make sure that your back and legs are straight from head to toe. Lower your body by bending your elbows 90 degrees. Return to the straight-arm position.

Wide push-ups: Intensity Level 2

HOW TO USE YOUR BODY WEIGHT IN A STRENGTH-TRAINING WORKOUT

- Warm up before your workout. Cool down after your workout.
- Choose the appropriate level of intensity for you.
- Perform each exercise 2 to 3 days per week.
- Begin with 1 set of 10 repetitions of each exercise. Increase sets and repetitions when the exercise becomes easy for you.
- Your goal should be to reach 3 sets of 15 repetitions of each exercise.

Wide push-ups: Intensity Level 3

List at least 1 response to each of the following questions about strength training.

Question	Response
What positive emotional response did you experience by participating in strength training?	
Why would the enjoyment of strength training lead you to a lifetime of fitness?	

RESEARCH INTEGRATION

Research and compare skeletal muscles with muscles that work your heart, digestion, and eye focus.

RESISTANCE BANDS

Resistance bands are elastic bands that are used to improve flexibility, muscular strength, muscular endurance, and body composition. When you first use resistance bands, start with the lightest resistance and then gradually increase to a higher resistance as you get stronger.

The purpose of this lesson is to encourage you to use resistance bands for strength training.

FITNESS TIP: Secure the resistance band in a way that the length is appropriate to give resistance for the entire exercise. Wrap the band around your hands if you need to increase your resistance level.

CAUTION: Check the resistance band for damage or wear before exercising. When you are exercising, secure the band before adding any resistance.

BENEFITS OF STRENGTH TRAINING WITH RESISTANCE BANDS

- is an effective overall strength workout that does not require weights
- offers a variety of resistance adjustments for beginner through advanced levels
- requires inexpensive pieces of equipment
- requires equipment that is easy to carry with you when you are traveling

Practice each of the following exercises, concentrating on proper form, prior to engaging in a workout.

SQUATS

muscle focus: quadriceps, hamstrings, and glutei maximi

- Stand on the middle of the band with your feet shoulder-width apart.
- Hold an end of the band in each hand. Bend your elbows and place your hands by your ears.
- Bend your legs as if you were sitting in a chair. Bend until your legs are at 90-degree angles. Do not let your knees go past your toes.
- Stand back up to the starting position. Do not lock your knees.

Squats

LEG EXTENSIONS

muscle focus: quadriceps, hamstrings, and glutei maximi

- Lay with your back flat on the ground and with your right knee bent to your chest.
- Wrap your band around the bottom of your right foot, holding an end in each hand.
- Keep your left leg flat on the ground.
- Hold the band firmly in your hands and push your right leg straight out without fully straightening your knee.
- Bring your leg slowly back to the starting position.
- After completing the set, switch to your left leg.

Leg extensions

OVERHEAD PRESSES

muscle focus: pectoralis majors, anterior deltoids, and triceps

- Sit in a chair on the middle of the resistance band so that you have an even amount of space on either side.
- Sit up straight and place an end of the band in each hand.
- Bend your elbows, bringing your hands up to your ears. The band should run parallel to your triceps.
- Extend both hands straight up and above your head.
- Bend your elbows, lowering your hands slowly back to the starting position.

Overhead presses

LATERAL RAISES

muscle focus: pectoralis majors, pectoralis minors, biceps, triceps, and front fibers of deltoids

- Place an end of the band under your right foot and the other end in your right hand.
- Keeping your right arm straight at your side, make sure that the tension of the band is at a good level. If the resistance is not enough, wrap the band around your hand until it feels comfortable.
- Keeping your right arm straight, raise it out to your side so that it is parallel to the ground.
- Bring your right arm slowly back to your side. Keep your arm straight during the entire exercise.
- After completing the repetitions, repeat the exercise with your left arm.

Lateral raises

TRICEPS EXTENSIONS

muscle focus: biceps and triceps

- Stand with your feet shoulder-width apart.
- Hold the band with an end in each hand.
- Bring the band behind your back so that your left hand is resting on your lower back and your right hand is just above your head with your elbow bent. The band should be parallel to your spine.
- Holding your left arm in place, extend your right arm straight above your right shoulder.
- Bend your right arm back to the starting position.
- After completing the repetitions, repeat the exercise with your left arm.
- If you need more resistance, wrap the band around your hands until it feels comfortable.

Tricep extensions

BICEPS HAMMER CURLS

muscle focus: biceps and triceps

- Stand on the middle of the exercise band with your feet shoulder-width apart.
- Hold both ends of the exercise band with your palms facing in toward your body.
- Bend at your elbows and slowly bring both hands toward the respective shoulder while keeping your elbows by your sides and your palms turned in toward your body.
- Return your arms slowly back to the starting position without fully straightening your elbows.

Biceps hammer curls

Have a trusted adult or friend evaluate you for correct form for the previous exercises. Did you respond positively to the feedback?

Reciprocate and evaluate your friend. Were you able to provide feedback in a positive manner?

How to Use Resistance Bands in a Strength-Training Workout

- Warm up before your workout. Cool down after your workout.
- Perform each resistance band exercise 2 to 3 days per week. Do not exercise the same muscle group on consecutive days.
- Begin with 1 set of 10 repetitions for each exercise. Increase sets and repetitions when the exercise becomes easy for you.
- Your goal should be to reach 3 sets of 10 to 15 repetitions.
- Wrap the band to increase resistance as necessary.

RESEARCH INTEGRATION

Research and discuss with a trusted adult the role of exercise and nutrition in weight management.

SPORTS-RELATED AND SKILL-RELATED ACTIVITIES

FITNESS TIP: Prior to beginning your physical education activities, read the following safety information that applies to every lesson, review the timeline, and review the assessment rubric.

SAFETY ALERT: Before you exercise, make sure that you are properly warmed up and have enough room to perform each activity. Wear proper equipment and follow activity-specific safety rules. Stay hydrated and take breaks as needed. Exercise only if you are healthy, and always exercise at your own pace. If an exercise starts to hurt, if you feel dizzy, or if you feel light-headed, stop the exercise completely and get help. Upon completion of any workout, cool down and stretch.

TIMELINE

Review all of the activity information before beginning. Use the scoring rubrics as assessment tools. You may ask a trusted adult or friend to observe your performance and provide feedback. Progress according to your skill level. The time that it takes you to complete a module will depend on your personal progress.

- **Practice and assess the first skill until competent.**
- **Continue to progress until you have practiced and assessed each skill until competent.**
- **Apply skills in a game situation.**

ASSESSMENT RUBRIC

You will find a rubric assessment tool following some of the basic skills. Use this tool to evaluate and score your progress in learning the elements of a new skill.

SKILL	PROGRESSING	COMPETENT	PROFICIENT
skill 1	1 or 2 of the elements	3 or 4 out of 5 elements	all elements met

BADMINTON

Badminton is a sport that is played by striking a shuttlecock, or birdie, with a racket over a net. This striking activity helps you develop concentration, hand-eye coordination, and footwork. You may play badminton as a competitive sport or as an opportunity for social play.

The purpose of this lesson is for you to practice badminton skills, participate in a badminton game, follow game rules, and communicate with others in a positive and effective manner.

⚠ **CAUTION:** Make sure that nobody is close to you before you swing your racket. Do not walk into the path of another person who is swinging a racket.

BADMINTON STROKES

READY POSITION

- Bending your knees, stand with your feet shoulder-width apart.
- Keep your head up and your weight on the balls of your feet.
- Hold the racket in your dominant hand.
- React quickly.
- Anticipate direction.

SKILL	PROGRESSING	COMPETENT	PROFICIENT
ready position	1 or 2 of the elements	3 or 4 out of 5 elements	all elements met

HANDSHAKE GRIP (V GRIP)

- Hold the handle of the racket in your dominant hand in a handshake grip.
- Form a V with your thumb and forefinger.
- Point the racket away from your body at waist height.
- Placing the head of the racket vertical to the ground, point the handle toward your belly button.
- Support the throat of racket lightly with your non-dominant hand.

SKILL	PROGRESSING	COMPETENT	PROFICIENT
handshake grip	1 or 2 of the elements	3 or 4 out of 5 elements	all elements met

UNDERHAND STROKE

- Hold the racket so that the head is facing the ground and is under the birdie.
- Step forward with your non-dominant foot.
- Flick your wrist to hit the birdie with the center of the racket.
- Rotate your forearm so that it faces upward on contact.
- Follow through to your target.

SKILL	PROGRESSING	COMPETENT	PROFICIENT
underhand stroke	1 or 2 of the elements	3 or 4 out of 5 elements	all elements met

OVERHAND STROKE

- Bend your elbow so that your racket is in a back-scratching position.
- Reach up and position the racket under the birdie.
- Flick your wrist to hit the birdie with the center of the racket. Extend your arm when you make contact.
- Follow through to your target.

SKILL	PROGRESSING	COMPETENT	PROFICIENT
overhand stroke	1 or 2 of the elements	3 out of 4 elements	all elements met

FOREHAND STROKE

- The racket should be on the same side of your body as your dominant hand.
- Face the palm of your hand forward.
- Rotate your hips in the direction that you are hitting.
- Extend your arm and flick your wrist to hit the birdie.
- Point the face of the racket up to get the birdie over the net.
- Follow through to your target.

SKILL	PROGRESSING	COMPETENT	PROFICIENT
forehand stroke	1, 2, or 3 of the elements	4 or 5 out of 6 elements	all elements met

BACKHAND STROKE

- Rotate the racket and extend it across your body.
- Rotate your feet, hips, and shoulders in the same direction as the racket.
- Face the back of your hand forward.
- Flick your wrist when you are hitting the birdie with the center of the racket.
- Follow through to your target.

SKILL	PROGRESSING	COMPETENT	PROFICIENT
backhand stroke	1 or 2 of the elements	3 or 4 out of 5 elements	all elements met

UNDERHAND SERVE

- Hold the racket in your dominant hand with the head of the racket pointed down toward the ground.
- Hold the birdie by the feathers in your non-dominant hand.
- Step forward with your non-dominant foot.
- Drop the birdie slightly below your waist.
- Hit the birdie with the center of the racket. Flick your wrist when you make contact.
- Follow through to your target.

SKILL	PROGRESSING	COMPETENT	PROFICIENT
underhand serve	1, 2, or 3 of the elements	4 or 5 out of 6 elements	all elements met

PRACTICE THE STROKES

Practice independently by holding the birdie by the feathers in your non-dominant hand. Hold the racket appropriately for the stroke. Drop the birdie and make contact with the racket.

- First, practice each stroke without using the birdie.
- Then, practice each stroke using the birdie.
- Practice the underhand stroke by holding the head of the racket down toward the floor. Drop the birdie and make contact with the racket slightly below your waist. Flick your wrist and make contact with the birdie. How many times you can hit the birdie in a row?
- Strike the birdie toward a target using the various strokes.
- Strike the birdie toward a target using different levels of force.
- Aim and strike the birdie to the left of a target.
- Aim and strike the birdie to the right of a target.
- Practice with a partner. Hit the birdie back and forth with a partner. How many times can you hit it back and forth?

BADMINTON SHOTS

CLEAR SHOT

The overhead and underhand defensive clear shots arc or lob the birdie high and push your opponent to the rear of the court. This slows down the game to give you a chance to get ready for your opponent's shot.

DROP SHOT

The overhand drop shot keeps the pace of the game the same. It is sent at a steep angle, forcing your opponent to rush forward.

SMASH SHOT

The overhand smash shot is a powerful hit at a severe angle. You need to contact the birdie high, which may even require you to jump to hit the birdie. This shot is often used to end a game.

PRACTICE THE SHOTS

Practice the shots independently by tossing the birdie at the appropriate height for each shot. Practice with a set-up net.

- Practice the clear shot with both the underhand and overhand strokes.
- Practice the drop shot.
- Practice the smash shot.
- Practice with a partner. Have a partner toss the birdie for you. Practice each shot and then switch roles. Be supportive and encouraging to your partner.

Copyright 2024 © Lincoln Learning Solutions. All rights reserved.

BADMINTON GAME

- Badminton is usually a singles game with 2 players or a doubles game with 4 players.
- Start with an underhand serve from the right side of the court. Serve from behind the end line to your opponent on the left.
- If you hit the birdie onto your opponent's side and your opponent cannot return it, you win the rally—which is the series of consecutive strokes back and forth until a point is earned—and get a point.
- Now, serve from the left side of the court.
- When your score is an even number, serve behind the right end line. When your score is an odd number, serve behind the left end line.
- In a doubles game, the same player on a team serves throughout a rally, alternating serving sides until losing the rally. The opponent then serves until the rally is lost. Partners alternate turns serving.
- You may only hit the birdie 1 time on each side.
- You lose a rally if you or your racket touch the net.
- You lose a rally if you hit the birdie into the net, hit it out of bounds, or miss it when you swing.

DEMONSTRATE POSITIVE GAME BEHAVIOR

- Follow rules.
- Call for the shot, when appropriate, to identify that you are going to hit the shot. This is for safety and game efficiency.
- Be supportive and encouraging to your teammate.
- Treat your opponents with respect.

SKILL	PROGRESSING	COMPETENT	PROFICIENT
game behavior	1 or 2 of the elements	3 or 4 out of 5 elements	all elements met

HOW TO SCORE

- You score a point when you hit the birdie over the net and onto your opponent's side before your opponent can return it. You also score a point when your opponent hits the birdie either into the net or out of bounds.
- A match consists of 3 games of 21 points.
- If you win a rally, you score 1 point.
- If the score is tied at 20 points, the first team to score 2 points wins the game.
- If the score is tied at 29 points, the first team to score its 30th point wins the game.
- The winning team serves first in the next game.

RATE YOUR ENJOYMENT OF BADMINTON

On a scale from 1 to 4, where 1 is not enjoyable and 4 is very enjoyable, rate this activity.

1	It was not enjoyable, and I will not participate again.
2	It was not enjoyable, but I will participate again for exercise.
3	It was enjoyable, and I will play again.
4	It was very enjoyable, and I will initiate future games.

🖥 RESEARCH INTEGRATION

Research badminton's country of origin, who invented the game, where badminton is played throughout the world, and the official rules of the game.

♥ HEALTH INTEGRATION

Count your pulse during and after playing badminton to determine if you are exercising in your personal target heart rate zone. Apply the results to your overall fitness plan. Keep in mind that many people choose to complete aerobic workouts by playing in casual games with friends.

BASKETBALL

Learning and practicing basketball helps you develop the skills necessary for playing games outside of PE class. Basketball enhances health-related and skill-related components of fitness. Learning basketball skills will not only help improve your basketball game but may also enhance your skills in other sports and activities. Playing basketball is a great aerobic workout.

The official game of basketball is played by 2 opposing teams that are each made up of 5 players. The players play on a basketball court. Points are scored when the ball goes through a basketball hoop. There are also other basketball games and activities that you can enjoy, such as independent shooting and dribbling challenges, shooting games, and half-court games of 1-on-1, 2-on-2, and 3-on-3 versions of the official game.

The purpose of this lesson is for you to participate in aerobic exercise and in skill-building activities. Game participation will depend upon the availability of a facility and players. Any time you play a game of basketball, be sure to follow game rules, communicate with teammates in a positive and effective manner, and exhibit appropriate behavior with your team and the opposing team.

⚠️ **CAUTION: Do not overinflate the basketball.**

DRIBBLING SKILLS

Learning to dribble efficiently with both your right hand and left hand is necessary for playing basketball.

BASIC STATIONARY DRIBBLING

- Using your dominant hand, spread your fingers and push the ball down gently toward the ground with your finger pads. Do not slap the ball.
- Let the ball bounce on the ground and come back to your hand. Do not let the ball bounce higher than your waist.
- Flex your wrist and push the ball back to the ground with your finger pads. This is a continuous movement; do not catch the ball after every bounce.
- Dribble with your head up.
- Keep your eyes looking forward, not watching the ball.
- Repeat dribbling the ball with your non-dominant hand.

Basic stationary dribbling

SKILL	PROGRESSING	COMPETENT	PROFICIENT
right-handed dribble	1 or 2 of the elements	3 or 4 out of 5 elements	all elements met
left-handed dribble	1 or 2 of the elements	3 or 4 out of 5 elements	all elements met

STATIONARY DRIBBLING

- See how many times you can dribble the ball with your dominant hand without losing control of the ball.
- Push the ball down with different amounts of force to make it bounce at different levels.
- Try pushing the ball with a soft force so that it bounces at a low level.
- Try pushing the ball with a hard force so that it bounces at a high level.
- Dribble with your dominant hand.
- Dribble with your non-dominant hand.
- Dribble the ball from 1 hand to the other.

DRIBBLING WHILE MOVING

- Dribble from 1 hand to the other while moving.
- Dribble while moving, increasing and decreasing speed.
- Dribble while moving and change directions.

CROSSOVER DRIBBLING

- Set up disc cones about 2 feet apart in a zigzag pattern.
- Start at the first cone and dribble the basketball to the next cone using the hand with which you are most comfortable.
- Reach the second cone and do a crossover (switch hands) in order to move on to the next cone.
- Complete a crossover at each cone until you have reached the last cone.
- Turn around and do the same thing back to the first cone.
- Continue this until you feel comfortable with dribbling and crossing over.

Crossover dribbling

CHALLENGE SKILLS

The following challenge skills are for those who are proficient in basic stationary dribbling. The challenge drills reinforce dribbling effectively with both the right hand and left hand. Practice as appropriate to your needs.

FIGURE-8 DRIBBLE

- Stand with your legs wide and your knees bent.
- Dribble the ball through your legs and around your ankles in a figure-8 pattern.
- Alternate hands while dribbling.
- Reverse directions for an advanced challenge.

Figure-8 dribble

FRONT 2, BACK 2 DRIBBLE

- Stand with your legs shoulder-width apart and your knees bent.
- Dribble twice in front of your body. Alternate hands while dribbling, but do not put both hands on the ball at the same time.
- Switch hands behind you, and dribble twice behind your body. This is a 1, 2, 3, 4 count.
- Move while making quarter turns for an advanced challenge.

Front, back 2 dribble

2-BALL DRIBBLE

- Dribble 2 balls at the same time.
- Keep the balls at the same height.

2 ball dribble

2-BALL HIGH-LOW DRIBBLE

- Dribble a ball with each hand.
- Dribble the ball on the right high while simultaneously dribbling the ball on the left low.
- Dribble the ball on the right low while simultaneously dribbling the ball on the left high.

2-ball high-low dribble

2-BALL FIGURE-8 DRIBBLE

- Dribble 1 ball between your legs while circling the other ball around 1 of your legs.
- When the ball that is circling your leg reaches the middle point between your legs, switch it with the ball between your legs.

2-ball figure-8 dribble

Check off the challenge skills that you have mastered.

_____FIGURE-8 DRIBBLE

_____FRONT 2, BACK 2 DRIBBLE

_____2-BALL DRIBBLE

_____2-BALL HIGH-LOW DRIBBLE

_____2-BALL FIGURE-8 DRIBBLE

PASSING SKILLS

There are 2 common passes that are used in the game of basketball. The bounce pass and chest pass are used to move the ball to your teammates. You can practice these passes with a partner or against a wall.

BOUNCE PASS AND CATCH

BOUNCE PASS

- Stand facing the target.
- Hold the ball with both hands at chest level and your elbows out.
- Step toward the target.
- Extend both arms toward the target. The ball should bounce on the floor between you and the target before it reaches the target.

Bounce Pass

CATCH

- When you are catching, watch the ball all the way until it reaches your hands.
- Move your hands toward the ball.
- Give with the ball (pull the ball slightly toward you) as it hits your hands to make a soft catch.

Catch

SKILL	PROGRESSING	COMPETENT	PROFICIENT
bounce pass	1 or 2 of the elements	3 out of 4 elements	all elements met
bounce-pass catch	1 of the elements	2 out of 3 elements	all elements met

CHEST PASS AND CATCH

CHEST PASS

- Stand facing the target.
- Hold the ball with both hands at chest level and your elbows out.
- Step toward the target.
- Extend both arms toward the target. The ball should not bounce on the floor.

Chest pass

CATCH

- When you are catching, watch the ball all the way until it reaches your hands.
- Move your hands toward the ball.
- Give with the ball (pull the ball slightly toward you) as it hits your hands to make a soft catch.

Catch

SKILL	PROGRESSING	COMPETENT	PROFICIENT
chest pass	1 or 2 of the elements	3 out of 4 elements	all elements met
chest-pass catch	1 of the elements	2 out of 3 elements	all elements met

PRACTICE PASSING WITH A PARTNER

- How many bounce passes can you and your partner do in a row?
- How many chest passes can you and your partner do in a row?
- Bounce pass to your partner. Your partner will send a chest pass back. Switch roles.
- Bounce pass as you and your partner move down the court.
- Chest pass as you and your partner move down the court.

BASIC SHOOTING SKILLS

BASIC SHOOTING

- Stand facing the hoop with your feet shoulder-width apart and your knees slightly bent.
- Place your dominant hand on the back of the basketball and bend your wrist. Place your non-dominant hand on the side of the ball.
- Place the ball on the finger pads of your dominant hand.
- Use your non-dominant hand as your guide.
- Position your elbow so that it is behind the ball, not out to the side.
- Look at the target—the front of the rim.
- Push your dominant hand toward the target while straightening your legs to give you more power to shoot.
- Shoot the ball toward the target and follow through with your arm and wrist. Snap your wrist as the ball leaves your hand.

Basic shooting skills

- Remember BEEF.
  - **Balance** the ball in your dominant hand.
  - Place your **elbow** behind the ball, not out to the side.
  - Keep your **eyes** on the target.
  - **Follow** through with a snap of your wrist.

SKILL	PROGRESSING	COMPETENT	PROFICIENT
BEEF elements	1 or 2 of the elements	3 out of 4 elements	all elements

SHOOTING DRILLS

PRACTICE SHOOTING

- Practice some shooting drills after you become comfortable shooting the basketball.
- Pick different spots on the court, both closer and farther away from the hoop.
- Map out a pattern in your mind as to what spots you will go to first, second, third, and so on.
- Practice shooting from each spot.
- Start on 1 side of the hoop and move around to the other side.
- Work back around to the starting position.

FOUL LINE SPELLING GAME

- You will need 2 or more players.
- Line up behind the foul line.
- The goal of the game is to be the first player to spell A-E-R-O-B-I-C.
- The first person takes a shot from behind the foul line.
- If the player makes the basket, the player gets a letter and goes to the back of the line to wait for their next turn.
- If the player misses, the player does not get a letter and goes to the back of the line.
- The next player in line repeats the above procedure.
- Continue to play until a player spells A-E-R-O-B-I-C.

OFFENSIVE AND DEFENSIVE SKILLS

Agile footwork is an essential component of basketball. Practice footwork skills to improve your offensive and defensive play.

OFFENSIVE SKILLS

Practice each of the following skills, concentrating on proper form, prior to using them in a game or other competition.

OFFENSIVE READY POSITION

The ready position allows a player to move quickly in any direction. It is used for both offense and defense.

- With your elbows out, hold the ball with both hands to the dominant side of your chest.
- Bend your knees to keep your body low.
- Stand with your feet shoulder-width apart.
- Keep your head up and your weight on the balls of your feet.

SKILL	PROGRESSING	COMPETENT	PROFICIENT
offensive ready position	1 or 2 of the elements	3 out of 4 elements	all elements met

PIVOT

The purpose of the pivot in a basketball game is for you to look around and decide to dribble, pass, or shoot.

- Plant 1 foot, which will be your pivot foot, in place on the ground.
- Place your weight on the balls of your feet.
- Slide your non-pivot foot and rotate your body 180 degrees.
- Repeat this exercise with your other foot.

SKILL	PROGRESSING	COMPETENT	PROFICIENT
pivot	1 of the elements	2 out of 3 elements	all elements

FAKE

- Look in 1 direction, and then pass or move in another direction.
- Stay on the balls of your feet.
- Move quickly.

SKILL	PROGRESSING	COMPETENT	PROFICIENT
fake	1 of the elements	2 out of 3 elements	all elements

GIVE AND GO

The purpose of the give and go in a basketball game is to for you to pass the ball to a teammate and to quickly relocate so that you can receive a pass.

- Pass the ball to a teammate.
- Move quickly to relocate and support your offense.
- Indicate (call out) that you are ready and open to receive the ball.
- Catch the ball.

SKILL	PROGRESSING	COMPETENT	PROFICIENT
give and go	1 or 2 of the elements	3 out of 4 elements	all elements

Copyright 2024 © Lincoln Learning Solutions. All rights reserved.

DEFENSIVE SKILLS

Practice each of the following skills, concentrating on proper form, prior to using them in a game or other competition.

DEFENSIVE SLIDES

The purpose of defensive slides in basketball is to keep up with your opponent and to legally take the ball or legally disrupt the opponent's pass or shot.

- Place your weight on the balls of your feet.
- Slide to the side with quick steps.
- Do not cross your feet.
- Keep your knees bent.
- Face your hips toward your opponent.
- Hold your hands up at chest level.
- Keep your eyes on your opponent's waistline.
- Stay with your opponent.
- Anticipate and react quickly to your opponent's movements.

SKILL	PROGRESSING	COMPETENT	PROFICIENT
defensive slides	1, 2, 3, 4, or 5 of the elements	6, 7, or 8 out of 9 elements	all elements met

PRACTICE OFFENSIVE AND DEFENSIVE SKILLS

- Practice the **pivot** by planting your right foot and rotating your left foot until you feel comfortable with the movement.
- Practice the **pivot** by planting your left foot and rotating your right foot until you feel comfortable with the movement.
- Practice the **give and go** with a partner and a defender. Pass the ball, quickly relocate, and then receive the pass, avoiding the defender.
- Practice the **fake** independently. Set up a cone as a decoy. Fake the pass toward the cone and then pass to your partner until you feel comfortable with the movement.
- Practice the **fake** with a partner defending you. Dribble, fake, and move in another direction to get around the defensive player. Do this until you feel comfortable with the fake.
- Practice the **defensive slide** with a partner. As your partner dribbles, defensive slide to try to prevent them from making a successful pass or shot. Do this until you feel comfortable with the defensive slide.

BASKETBALL GAME

- The game is played by 2 opposing teams of 5 players each. Each team has a point guard, a shooting guard, a small forward, a power forward, and a center.
- The game is played on a basketball court 92 feet long and 50 feet wide.
- A 10-foot-high basketball hoop with a net is at each end of the court.
- The object of the game is to move the ball down the court by passing or dribbling and to score by shooting the ball through the opposing team's hoop.

- A high school game is divided into 8-minute quarters of play time with a rest period after 2 quarters of play.
- The team with the most points is the winning team.
- The game begins with a jump ball at mid-court. A referee tosses the ball between 2 opposing players.
- The team that possesses the ball is on offense, and the other team is on defense.
- The player with the ball must dribble, pass, or shoot.
- When they are moving with the ball, the player must dribble. When the player stops dribbling, they cannot take any more steps.
- If a player walks without dribbling, the ball is turned over to the opposing team.
- The players on defense try to intercept, or take away, the ball.

DEMONSTRATE POSITIVE GAME BEHAVIOR

- Follow the rules of the game.
- Do not commit a foul or make illegal physical contact against an opposing player.
    - A foul against a non-shooting player results in a turnover, which is a change in possession of the ball between teams.
    - A foul against a shooting player results in the team getting free shots—2 shots for a foul on a player shooting a 2-point shot and 3 shots for a player shooting a 3-point shot.
    - A player who commits 5 fouls is removed from the game.
- Be supportive and encouraging to your teammates.
- Treat your opponents with respect.

SKILL	PROGRESSING	COMPETENT	PROFICIENT
game behavior	1 or 2 of the elements	3 out of 4 elements	all elements met

HOW TO SCORE

- An arc line, referred to as a 3-point line, is marked on the basketball court.
    - A player who makes a basket from behind the 3-point line is awarded 3 points.
    - A player who makes a basket from inside the 3-point line is awarded 2 points.
- Foul shots are worth 1 point each.

OPTIONAL 1-ON-1 GAME

Playing 1-on-1 allows you to play basketball and complete an aerobic workout when you only have 2 players. This is an example of how to break down the barrier of not having enough players for an official game and create a solution.

- You can play a 1-on-1 half-court game with 2 players.
- Determine the boundaries.
- Determine who starts with the ball.
- Begin behind the half-court line of your established boundary.
- After a score, the opposing player takes the ball out to the half-court line and tries to score.
- Scoring is the same as in the official rules.
- You will have to call your own fouls or have another person referee.
- Treat your opponent with respect.
- If there are more players, you can play 2-on-2 or 3-on-3 games.

Prior to playing 1-on-1, establish and review the game rules so that you and your opponent understand them. If problems arise, work to solve them in a positive and effective manner. Appreciate different players' abilities. An example of a rule that you may want to decide upon is the boundaries.

Below are our game rules for safety and fairness.
1.
2.
3.
4.
5.

RATE YOUR ENJOYMENT OF THE BASKETBALL ACTIVITY THAT YOU ENJOYED MOST

On a scale from 1 to 4, where 1 is not enjoyable and 4 is very enjoyable, rate this activity.

1	It was not enjoyable, and I will not participate again.
2	It was not enjoyable, but I will participate again for exercise.
3	It was enjoyable, and I will play again.
4	It was very enjoyable, and I will initiate future games.

RESEARCH INTEGRATION

1. Research the official rules and regulations of high school basketball for additional official basketball information.
2. Attend a basketball game or watch a basketball game on television. It can be men's, women's, or co-ed basketball at any level—youth, high school, college, or professional. Identify the basketball skills you have learned that are used by the players throughout the game.

HEALTH INTEGRATION

Count your pulse during and after playing basketball to determine if you are exercising in your personal target heart rate zone. Apply the results to your overall fitness plan. Many people choose to complete aerobic workouts by playing in fast-paced games like basketball.

GOLF

The game of golf can be played as a competitive sport or as a casual game. Golf is played around the world by people of all ages for exercise and for the enjoyment of the social and competitive aspects of the game. The object of the game is to use clubs to hit a ball into each hole in a course. The player who hits their ball the fewest times is the winner of the game.

Golf is played on an open outdoor course. A typical course has 18 holes. A hole consists of a starting tee, a putting green of short and smooth grass where the hole is located, and a long area of grass between the tee and putting green called a fairway. A variety of up to 14 long-handled clubs are used to hit a small, hard ball into the holes. Common types of clubs include drivers, woods, irons, hybrids, and putters. Part of the game is knowing which club to use for each hit.

The mechanics of a golf swing are similar for most clubs, with adjustments for distance and direction. The clubs are used to launch the ball into the air toward the hole. The putter is a club that is used differently than the other clubs. It is used to hit the ball when it is on a green into the hole with a stroke called a putt, which is a small, close, controlled strike that causes the ball to roll on the ground.

The purpose of this lesson is for you to learn the mechanics of the full golf swing and to encourage you to participate in the game of golf.

⚠ **CAUTION: Make sure that nobody is close to you before you swing a golf club. Do not walk into the path of another person who is swinging a golf club.**

GOLF SKILLS

GRIP AND STANCE

OVERLAPPING GRIP: RIGHT-HANDED

- Hold the golf club with the head of the club on the ground.
- Grasp the grip of the golf club with your left hand as if you were shaking hands with the club, laying your left thumb flat on the front of the grip and pointing it toward the head of the golf club. If you were looking at direction like the face of a clock, your thumb would be pointing at 1:00.
- Place your right hand over your left hand, covering your left thumb with your right middle fingers.
- Overlap your right pinky so that it is behind your left hand and between the pointer finger and middle finger of your left hand.
- When you are gripping the golf club, the back of your left hand and the palm of your right hand should be facing the target.

OVERLAPPING GRIP: LEFT-HANDED

- Hold the golf club with the head of the club on the ground.
- Grasp the grip of the golf club with your right hand as if you were shaking hands with the club, laying your right thumb flat on the front of the grip and pointing it toward the head of the golf club. If you were looking at direction like the face of a clock, your thumb would be pointing at 11:00.
- Place your left hand over your right hand, covering your right thumb with your left middle finger.
- Overlap your left pinky so that it is behind your right hand and between the pointer finger and middle finger of your right hand.

Copyright 2024 © Lincoln Learning Solutions. All rights reserved.

- When you are gripping the golf club, the back of your right hand and the palm of your left hand should be facing the target.

SKILL	PROGRESSING	COMPETENT	PROFICIENT
grip	1, 2, or 3 of the elements	4 out of 5 elements	all elements met

STANCE

- Stand with your feet shoulder-width apart with your knees slightly bent. Bend at your waist, but keep your back straight.
- Your head should be angled down slightly to see the ball.
- Maintain balance, keeping your center of gravity over your feet.

SKILL	PROGRESSING	COMPETENT	PROFICIENT
stance	1 of the elements	2 out of 3 elements	all elements met

GOLF SWING

THE FULL GOLF SWING IN 3 PARTS

Practice each step of the full swing without golf balls repeatedly before using golf balls.

1. BACKSWING

- Position the clubhead so that it is on the ground and slightly behind the ball.
- In the backswing, the clubhead, your hands, and your shoulders must start in a single motion.
- Bring your head back slowly to make sure that your left shoulder is slightly higher than your right shoulder. During the backswing, rotate at your hips, keeping your arms straight and your upper body and shoulders in line.
- The weight of your feet in the stance shifts laterally from your front foot to your back foot. This helps with hip rotation.
- As your weight is shifted to your back foot, lateral rotation at your left hip turns your pelvis away from the ball.
- Keep your head forward and your eyes on the ball.

These steps are for a right-handed golfer. Switch directions in each step for a left-handed golfer.

SKILL	PROGRESSING	COMPETENT	PROFICIENT
backswing	1, 2, or 3 of the elements	4 or 5 out of 6 elements	all elements met

2. DOWNSWING

- Swing the club forward by first twisting your hips toward the target and then following through with your arms.
- As your body shifts to uncoil, make sure that your weight starts to shift from your right foot to your left foot.
- Your arms should return to their original position at the point of contact with the ball.
- Your wrists should stay strong but should rotate in the direction of your swing when the club contacts the ball; so, you should finish your swing with the back of your wrist slightly more toward your target than the front of your wrist.

These steps are for a right-handed golfer. Switch directions in each step for a left-handed golfer.

SKILL	PROGRESSING	COMPETENT	PROFICIENT
downswing	1 or 2 of the elements	3 out of 4 elements	all elements met

3. FOLLOW-THROUGH

- The follow-through is what your body and club do after making contact with the ball.
- Bring your club all the way through the swing, with the club finishing over your front shoulder.
- Twist your upper body so that it ends up being squared with your target. Keep your front leg in the starting position. The knee of your back leg should be bent, and your toes should be on the ground.
- Turn your hips enough to allow your belly button to face your target.
- The club itself should wrap behind your shoulders while you maintain a straight back.
- Freeze your body in a finishing position for a few seconds while watching the flight of the ball.

SKILL	PROGRESSING	COMPETENT	PROFICIENT
follow-through	1, 2, or 3 of the elements	4 or 5 out of 6 elements	all elements met

TARGET PRACTICE

- For this activity, make sure that you are in a large, open space.
- Set up discs so that they are spread out at a variety of distances, like shown in the picture.
- Stand about 10 feet from the closest disc. From that spot, practice chipping the ball as close to the different discs as you can.
- As you get better, increase your distance from the discs.
- Make a game by assigning a point value to each of the different discs. The closer discs can be worth 1 or 2 points each, and the further discs can be worth 3 to 5 points each.

RATE YOUR ENJOYMENT OF GOLF

On a scale from 1 to 4, where 1 is not enjoyable and 4 is very enjoyable, rate this activity.

1	It was not enjoyable, and I will not participate again.
2	It was not enjoyable, but I will participate again for exercise.
3	It was enjoyable, and I will play again.
4	It was very enjoyable, and I will initiate future games.

RESEARCH INTEGRATION

1. Research the 3 common golf grips: the overlapping (Vardon) grip, the interlocking grip, and the baseball grip. Try each grip to determine the grip that you prefer.
2. Play a round of golf with a seasoned golfer or watch golf on television.

HEALTH INTEGRATION

Discuss with a trusted adult or friend how someone could reduce their stress levels by playing golf through concentrating on the task, socializing, exercising, and so on.

PLAYGROUND BALL GAMES

You can use a playground ball to play many fun games and activities that can help you develop your skills and participate in cardiovascular conditioning.

A popular playground game is 4 square. This game is played on a square court that is divided into 4 quadrants and with a playground ball.

Playing the game utilizes and improves the skill-related components of agility, balance, coordination, speed, and reaction. Playing 4 square with moderate intensity also serves as an aerobic workout. Finally, the game provides the opportunity to interact with others in a competitive and social manner.

The purpose of this lesson is to encourage you to participate in a game of 4 square with other players, follow game rules, and exhibit appropriate behavior.

⚠ **CAUTION: Do not overinflate the ball.**

4 SQUARE GAME

Using chalk or ropes, divide a 10-foot by 10-foot space into 4 even squares. You will need 4 players for this game. Number the squares 1, 2, 3, and 4. The goal of the game is to reach square 4 and be the server. Players move in numerical order to get to square 4.

RULES

- Each player stands in a square. Extra players stand in the waiting line near square 1.
- The player in square 4 is the server.
- If you are the server, serve underhand to the square of your choice. You must bounce the ball before you strike it to serve.
- Serve again if the ball lands on a line.
- A miss results in the player who missed moving to the end of the waiting line or to square 1 if there are only 4 players total.
- Misses include double bounces, out of bounds bounces, and catches.

Prior to playing the game, establish and review the game rules so that all participants understand them. If problems arise, work as a group to solve them in a positive and effective manner. Appreciate different players' abilities. An example of a rule that you that may want to decide upon is whether or not overhand strikes are allowed in your game.

Below are our game rules for safety and fairness.
1.
2.
3.
4.
5.

RATE YOUR ENJOYMENT OF 4 SQUARE

On a scale from 1 to 4, where 1 is not enjoyable and 4 is very enjoyable, rate this **activity**.

1	It was not enjoyable, and I will not participate again.
2	It was not enjoyable, but I will participate again for exercise.
3	It was enjoyable, and I will play again.
4	It was very enjoyable, and I will initiate future games.

RESEARCH INTEGRATION

Research 4 square's country of origin, who invented the game, where it is played throughout the world, and the official rules of the game.

HEALTH INTEGRATION

Count your pulse during and after playing 4 square to determine if you are exercising in your personal target heart rate zone. Many people choose to complete aerobic workouts by playing in casual games with friends.

TEAM HANDBALL: A PASSING GAME

Team handball is a game that is played by 2 teams of 7 players on a rectangular court with a lightweight ball. The object of the game is to pass the ball into the goal to score more points than your opponent in 2 periods of 30 minutes. It is an Olympic sport and is gaining popularity worldwide.

Playing the game requires you to utilize and helps you to make improvements in the skill-related components of agility, balance, coordination, speed, power, and reaction. Playing team handball at a moderate intensity level is an aerobic workout. The game also provides the opportunity to work as a team to develop offensive and defensive strategies and the ability to transition quickly from each. It is a game that improves mental focus.

The purpose of this lesson is for you to participate in aerobic exercise and in skill-building activities. Game participation will depend upon the availability of a facility and players. Any time you play team handball, be sure to follow game rules, communicate with teammates in a positive and effective manner, and exhibit appropriate behavior with your team and the opposing team.

OFFICIAL TEAM HANDBALL COURT

Court dimensions: 20m by 40m (22 yd. by 44 yd.)

Goal line: 6m (6.2 yd.)

Goal net: 3m by 2m (3.2 yd. by 2.2 yd.)

Penalty line: 9m (9.3 yd.)

⚠ **CAUTION: Do not overinflate the ball.**

TEAM HANDBALL SKILLS

The following skills are used to play team handball. Practice each skill prior to playing a game. Practicing the skills will lead to better performance and more confidence when you are playing the game.

OVERHEAD PASS

- Grip the ball with your hands.
- Step toward your target and transfer your weight to your front foot.
- Move your arms forward in the direction of your target.
- Snap your wrists.
- Aim and pass to your target by releasing the ball, using the appropriate force to reach your target.

SKILL	PROGRESSING	COMPETENT	PROFICIENT
overhead pass	1 or 2 of the elements	3 or 4 out of 5 elements	all elements met

RECEIVING

- Spread your fingers to catch the ball.
- Catch the ball firmly using only your hands.
- Gain control of the ball.
- Maintain your balance throughout the catch.
- Make the necessary pass or run with the ball after the catch.

SKILL	PROGRESSING	COMPETENT	PROFICIENT
receiving	1 or 2 of the elements	3 or 4 out of 5 elements	all elements met

RECEIVING WHILE RUNNING

- Keep your eyes on the ball.
- Anticipate the throw. Change your speed and direction to accommodate the throw.
- Use speed and direction to create an opening.
- Catch the majority of throws.

SKILL	PROGRESSING	COMPETENT	PROFICIENT
receiving while running	1 or 2 of the elements	3 out of 4 elements	all elements met

PIVOT

The purpose of the pivot in a handball game is for you to look around and decide to pass or to attempt to score.

- Plant 1 foot, which will be your pivot foot, in place on the ground.
- Place your weight on the balls of your feet.
- Slide your non-pivot foot and rotate your body 180 degrees.

Repeat this exercise with your other foot.

SKILL	PROGRESSING	COMPETENT	PROFICIENT
pivot	1 of the elements	2 out of 3 elements	all elements

DEFENSIVE SLIDES

The purpose of performing defensive slides is to keep up with your opponent and to legally disrupt your opponent's pass or shot on goal.

- Place your weight on the balls of your feet.
- Slide to the side with quick steps.
- Do not cross your feet.
- Keep your knees bent.
- Square your hips so that they are facing your opponent.
- Hold your hands at chest level.
- Keep your eyes on your opponent's waistline.

Copyright 2024 © Lincoln Learning Solutions. All rights reserved.

- Stay with your opponent.
- Anticipate and react quickly to your opponent's movements.

SKILL	PROGRESSING	COMPETENT	PROFICIENT
defensive slides	1, 2, 3, 4, or 5 of the elements	6, 7, or 8 out of 9 elements	all elements met

TEAM HANDBALL PICK-UP GAME

OBJECT OF THE GAME

A pick-up game is like an official game except that it has adjustments to accommodate your environment. Team handball is a passing game that is played by 2 teams. Players can take up to 3 steps while in possession of the ball and can hold onto the ball for 3 seconds before passing to a teammate or shooting. Players continue passing to each other until a goal is scored, the ball is turned over to the other team, or a penalty occurs.

HANDBALL SETUP

- It is recommended that you have a trusted adult supervise the game.
- Use a playground ball to play the game.
- There are 7 players on each team including 1 goalie. Player numbers can be adjusted for pick-up games according to how many players are available.
- A rectangular handball court is comparable to a basketball court; however, you have the option of playing indoors on a court or outdoors on a field. No matter where you play, establish the size and boundaries for a safe play area.
- Set up 2 goals, each with a marked semicircle boundary from the goal line that only the goalie can be in. A net or cones can be used to mark off each goal. Also mark a penalty area beyond each semicircle.
- The above lines aren't bulleting for whatever reason, but they should be bulleted just as the points in the other sections are.

RULES OF THE GAME

- Establish the time of your game or the total points of your game.
- Establish who will be the goalie on your team.
- The other 6 players on your team should be arranged in 2 lines of 3 on your side of the court—a front line and a back line. Establish who will play on the right and left sides and who will cover the middle of the court.

	X back	X wing
X goalie	X center back	X center line
	X back	X wing

- Begin the game at midcourt with a jump ball. A neutral person should toss the ball between 2 designated opposing players.
  - In the event that there is not a neutral person available to toss the ball, use a coin toss to decide who has first possession of the ball.
- The goalies are the only players who are allowed to touch the ball with their feet.
- A goalie can come out of their goal area only without possession of the ball.
- The goalie throws the ball back into play immediately after a score.

- A player can only hold onto the ball for 3 seconds before moving or passing.
- A player can only take 3 steps while in possession of the ball.
- A turnover, which is a change in possession of the ball between teams, occurs whenever an incomplete pass or an interception is made.
- Players are not allowed to make physical contact.
- Physical contact that is made by the team on defense is a penalty that results in a throw-in by the player on offense.
- Physical contact that is made by the team on offense is a penalty that results in a turnover.

Prior to playing the game, establish and review the game rules so that all participants understand them. If problems arise, work as a group to solve them in a positive and effective manner. Appreciate different players' abilities. An example of a rule that you may want to decide upon is when to switch out the player in the goalie position so that everyone has equal play time.

Below are our game rules for safety and fairness.
1.
2.
3.
4.
5.

RATE YOUR ENJOYMENT OF HANDBALL

On a scale from 1 to 4, where 1 is not enjoyable and 4 is very enjoyable, rate this activity.

1	It was not enjoyable, and I will not participate again.
2	It was not enjoyable, but I will participate again for exercise.
3	It was enjoyable, and I will play again.
4	It was very enjoyable, and I will initiate future games.

RESEARCH INTEGRATION

Research the official rules and regulations of handball and compare them to the pick-up game rules that are given in this lesson.

HEALTH INTEGRATION

Count your pulse during and after playing handball to determine if you are exercising in your personal target heart rate zone. Predict and then compare the difference between your heart rate after playing in the goalie position and your heart rate after playing in a running position. Apply your results to your overall fitness plan. Many people choose to complete aerobic workouts by playing in fun pick-up games of sports like handball.

SOCCER

Soccer is a sport that is popular around the globe. The object of the game is to use your feet to dribble, pass, and kick a ball in order to score goals by getting the ball into your opponent's net.

People of all skill levels enjoy playing casual or competitive games of soccer. In most communities, there are soccer leagues for everyone from preschoolers to adults. Playing soccer is a great way to improve footwork, interact with others, have fun, and complete an aerobic workout.

The purpose of this lesson is for you to participate in soccer activities. Students who practice soccer skills are more likely to join a game and exercise outside of PE class. You will practice skills, learn game rules, be encouraged to communicate with teammates in a positive and effective manner, and be reminded to exhibit appropriate behavior with your team and the opposing team.

⚠️ **CAUTION: Wear appropriate safety equipment. Do not overinflate the ball.**

SOCCER SKILLS

DRIBBLING

Use your peripheral vision, or your side vision, to watch the ball as you dribble it. Dribbling is a series of small, controlled touches that you complete in order to move with the ball in your possession. Dribble the ball with the insides and outsides of your feet as well as with the tops of your feet, where your shoelaces lay. Do not dribble the ball with your toes, otherwise, you risk losing control of the ball.

- Start with the ball positioned in front of you on the ground.
- Dribble forward, keeping the ball close—no more than 3 to 5 feet in front of you.
- Move the ball with the insides, outsides, and/or tops of both of your feet.
- Keep your head up.
- Match your speed to your skill.
- Change directions.

SKILL	PROGRESSING	COMPETENT	PROFICIENT
dribbling	1, 2, or 3 of the elements	4 or 5 out of 6 elements	all elements

PASSING

Passing the ball is an important part of soccer. Players pass the ball to each other in order to keep the other team from gaining control of the ball and to progress the ball up the field toward the other team's goal.

- Start with the soccer ball on the ground, next to the inside of your dominant foot.
- Position the inside of your kicking foot behind the middle of the soccer ball.
- Establish your non-kicking foot slightly behind you.
- Swing your kicking leg back, keeping it straight throughout your entire kick.
- Contact the middle of the ball with the inside of your foot. Follow through your kick with your foot and leg.
- Use appropriate force and direction to keep your pass on target.

SKILL	PROGRESSING	COMPETENT	PROFICIENT
passing	1, 2, or 3 of the elements	4 or 5 out of 6 elements	all elements

TRAPPING: OPTION 1

Trapping is a way of stopping the ball, receiving a pass, or gaining control of the ball.

- Start with the ball positioned in front of you on the ground.
- Place your dominant foot on top of the ball. To do this, lift your foot slightly off the ground, keeping your ankle locked and your toes up.
- Repeat this with your non-dominant foot.

SKILL	PROGRESSING	COMPETENT	PROFICIENT
trapping: option 1	1 of the elements	2 out of 3 elements	all elements

TRAPPING: OPTION 2

Trapping is also a way to stop the ball in order to quickly gain control and transition to your next move.

- When the soccer ball comes toward you, turn the ankle of whichever foot you are trapping with so that your instep, or the inside of your foot, is facing forward.
- Cushion the ball with your foot as you stop it lightly, as if you were catching an egg.
- Repeat this with your other foot.

SKILL	PROGRESSING	COMPETENT	PROFICIENT
trapping: option 2	1 of the elements	2 out of 3 elements	all elements

SHOOTING

The purpose of shooting is to get the soccer ball into your opponent's goal by striking it with your foot.

- Place 2 discs about 4 feet apart and 5 feet in front of you. Place the soccer ball on the ground in front of you.
- Stand so that your dominant leg, or kicking leg, is pulled back behind you.
- Place your non-kicking foot alongside the soccer ball, with your toes pointing at the goal that you made.
- Bend the knee of your kicking leg by pulling your foot back. Then, in a single motion, swing your leg forward, straightening your leg and pointing your toes to kick the soccer ball with the top of your foot. Kick the center of the soccer ball with the laces of your shoe, pointing your toes down. You do not want to kick the soccer ball with your toes.
- Follow through your kick, making sure that you finish with your toes pointing toward the goal.

SKILL	PROGRESSING	COMPETENT	PROFICIENT
shooting	1 or 2 of the elements	3 or 4 out of 5 elements	all elements

PRACTICE THE SKILLS

After mastering the basic soccer skills, put them all together in practice activities.

DRIBBLE

- Practice dribbling by placing discs in various locations around your practice area. As you are dribbling, weave in and out of the discs.

Copyright 2024 © Lincoln Learning Solutions. All rights reserved.

TRAP

- Place 2 discs about 4 feet apart to create a goal. Make your goal 10 to 20 feet away from you.
- Toss the ball up in the air, trapping it with your foot and guiding it to the ground just in front of you.
    - After mastering trapping the soccer ball with your feet, try trapping it using your thigh. Throw the soccer ball up in the air and bend your knee so that your thigh is just under the soccer ball. As the soccer ball comes back down, cushion it with your thigh. Allow the ball to hit your thigh and then guide it with your thigh as it falls to the ground.
- Dribble the soccer ball toward the goal.
- When you get about 5 feet away from the goal, shoot the ball through the discs.

Trap

PASS

- Set up 2 discs about 3 feet apart. Aim to kick the soccer ball between the discs.
- If you kick the soccer ball in the middle, the soccer ball will go straight.
- Move to the left of the discs. Try passing the soccer ball between the discs from the left. Kick the right side of the ball with the instep of your right foot to make the soccer ball go to the left.
- Move to the right of the discs. Try passing the soccer ball between the discs from the right. Kick the left side of the ball with the instep of your left foot to make the ball go to the left.

Pass

SHOOT ON GOAL

- Place 2 discs about 4 feet apart to use as your goal.
- Shoot the soccer ball between the discs that you set up as a goal.
- Dribble the soccer ball toward the goal and shoot. You can add extra discs between you and the goal to act as pathways that you can dribble through or points where you can change directions before shooting on goal.

STRATEGIES TO REMEMBER

- When you are dribbling the soccer ball, keep it close to you.
- When you are passing the ball, kick with the instep of your foot.
- When you are trapping the ball, cushion it as if you were catching an egg.
- When you are shooting the soccer ball, point your toes down and kick the middle of the ball with the top of your foot. Your non-kicking foot should be next to the ball, pointing toward the target. When you follow through, make sure that your kicking toes end up pointing toward the target as well.

CHALLENGE SKILLS

The following advanced skills are for those who have mastered the basic skills. The challenge skills are recommended for those who want to improve their footwork.

TOE TAPS

With the ball stationary on the ground, hop onto your right foot and tap the top of the ball with the toes of your left foot. Then, hop onto your left foot and tap the top of the ball with the toes of your right foot. Continue this pattern. How fast can you go?

Toe taps

SIDE TO SIDE

With the ball between your feet, move the ball from side to side with the insteps of your feet while taking small hops.

Side to side

PULL BACK/REVERSE DIRECTION

Place your foot on top of the ball. Pull your foot back so that the ball rolls along the bottom of your foot from back to front. This will pull the ball back so that you can make a quick turn to dribble or pass in the opposite direction.

Pull back/Reverse direction

BACKSPIN/CATCH

Position your toes on the top of the ball to start. In a single motion, roll your toes backward and down along the ball to roll the ball back onto your toes.

Backspin/Catch

SCISSORS

Swing 1 foot around the ball. Then, swing your other foot around the ball in the opposite direction. Try again, switching the directions that you swing your feet.

Scissors

KNEE JUGGLE

Drop the ball onto your knee, softly bouncing it back up. Use the same knee or your other knee to bounce the ball. See how many times you can bounce the ball on your knees to keep it from hitting the ground.

Knee juggle

INSIDE FOOT JUGGLE

Hold up 1 of your feet, bending at the knee to angle the instep of your foot up. Drop the ball and bounce it back up with the instep of your foot. Use the same foot or the instep of your other foot to bounce the ball back up again before it hits the ground. How many times can you juggle the ball with the insides of your feet before it touches the ground?

Inside foot juggle

OUTSIDE FOOT JUGGLE

Drop the ball softly. Use the outside of 1 of your feet, angling your ankle down, to kick the ball back up. Repeat this with 1 or both of your feet. How long can you juggle the ball without it hitting the ground?

Outside foot juggle

TOE JUGGLE

Drop the ball slightly in front of you. Gently kick the ball back up with the top part of your foot. Continue this with 1 or both of your feet to juggle the ball without letting it hit the ground for as long as you can.

Toe juggle

COMBINATION JUGGLE

Use a combination of your knees and the insides, outsides, and tops of your feet to keep the ball up for as long as you can.

Copyright 2024 © Lincoln Learning Solutions. All rights reserved.

OFFENSIVE AND DEFENSIVE SKILLS

Quick, fast, agile footwork is an essential component of a soccer game. Practice footwork skills to improve offensive and defensive play.

OFFENSIVE SKILLS

FAKE

- Look 1 direction, but pass or move the ball in another direction.
- Stay on the balls of your feet.
- Move quickly.

SKILL	PROGRESSING	COMPETENT	PROFICIENT
fake	1 of the elements	2 out of 3 elements	all elements

GIVE AND GO

The purpose of the give and go in a soccer game is for you to pass the ball to a teammate and quickly relocate so that you can receive a pass.

- Pass the ball to a teammate.
- Move quickly to relocate and support your offense.
- Indicate (call out) that you are ready and open to receive the ball.
- Receive the ball.

SKILL	PROGRESSING	COMPETENT	PROFICIENT
give and go	1 or 2 of the elements	3 out of 4 elements	all elements

THROW-IN

The only time that a player other than a goalie can use their hands to touch the ball in a game is to perform a throw-in. A throw-in occurs when the ball goes out of bounds on either of the long sides of the field. The team that sends the ball out of bounds loses possession of the ball. The other team gains control of the ball and throws it in from the point where it went out of bounds.

- Hold the ball in front of your body with both hands.
- Lift the ball over and behind your head.
- Step forward and throw the ball to a teammate. You cannot be the first person to touch the ball after you throw it in; or, you cannot throw-in to yourself.
- Follow through toward your target.
- Both of your feet must remain on the ground when you complete a throw-in. You can drag your back foot, but you cannot hop.

SKILL	PROGRESSING	COMPETENT	PROFICIENT
throw-in	1 or 2 of the elements	3 or 4 out of 5 elements	all elements

DEFENSIVE SKILLS

DEFENSIVE READY POSITION

The ready position allows a player to move quickly in any direction. It is used for both offense and defense.

- Bend your knees to keep your body low.
- Stand with your feet shoulder-width apart.
- Keep your head up and your weight on the balls of your feet.
- Hold your arms extended out above waist height.
- Be ready to move and react quickly.
- Anticipate direction.

SKILL	PROGRESSING	COMPETENT	PROFICIENT
defensive ready position	1, 2, or 3 of the elements	4 or 5 out of 6 elements	all elements met

DEFENSIVE SLIDES

The purpose of the defensive slides in soccer is to keep up with your opponent and to legally take the ball or legally disrupt the opponent's pass or shot.

- Place your weight on the balls of your feet.
- Slide to the side with quick steps.
- Do not cross your feet.
- Keep your knees bent.
- Square your hips so that they face your opponent.
- Hold your hands up at chest level.
- Keep your eyes on your opponent's waistline.
- Stay with your opponent.
- Anticipate and react quickly to your opponent's movements.

SKILL	PROGRESSING	COMPETENT	PROFICIENT
defensive slides	1, 2, 3, 4, or 5 of the elements	6, 7, or 8 out of 9 elements	all elements met

PRACTICING OFFENSIVE AND DEFENSIVE SKILLS

- Practice the **give and go** with a partner and a defender. Pass the ball, quickly relocate, and then receive the pass, avoiding the defender.
- Practice the **fake** independently. Set up a cone as a decoy. Fake the pass toward the cone, and then pass to your partner. Practice until you feel comfortable with the movement.
- Practice the **fake** with a partner defending you. Dribble, fake, and then move in another direction to get around the defensive player. Practice until you feel comfortable with the fake.
- Practice the **defensive slides** with a partner. As your partner dribbles, defensive slide to try to prevent the player from making a successful pass or shot. Practice until you feel comfortable with the defensive slide.

SOCCER GAMES

KEEP AWAY

Keep away is an activity that lets you practice your soccer skills, even if you do not have enough players to play a full game of soccer.

- You need at least 5 players to play this game.
- Make a circle with all but 1 of the players. The remaining 1 person goes in the middle of the circle.
- The players on the outside, or making up the circle, can touch the ball twice to keep it away from the person in the middle.
- If the person in the middle touches the ball, they switch with the person the ball was stolen from.
- If the players on the outside touch the ball 21 times before the person in the middle touches it, the outside players win and the person in the middle stays in the middle for another round.

ABOUT THE GAME

- To begin, 2 opposing teams of 11 players each including a goalie are established.
- All players must wear shin guards, socks that cover their shin guards, and appropriate cleats.
- The game is played on a rectangular grass or turf field.
- A goal is located at each end of the field.
- The object of the game is to move the ball down the field by passing or dribbling with your feet and to score by getting the ball into your opponent's goal.
- A game is divided into 45-minute halves.
- A goal is worth 1 point.
- The team with the most points at the end of the second half wins.

PLAYING THE GAME

- The game begins with a coin toss made by a referee at midfield.
- The team that possesses the ball is on offense and the other team is on defense.
- The first player to touch the ball at kickoff can only touch the ball once. They must kick the ball or pass it to another player who can dribble, pass, or kick the ball.
- No players except for the goalies or a player who is performing a throw-in can touch the ball with their hands. The entire arm counts as a hand in soccer, which means that a player cannot touch the ball anywhere from their fingertips to their upper arm.
- It is legal to use any body part other than a hand to contact the ball.
- If a player illegally uses their hands, which is referred to as a handball, the ball is turned over to the opposing team.
- The players on defense try to intercept, or take away, the ball from the offensive team to gain possession of the ball.

DEMONSTRATE POSITIVE GAME BEHAVIOR

- Follow all game rules.
- Do not conduct any fouls against another player (do not make illegal physical contact) and do not exhibit any unsportsmanlike behavior.
  - Fouls and unsportsmanlike behavior can result in a free kick, a yellow card warning, or a red card ejection from the game for the offending player.
- Be supportive and encouraging to your teammates.
- Treat your opponents with respect.

SKILL	PROGRESSING	COMPETENT	PROFICIENT
game behavior	1 or 2 of the elements	3 out of 4 elements	all elements met

MODIFIED 5-ON-5 GAME

Play a casual game of soccer according to the number of available players. Play a game of 3-on-3, 4-on-4, 5-on-5, or whatever you are able with your available players. The following information is for a 5-on-5 game.

```
^^^^^^^^^^^^^^^^^^^^^^
^    2   4 | 4   2    ^
1                     1
^    3   5 | 5   3    ^
^^^^^^^^^^^^^^^^^^^^^^
```

- Establish 2 teams, each consisting of 1 goalie, 2 defensive players, and 2 offensive players.
- Establish boundaries and set up a goal for each team.
- Establish the perimeters that the 5 players on each team adhere to. Establishing perimeters encourages teamwork and passing. The following are suggestions.
  - The goalie remains in the goalie area.
  - The defenders are allowed up to midfield.
  - The offensive players are allowed from ¾ of the way back on their side to the opposing goal.
- Establish rules for your game. The following are suggestions.
  - For out-of-bounds balls, a player from the opposing team throws the ball back into play.
  - Goalies throw the ball in after a score.
  - Goalie and players may use their hands to throw the ball in.

RATE YOUR ENJOYMENT OF THE SOCCER ACTIVITY THAT YOU ENJOYED MOST

On a scale from 1 to 4, where 1 is not enjoyable and 4 is very enjoyable, rate this activity.

1	It was not enjoyable, and I will not participate again.
2	It was not enjoyable, but I will participate again for exercise.
3	It was enjoyable, and I will play again.
4	It was very enjoyable, and I will initiate future games.

RESEARCH INTEGRATION

1. Research soccer's country of origin, who invented soccer, where soccer is played throughout the world, alternate names for soccer, and the official rules and regulations of soccer.
2. Attend a soccer game or watch a soccer game on television. It can be men's, women's, or co-ed soccer at any level—youth, high school, college, or professional. Identify the soccer skills you have learned that are used by the players throughout the game.

HEALTH INTEGRATION

1. Count your pulse after practicing skills and after playing in a game to determine if you are exercising in your personal target heart rate zone. Predict and then compare the difference between your heart rate after playing in the goalie position and your heart rate after playing in a running, or field, position. Apply the results to your overall fitness plan. Many people choose to complete aerobic workouts by playing in fast-paced games like soccer.
2. Have a discussion about the protective gear that is worn by a soccer player and why they wear this gear.

SHORT-HANDLED RACKET TENNIS

Tennis is a sport that is played by striking a ball with a racket over a net. It is played by 2 opposing players or by 2 teams of 2 as a doubles game. The required striking activity helps you develop concentration, hand-eye coordination, and footwork. You can play tennis as a competitive sport or as an opportunity for social play.

The purpose of this lesson is for you to learn to use a short-handled tennis racket by learning the mechanics of the tennis strokes, to participate in tennis games, and to get an aerobic workout.

CAUTION: Make sure that nobody is close to you before you swing the racket. Do not walk into the path of another person who is swinging a racket.

RACKET SKILLS

READY POSITION

The ready position allows a player to move quickly in any direction.

- Bending your knees, stand with your feet shoulder-width apart.
- Keep your head up.
- Keep your weight on the balls of your feet.
- Hold the racket in your dominant hand.

SKILL	PROGRESSING	COMPETENT	PROFICIENT
ready position	1 or 2 of the elements	3 out of 4 elements	all elements met

HANDSHAKE GRIP

- Hold the racket in your dominant hand as if you were about to shake someone's hand.
- Place your 4 fingers around the racket; then, wrap your thumb around the racket in the opposite direction.
- Hold the racket so that the head is vertical to the ground. Make sure that the strings on the racket head are facing front and back.
- Point the handle toward your belly button.

SKILL	PROGRESSING	COMPETENT	PROFICIENT
handshake grip	1 or 2 of the elements	3 out of 4 elements	all elements met

FOREHAND STROKE

- Begin in the ready position.
- Pivot to bring the racket back on the same side of your body as your dominant hand.
- Face the palm of your hand forward.
- While swinging the racket with your dominant hand, shift your weight from your back foot to your front foot as you step forward.
- Extend your arm and flick your wrist to hit the ball, pointing the face of the racket up to get the ball over the net.
- Follow through to your target.

SKILL	PROGRESSING	COMPETENT	PROFICIENT
forehand stroke	1, 2, or 3 of the elements	4 or 5 out of 6 elements	all elements met

BACKHAND STROKE

- Begin in the ready position.
- Rotate the racket and extend it across your body.
- Rotate your feet and shoulders in the same direction as the racket.
- Face the back of your hand (the side that your knuckles are on) forward.
- As you swing the racket, step forward with your non-dominant foot.
- Flick your wrist as you are hitting the ball with the center of the racket.
- Follow through to your target.

SKILL	PROGRESSING	COMPETENT	PROFICIENT
backhand stroke	1, 2, or 3 of the elements	4, 5, or 6 out of 7 elements	all elements met

2-HANDED BACKHAND STROKE

- Place your non-dominant hand below your dominant hand on the racket handle.
- Rotate the racket and extend it across your body.
- Rotate your feet and shoulders in the same direction as the racket.
- Flick your wrists when you are hitting the ball with the center of the racket.
- Follow through to your target.

OVERHAND STROKE

- Bend your elbow slightly and position the racket under the ball.
- Flick your wrist to hit the ball with the center of the racket.
- Extend your arm as you are making contact.
- Follow through to your target.

SKILL	PROGRESSING	COMPETENT	PROFICIENT
overhand stroke	1 or 2 of the elements	3 out of 4 elements	all elements met

SERVES

Every game starts with a serve.

PUNCH SERVE

Stand behind the service line at a 45-degree angle to the net. A punch serve is an excellent stroke to use as a beginner.

- If you are right-handed, place your left foot forward; if you are left-handed, place your right foot forward. Put your weight on your back foot.
- Hold the racket with a forehand grip in your dominant hand. Raise the racket over your head and slightly back.
- Hold the ball with your fingertips in your non-dominant hand.
- Toss the ball slightly in front of you and high above the racket. Look up at the ball.
- As the ball comes back down, hit it up and forward with the racket. Extend your arm and the racket while you are hitting the ball.
- Follow through to your target. Swing out, across, and down.

SKILL	PROGRESSING	COMPETENT	PROFICIENT
punch serve	1, 2, or 3 of the elements	4 or 5 out of 6 elements	all elements met

OVERHAND SERVE

- Hold the racket with your dominant hand.
- Place your non-dominant foot so that it is pointing toward the opposite post of the net and your dominant foot so that it is parallel to the court.
- Toss the ball into the air just above your head.
- Bring your dominant arm back with the head of the racket pointing toward the sky.
- Watch for the ball to begin to fall.
- Extend your arm up over your head and contact the ball with the head of the racket.

SKILL	PROGRESSING	COMPETENT	PROFICIENT
overhand serve	1, 2, or 3 of the elements	4 or 5 out of 6 elements	all elements met

SKILL PRACTICE

AGAINST A WALL

- Practice the various strokes and serves by hitting the ball against a wall with the racket. Catch the ball each time and repeat.
- Allow the ball to bounce before hitting it against the wall.
- Volley against the wall, aiming and hitting different spots on the wall.

WITH A PARTNER

You can use a jump rope to separate each side if a net is unavailable.

- Have a partner stand on 1 side of the net and toss the ball toward your forehand. Return with a proper forehand stroke.
- Have a partner stand on 1 side of the net and toss the ball toward your backhand. Return with a proper backhand stroke.

- Have a partner stand on 1 side of the net and toss the ball, mixing up forehand and backhand shots. Return with proper forehand strokes or backhand strokes.
- Use the various strokes to hit the ball back and forth with a partner. Stand 15 feet away from your partner when you are volleying back and forth.

GAMES

INDEPENDENT RACKET DRIBBLE CHALLENGE

- Place the palm of your dominant hand on top of the racket and turn the face of the racket toward the ground.
- Hold the ball in your non-dominant hand.
- Bump the ball with the racket.
- Let the ball bounce back up to the racket.
- Continue dribbling the ball. How many consecutive dribbles can you do in a row?
- To increase difficulty, stand near a line and try to make the ball hit the line each time you dribble it. How many consecutive line dribbles can you do in a row?
- Practice air dribbling. Hit the ball consecutively up in the air with the racket. Do not let the ball touch the ground between hits. How many hits can you do in a row?

COOPERATIVE SCORING GAME

- Begin with 1 person standing on either side of the net. If a net is unavailable, separate the sides with a jump rope.
- Conduct a coin toss to determine who will serve first.
- Rally the ball back and forth following the serve.
- Count each time a player strikes the ball and keeps it in play, not counting the serve.
- The ball can only be hit once per side. So, each player can only use 1 hit on their own side of the court to return the ball to the other side of the court.
- The ball can be returned after 1 bounce or on a fly, which means that the player can strike the ball before it hits the ground.
- Continue until the ball is not in play.
- Indicate the score.
- Switch servers.
- Play again and try to beat your previous score.

OFFICIAL SINGLES GAME

You will need traditional tennis balls for this game.

- Start with an overhand serve from the right side of the court. Serve from behind the baseline to your opponent on the left.
- You must get the ball into your opponent's service box. You have 2 tries to get the ball into the service box.
- If you hit the ball into your opponent's service box and your opponent cannot return it, you win that volley and get a point.
- Now, serve from the left side of the court.

- When your score is an even number, serve from the right side of the court. When your score is an odd number, serve from the left side of the court.
- Continue serving the ball until the game is over. The receiver becomes the server during the next game.
- You may only hit the ball 1 time on each side.
- You score if your opponent does not have a successful serve, fails to return a serve, or hits the ball out of bounds.
- You lose a volley if you or the racket touch the net.

SCORING
- The server's score is always announced first.
- The point system is given below.
    - 0 points (love) = 0 points
    - 1 point = 15 points
    - 2 points = 30 points
    - 3 points = 40 points
    - 4 points = win
- To win a game, you must lead by at least 2 points.
- If the score is tied at 40 points (a deuce), you must earn 2 consecutive points (an advantage point) to win the game.
- You must win at least 6 games in a set. You must lead by 2 sets to win a match.

RATE YOUR ENJOYMENT OF THE TENNIS ACTIVITY THAT YOU ENJOYED MOST
On a scale from 1 to 4, where 1 is not enjoyable and 4 is very enjoyable, rate this activity.

1	It was not enjoyable, and I will not participate again.
2	It was not enjoyable, but I will participate again for exercise.
3	It was enjoyable, and I will play again.
4	It was very enjoyable, and I will initiate future games.

RESEARCH INTEGRATION
1. Research tennis's country of origin, who invented tennis, and the official rules and regulations of tennis.
2. Attend a tennis game or watch a tennis game on television.

HEALTH INTEGRATION
Count your pulse to determine if you are exercising in your personal target heart rate zone. Count your pulse after practicing skills and after playing a game. Apply the results to your overall fitness plan. Many people choose to complete aerobic workouts by playing in social, competitive games with friends.

WIFFLE® BALL

Wiffle® ball is a game played by 2 teams of 1 to 10 players each on a small version of a baseball field with a plastic bat and ball. The object of the game is to scores more runs than the opposing team. People of all ages play Wiffle® ball to get exercise and to enjoy the social aspect of the game.

Playing the game allows you to utilize and improve the skill-related components of agility, balance, coordination, speed, power, and reaction. Wiffle® ball also provides the opportunity to work as a team to develop offensive and defensive strategies as well as the ability to transition quickly between them.

The purpose of this lesson is to practice the skills necessary for you to participate in a team game, follow game rules, communicate with teammates in a positive and effective manner, and exhibit appropriate behavior with your team and the opposing team.

⚠️ **CAUTION: Make sure that nobody is close to you before you swing the bat. Do not walk into the path of another person who is swinging a bat. Do not throw the bat.**

WIFFLE® BALL SKILLS

STRIKING AND BASE-RUNNING SKILLS

GRIP AND STANCE

GRIP

- If you are right-handed, wrap your left hand below your right hand at the bottom of the bat. If you are left-handed, wrap your right hand below your left hand at the bottom of the bat.
    - Smaller batters may benefit from choking up on the bat, or holding the bat a little higher up from the base of the handle.
- Your hands should be touching each other.

STANCE

- Position your body perpendicular to the plate.
- Bending your knees slightly, place your feet so that they are shoulder-width apart. Your hips, knees, and shoulders should be squared. This stance should be comfortable.
- Once your feet are inside the batter's box, face your shoulder toward the pitcher and point the tip of the bat up toward the sky. If you are right-handed, face your left shoulder toward the pitcher. If you are left-handed, face your right shoulder toward the pitcher.

SKILL	PROGRESSING	COMPETENT	PROFICIENT
grip and stance	1 or 2 of the elements	3 or 4 out of 5 elements	all elements met

STRIKING A BALL FROM A PITCH

- Check your position to see if your swing will cross over the plate. Stand in the batter's box and touch the opposite side of the plate with the bat. Adjust your stance if necessary.
- While in the correct position, practice swinging all the way through, keeping the bat level with the ground and twisting your body as you hit the ball.
- The whole swing should be in your hips. Try to get in the habit of twisting your whole body rather than just swinging your arms.
- Take a small step toward the pitcher as they throw the ball. Rotate your hips toward the pitcher, moving your hands through the strike zone and over the plate. Watch the ball as it comes toward you and over the plate before you hit it into the outfield.
- After swinging the bat, face your hips toward the pitcher. Pivot your back foot, but do not let it come off the ground.
- During a game, after you hit the ball, drop the bat to the ground and run to first base.

SKILL	PROGRESSING	COMPETENT	PROFICIENT
striking	1 or 2 of the elements	3 or 4 out of 5 elements	all elements met

BASE RUNNING

- Drop the bat to the ground after you hit the ball.
- Immediately sprint as fast as you can to first base.
- Run on and through the base.

SKILL	PROGRESSING	COMPETENT	PROFICIENT
base running	1 of the elements	2 out of 3 elements	all elements met

THROWING, CATCHING, AND FIELDING SKILLS

OVERHAND THROW

An overhand throw can be used by the field players and the pitcher.

- Take a first step, such as a hop or shuffle step, toward your target.
- Bring your throwing arm back, up, and around.
- Step with your opposite foot.
- Rotate your hips as you twist with your throw.
- Release the ball high in your throw, when your throwing arm is in an L shape near your ear.
- Follow through your throw to make it accurate.

SKILL	PROGRESSING	COMPETENT	PROFICIENT
overhand throw	1, 2, or 3 of the elements	4 or 5 out of 6 elements	all elements met

CATCHING

- Track the ball with your eyes.
- Step toward your target.
- Extend your hands to the level of the ball.
- Give with the ball (pull it slightly toward you) as it hits your hands for a soft catch.

SKILL	PROGRESSING	COMPETENT	PROFICIENT
catching	1 or 2 of the elements	3 out of 4 elements	all elements met

FIELDING GROUND BALLS

- Keep your body low and ready.
- Scoop up the ball as it rolls.
- Look to your target.
- Throw accurately to your target.

SKILL	PROGRESSING	COMPETENT	PROFICIENT
fielding	1 or 2 of the elements	3 out of 4 elements	all elements met

SKILL PRACTICE

THROW AND CATCH

- Throw and catch a ball against a wall.
- Throw and catch a ball with a partner.
- Throw and catch a ball with a partner while moving.

BATTING FOR DISTANCE

- As a batter, hit a pitch that is thrown to you by a partner.
- The pitcher will place a disc cone where the ball landed, marking the distance it traveled.
- Hit another pitch, trying to increase the distance you hit the ball from your last hit.
- Take turns batting and pitching with your partner.

BATTING FOR DIRECTION

- Place disc cones in the right, left, and center field.
- Before you bat, call out the direction in which your hit will go: right field, left field, or center field.
- Hit a pitch from your partner in the determined direction.
- Take turns batting and pitching with your partner.

BATTING FOR FORCE

- Before you bat, call out what the force of your hit will be—soft, medium, or hard.
- Hit a pitch from your partner with the force that you called out.
- Take turns batting and pitching with your partner.

3 PLAYERS PRACTICE GAME: STRIKING, FIELDING, AND BASE RUNNING

- Set up a playing field with first base, second base, third base, home base, and a pitching mound.
- Choose 1 player to be the pitcher, 1 player to be the batter, and the remaining players to be outfielders.
- If you are the pitcher, pitch the ball to the batter until the batter gets a hit. Retrieve the ball and run to home base before the batter gets there.
- If you are the batter, run the bases after you hit the ball. If the pitcher gets to home base before you, you are out.
- If you are an outfielder, retrieve the ball and give it back to the pitcher before the batter gets to home base.
- Take turns in the different positions.

WIFFLE® BALL GAME

- Wiffle® ball teams can range from being made up of 1 to 10 players.
- The pitcher throws 3 balls to each batter, and the batter must attempt to hit them.
- If you fail to hit the ball within 3 pitches, you strike out.
- Do not run to the next base until the batter hits the ball.
- If you hit the ball into the single zone, you advance 1 base. If you hit the ball into the double zone, you advance 2 bases. If you hit the ball past the triple zone, you get a home run.
- Every player who makes it around the bases scores a run for their team.
- You are out if the batted ball is caught in the air, a fielder tags you when you are running to a base, or the ball is fielded and thrown to a base before you get there.
- An inning is over when all the batters have had their turns or if 3 batters strike out.
- At the end of the game, the team with the most runs is the winner. Games may last a set time or last a set number of innings.

GAME NOTES

1. A **foul ball** is a ball that the batter hits outside of the baseline. The batter gets another pitch if this happens. There are unlimited foul balls unless a defensive player catches a fly ball.
2. The field is split up into different **zones**. The suggested sizes of these zones are given below, but the zones can be adjusted according to your play area.
   - The single zone is 24 feet from home base.
   - The double zone is 20 feet from the single zone.
   - The triple zone is 20 feet from the double zone.
   - The home run zone is 20 feet from the triple zone.

3. A **strike** occurs when the batter swings and misses the ball. The batter is out after 3 strikes.
4. A **fly ball** is a ball that is hit up in the air. Fly balls are often caught to strike a player out.
5. The **pitcher** is the defensive player who stands on the pitching mound and pitches (throws) the ball to the batter.

6. The **catcher** is the defensive player who plays behind home base. The catcher returns the ball to the pitcher and tags players out at home base.

7. An **outfielder** is a defensive player who plays behind the baseline to retrieve the ball when it is hit far.

8. A **baseman** is a defensive player who plays on first, second, or third base. The 3 basemen should stand near their bases. To prevent colliding with a runner, the basemen should not stand on their bases; however, the basemen can touch their bases to strike a runner out.

RATE YOUR ENJOYMENT OF WIFFLE® BALL

On a scale from 1 to 4, where 1 is not enjoyable and 4 is very enjoyable, rate this activity.

1	It was not enjoyable, and I will not participate again.
2	It was not enjoyable, but I will participate again for exercise.
3	It was enjoyable, and I will play again.
4	It was very enjoyable, and I will initiate future games.

RESEARCH INTEGRATION

1. Research who invented the game of Wiffle® ball and the rules and regulations of the game.
2. Attend a baseball game or watch a baseball game on television and compare the skills that you have practiced for the game of Wiffle® ball with the skills that the baseball players use.

HEALTH INTEGRATION

Count your pulse after practicing Wiffle® ball skills and after playing in a Wiffle® ball game to determine if you are exercising in your personal target heart rate zone. Apply the results to your overall fitness plan. Often, when you are playing in games that require you to take turns, you may find that your pulse rate is not in your aerobic target zone. If that is the case for you, remember that you still need to get your aerobic exercise in for the week. Enjoy the game and count it toward your 60 minutes per day of being active.

GRADE 8
PE EQUIPMENT KIT

SAFETY ALERT!

Before you exercise, make sure that you are properly warmed up and have enough room to perform each activity. Wear proper equipment and follow activity-specific safety rules. Stay hydrated and take breaks as needed. Exercise only if you are healthy, and always exercise at your own pace. If an exercise starts to hurt, if you feel dizzy, or if you feel light-headed, stop the exercise completely and get help. Upon completion of any workout, cool down and stretch.

WARM-UP AND COOL-DOWN

⚠ **CAUTION: Stretching should not be painful; ease up if stretching hurts. See the Flexibility section of your PE Manual for more information.**

WARM-UP

The purpose of a warm-up is to gradually increase heart rate, breathing rate, body temperature, and muscle temperature. Warming up prior to exercising increases circulation and blood flow to your muscles. When your muscles are warmed up, their performance—such as in the areas of strength and speed—is enhanced and risk of injury is decreased.

Before you begin any workout, you should always warm up. Getting your heart and muscles prepared for exercise is important. There are numerous ways to get your body ready to participate in physical activity. **The Flexibility section of your PE Manual includes a variety of dynamic and static stretches for each major body part that will help you increase your flexibility.**

Elements of a Warm-Up

1. **Low-intensity cardio**: Walk, slow jog, or slow swim for 5 to 10 minutes to increase your heart rate, breathing rate, and body temperature before your workout.
2. **Dynamic stretch**: Perform a repeated motion—such as kicks, high knees, lunges, or arm circles—that will loosen up your joints and prepare your muscles for the exercise that you are about to do. Perform each dynamic stretch for at least 30 seconds.
3. **Static stretch**: Stretch your muscles slowly and hold each stretch for 20 to 30 seconds without bouncing in order to lengthen your muscles and increase your flexibility. Some important areas to stretch as a part of your warm-up are your neck, sides, shoulders, triceps, back, hamstrings, quadriceps, and groin.

Example + + = EFFECTIVE WARM-UP

PERSONAL WARM-UP ACTIVITY

1. Select an exercise activity to participate in.
2. Design your personal warm-up plan for the activity that you selected. Any dynamic and static stretches that you choose to complete should be specific to the exercise activity that you chose.
3. Have a trusted adult or friend assess your stretches to make sure that you are using proper form.
4. Explain how the warm-up will decrease your risk of injury for this activity. _____

Procedure	Enter your personal warm-up regimen below.
1. **Low-intensity cardiovascular exercise:** Exercise for 5 to 10 minutes.	
2. **Dynamic stretches:** Perform dynamic stretches specifically for the selected activity.	
3. **Static stretches:** Perform static stretches specifically for the selected activity.	

COOL-DOWN

After you have finished your workout, exercise, or activity, it is imperative that your body returns to its normal state. You want to avoid stopping immediately and sitting down **unless you are in pain, dizzy, or injured**. Be sure to slow your heart rate and breathing rate back to or slightly above their resting rates. There are several ways to do this. You can simply walk or slow down your exercise for a few minutes, or you can find your own way to slow your body back down. You also may want to incorporate static stretches to increase flexibility and to avoid your muscles tightening. **The Flexibility section of your PE Manual includes a variety of static stretches for each major body part.** Always keep hydrated by drinking water before, during, and after exercise.

Elements of a Cool-Down

1. **Slow down**: Walk or gradually slow down your exercise—such as returning to a slow swim if you are swimming—until your heart rate, breathing rate, and body temperature are back to normal.
2. **Static stretch**: Stretch your muscles slowly and hold each stretch for 20 to 30 seconds without bouncing in order to lengthen your muscles and increase flexibility. Some important areas to stretch as part of your cool-down are your neck, sides, shoulders, triceps, back, hamstrings, quadriceps, and groin.

WALK + STATIC STRETCHES = EFFECTIVE COOL-DOWN

Design your personal cool-down plan. You can perform the same cool-down each time you finish a physical activity or you can change each time in order to reflect the exercise activity, such as by slowing your pedaling if you are biking.

Procedure	Enter your personal cool-down regimen below.
1. **Slow down:** Perform this slowed activity for 5 to 10 minutes.	
2. **Static stretches:** Perform several lower-body and upper-body stretches.	

AEROBIC EXERCISE

Aerobic exercise—also referred to as cardio or cardiovascular exercise—is any exercise that is done in your target heart rate zone and is performed for an extended period. Aerobic exercise is important for strengthening your heart muscle. Your heart pumps nutrient-rich, oxygenated blood to the cells of your body. Your skin, hair, bones, muscles, brain, and internal organs benefit from the increased nutrition and oxygen provided during regular aerobic workouts.

The purpose of this lesson is to encourage you to do an aerobic workout for at least 30 minutes 3 to 5 days per week in order to experience health benefits. An aerobic workout can be included as part of your recommended 60 minutes of daily physical activity. **The Cardiovascular Endurance section of your PE Manual includes the target heart rate zone formula and the Borg Rating of Perceived Exertion Scale to help you to determine if you are exercising for heart health.** You can also use available technology to monitor your pulse rate and workout intensity.

⚠ **CAUTION: Wear proper equipment and follow activity-specific safety rules.**

AEROBIC EXERCISE

There are a variety of exercises to choose from. Choose aerobic exercises that will fit into your lifestyle and that you enjoy. Limit excuses and make a commitment to exercise!

TYPES OF AEROBIC EXERCISE

Sports: Playing a sport or sport-related game provides the opportunity to complete an aerobic workout and interact with others. Examples include soccer, basketball, volleyball, swimming, hockey, lacrosse, tennis, badminton, pickleball, handball, gymnastics, dance, martial arts, wrestling, track and field, and so on.

Outdoor pursuits: Examples include walking, jogging, biking, canoeing, kayaking, golfing, fly fishing, hiking, rock climbing, horseback riding, skiing, and so on.

Fitness gyms: Find a gym that is convenient for you to attend where you can complete circuit exercises, use aerobic machines, take classes, and more.

Stationary exercise equipment: Examples include using a jump rope, treadmill, elliptical trainer, bike, mini trampoline, and so on.

Exercise apps or videos: Use a workout tutorial on an app, website, video, or other digital source.

Your own sequence workouts: You can also design your own workout sequences by following the steps below.

- Create your personal aerobic workout routines by blending activities that involve basic locomotor skills such as jogging in place, jumping jacks, high knees, and so on.
- Design the intensity and duration of the exercise according to your level of fitness.
- Consider setting your routine to music.
- Perform your personal routine for some or all your aerobic workouts.

When you are beginning any exercise program, begin with workouts that match your fitness level and then build accordingly. You want to feel refreshed after each exercise session, not exhausted. Use your pulse rate to monitor aerobic workouts.

EXAMPLE OF HOW TO BUILD CARDIOVASCULAR ENDURANCE AT A STANDARD TRACK

Warm-up: Walk 1 lap and jog 1 lap. If your heart rate, breathing rate, and body temperature have not increased, repeat this.

Day of the Week	Monday/Wednesday/Friday		Tuesday/Thursday	
	Exercise	**Duration**	**Exercise**	**Duration**
	Walk the straight section of the track and sprint the curves.	4 laps	Walk or jog lightly.	3 laps
	Walk or jog lightly.	2 laps	Run or sprint.	1 lap
	Walk the straight section of the track and sprint the curves.	4 laps	Walk or jog lightly.	3 laps
	Walk or jog lightly.	2 laps	Run or sprint.	1 lap

Cool-down: Slowing your pace, continue to walk around the track until your heart rate, breathing rate, and body temperature have returned to baseline.

Record at least 3 aerobic exercise sessions that you participated in outside of PE class for 1 week. Record the time of each session.

An exercise can be any of the following.

1. a sport-related game
2. an outdoor pursuit
3. a self-created workout routine set to music

	Monday	Tuesday	Wednesday	Thursday	Friday	Saturday	Sunday
Exercise							
Time							
Exercise Heartrate							

List at least 1 response to each the following questions about aerobic exercise.

Question	Response
What positive emotional response did you experience by participating in aerobic exercise?	
What aerobic exercise activity did you enjoy the most?	
Why would the enjoyment of your favorite aerobic exercise activity lead to a lifetime of fitness for you?	

RESEARCH INTEGRATION

Review the 7th-grade Aerobic Exercise section in your PE Manual to practice the correct form for the basic locomotor skills before creating your movement sequence.

HEALTH INTEGRATION

Use available technology to monitor your pulse rate and workout intensity. Apply the results to your overall fitness plan.

HIP-HOP DANCE

Dancing is an exercise option for aerobic workout, for competition, or just for fun. You can dance on your own or with others. Dancing is expressing yourself through repeated patterns of movement which are usually set to music. Some forms of dance include creative, tap, ballet, hip-hop, modern, folk, square, jazz, line, Latin, ballroom, and social.

Hip-hop is an energetic dance type that originated when the hip-hop style of music surfaced. Hip-hop dancing was first performed within a subculture and is now also practiced in dance studios.

The purpose of this lesson is for you to perform basic hip-hop steps and locomotor movements using common dance concepts in rhythmic patterns to create your own dance for aerobic exercise.

HIP-HOP DANCE: CREATE YOUR PERSONAL DANCE ROUTINE

COMMON CONCEPTS OF DANCE TO USE FOR YOUR PERSONAL DANCE

- The concept of space includes the following.
  - high, medium, or low **levels**
  - forward, backward, right, or left **directions**
  - curved, zigzag, straight, circle, or square **pathways**
- The concept of time includes the following.
  - slow, medium, or fast **speeds**
  - a pattern for **rhythm**
- The concept of force includes the following
  - applying light, moderate, or strong **weights**

CREATE YOUR OWN DANCE

Start with the dance steps below. Then, complete the routine by adding your own dance steps. Set your dance to music.

1. Learn a scoop.
   - Face forward, with your feet a little more than shoulder-width apart.
   - Place your hands lightly on your thighs.
   - Simultaneously bend your knees and lean to the right.
   - Repeat this to the left.
   - Do these 4 times.
2. Learn a circle.
   - Face forward, with your feet a little more than shoulder-width apart.
   - Place your hands lightly on your thighs.
   - Simultaneously bend your knees, lean to the right, and do a complete circle to the right with your upper body.
   - Repeat this to the left.
   - Do these 4 times.

3. Learn a walk step with an arm pump.
   - Walk to the right with your right foot leading; step right, left, right, left.
   - At the last left step, simultaneously pump your right arm; reach above your head and pull your hand down to shoulder level with your elbow bent.
   - Repeat this to the left.
   - Do these 4 times.
4. Combine the scoop, circle, and walk step, doing them 4 times each.
5. Next, choreograph your dance steps to complete the dance. Create the steps, write a description of each step, and practice the steps.
   - Choose locomotor skills to blend (steps, jumps, slides, turns, and so on).
   - Use your arms to accompany the footwork, for example: step, cross, step, clap.
   - Perform each skill at different levels.
   - Move in different directions.
   - Move in different pathways.
   - Move at slow, medium, and fast speeds.
   - Use light, moderate, and strong force to move your body.
   - Create a pattern.
   - Use an 8 count for each move.

Option: Dance with a partner or small group for a social experience. You can also perform your dance for friends or family.

RATE YOUR ENJOYMENT OF HIP-HOP DANCE

On a scale from 1 to 4, where 1 is not enjoyable and 4 is very enjoyable, rate this activity.

1	It was not enjoyable, and I will not participate again.
2	It was not enjoyable, but I will participate again for exercise.
3	It was enjoyable, and I will dance again.
4	It was very enjoyable, and I will create more dances.

RESEARCH INTEGRATION

1. Research hip-hop dance and some hip-hop moves that you can safely use in your dance.
2. Join a dance class or dance with a dance video.
3. Join a dance from the USB if provided in your PE program.

HEALTH INTEGRATION

Count your pulse to determine if you are exercising in your personal target heart rate zone. Apply the results to your overall fitness plan. Many people choose to complete aerobic workouts through dance.

JUMP ROPE

Jumping rope is an exercise that meets components of both skill-related fitness and health-related fitness. It helps you develop coordination, balance, rhythm, agility, and timing. Jumping rope is an efficient way to perform aerobic exercise and build muscular strength and endurance in your legs. It can be done daily and in a small space almost anywhere there is a safe, stable surface.

The purpose of this lesson is to provide you with the skills that you need to establish and implement your goal: to improve sport-related skills, to improve cardiovascular endurance, or both.

JUMP ROPE BASICS

FITTING THE JUMP ROPE TO YOUR HEIGHT

- Place a jump rope handle in each hand.
- Stand on the middle of the rope with 1 foot.
- Move the handles straight up, making sure that the rope is straight and pulled tight.
- The tops of the handles should reach close to your shoulders.

ELEMENTS OF JUMP ROPE

- Keep your eyes forward.
- When you are turning the rope, keep your elbows near your sides, maintaining a 45-degree angle and making 2-inch circles with your wrists.
- Leave just enough space for the rope to pass under your feet when you jump.
- Stay on the balls of your feet.
- Land softly, keeping your knees slightly bent.

BASIC SKILLS

BASIC JUMP

- Pick up the rope. Holding a handle in each hand, rest the rope behind your feet. Stand on the balls of your feet. This is the ready position.
- Your hands should be just above the height of your waist.
- Swing the rope up and over your head.
- Jump over the rope when it approaches your toes.
- Continue as long as you can without stopping.

Basic jump

BACKWARD JUMP

- Begin with the rope in front of your feet.
- Swing the rope up and over your head.
- Jump over the rope when it approaches your feet.
- Continue as long as you can without stopping.

Backward jump

ALTERNATE-FOOT JUMP

- Pick up the rope. Holding a handle in each hand, rest the rope behind your feet. Stand on the balls of your feet. This is the ready position. Note that 1 foot will be lifted off the ground during each turn of the rope before the other foot jumps.
- Turn the rope from behind you up over your head. When the rope reaches your toes, jump over it with your right foot.
- Turn the rope again from behind you up over your head. When the rope reaches your toes this time, jump over it with your left foot.
- Continue turning the rope and alternating feet as if you were running in place. Try it jumping backward.

Alternate-foot jump

SAMPLE OF A CARDIOVASCULAR CONDITIONING WORKOUT	SAMPLE OF A WORKOUT TO IMPROVE FOOTWORK SPEED
• basic jump 2 minutes • march or jog in place 30 seconds • backward jump 2 minutes • march or jog in place 30 seconds • alternate-foot jump 2 minutes • walk or jog in place 30 seconds • basic jump 2 minutes • march or jog in place 30 seconds • repeat for a 20-minute workout	• basic jump 1 minute at a medium pace • basic jump 30 seconds at a fast pace • rest 30 seconds • back jump 1 minute at a medium pace • back jump 30 seconds at a fast pace • rest 30 seconds • alternate-foot jump 1 minute at a medium pace • alternate-foot jump 30 seconds at a fast pace • rest 30 seconds • repeat as needed
DESIGN YOUR PERSONAL CARDIOVASCULAR JUMP ROPE ROUTINE AND SET IT TO MUSIC **(You can include basic, challenge, and partner skills after you have completed the module.)**	**DESIGN YOUR PERSONAL FOOTWORK SPEED ROUTINE**

CHALLENGE SKILLS

The following challenges are for students who have mastered the basic jump rope skills. The challenge level is recommended if you want to improve agility and further explore jump rope activities.

Hop on 1 foot (switch)

HOP ON 1 FOOT

Perform the basic jump on your right foot.

Perform the basic jump on your left foot.

SKIER

With both feet together, hop side to side while turning the rope.

Skier

CROSSOVERS

- After the rope moves over your head, cross the rope in front of you, jump, and uncross the rope.

Crossovers

FRONT KICKS

- Kick 1 foot forward as the rope passes under your feet with a skip-step in between.
- Alternate kicks.

SIDE KICKS

- Kick 1 foot and then the other out to the side with a skip-step in between.

Front kicks

Practice the challenge jump rope skills until competent. Next, design your personal aerobic jump rope routine by blending the basic jump rope skills and the challenge skills. Set your routine to music. Monitor your pulse rate.

BLENDING: Perform 1 jump rope skill and transition smoothly to another jump rope skill without stopping between moves.

BLENDED 3 SKILLS CHECKLIST SAMPLE

Check off the blended challenge skills that you have successfully completed at least 3 consecutive times.

_____ Blend forward consecutive jumps, crossovers, and skiers.

_____ Blend backward consecutive jumps, right-foot hops, and left-foot hops, all while backward turning.

_____ Blend forward consecutive jumps, front kicks, and side kicks.

_____ Create your personal blend.

_____ Combine blends for an aerobic workout.

Side kicks

PARTNER SKILLS

Jump rope can have a social component. Individual jumping with a friend may motivate you and may make your workout more fun. Partner or long jump rope requires 2 or more participants.

PARTNER JUMP ROPE SKILLS

PARTNER CHAIN JUMP

- Make sure that each person has their own rope.
- Standing side by side, face forward in the ready position.
- Exchange inside handles with your partner; hold your handle with your outside hand and your partner's handle with your inside hand.
- Turn the rope over your head and jump together.
- Establish a rhythm with your partner. Jump rope together to that rhythm.

Partner chain jump

3-PERSON CHAIN JUMP

- This is like the partner chain jump except that 3 people participate.
- Try adding another person to the group of 3 to make it a 4-person chain jump.

3-person chain jump

FACING YOUR PARTNER JUMP

- You will need 1 rope.
- Stand face-to-face with your partner.
- Have 1 person hold the rope.
- If you are holding the rope, stand facing your partner and turn the rope.
- If you are not holding the rope, stand facing your partner and jump rope with your partner as they turn the rope.
- No matter who is holding and turning the rope, establish a rhythm with your partner and jump rope together.

Facing your partner jump

FACE THE SAME WAY

- Either stand in front of your partner with your back turned to them or stand behind your partner and face their back. Both you and your partner should be facing the same way.
- If you are not holding the rope, stand in front of your partner and jump rope together.
- If you are holding the rope, stand behind your partner and turn the rope. Jump rope together.
- Establish a rhythm with your partner. Jump rope together to that rhythm.

Facing the same way

SIDE BY SIDE JUMP

- You will need 1 rope.
- Stand beside your partner.
- Hold a handle of the rope with your outside hand. Your partner should hold the other handle in their outside hand.
- Jump rope together as you work together to turn the rope.

Side by side jump

List at least 1 response to each of the following questions about jumping rope.

Question	Response
What jump rope activity do you enjoy the most?	
Why did you enjoy the above-mentioned activity the most?	

RESEARCH INTEGRATION

Research how jump rope is used in training for a sport.

HEALTH INTEGRATION

Count your pulse to determine if you are exercising in your personal target heart rate zone. Apply the results to your overall fitness plan.

STRENGTH TRAINING

Your body is made up of over 600 muscles. Muscles work in pairs to pull on bones to create movement. Opposing muscles, or antagonistic muscles, should be equally trained because they work together. For example, the quadriceps and hamstring muscles work together, 1 contracting while the other relaxes to bend and straighten your knee.

The saying "if you don't use it you will lose it" can be applied to your skeletal muscles. Muscles that are not used and not exercised become weak. Muscles are important for posture, movement, and maintaining body temperature. Strength training, also known as resistance training, builds muscular strength and endurance.

The purpose of this lesson is to encourage you to design your personal strength-training program and to perform exercises 2 to 3 days per week to experience health benefits.

⚠ **CAUTION: Have a certified trainer plan for you and supervise you when you are working with weights.**

STRENGTH-TRAINING EXERCISES

There are a variety of exercises from which to choose. Do strength exercises for the muscles of your upper body, lower body, and core. Choose the intensity of each exercise to fit your fitness level. For example, if you are struggling to do a right-angle push-up, switch to a knee push-up. Limit excuses and make a commitment to exercise!

STRENGTH-TRAINING EXERCISE IDEAS

Weightlifting machines: You can use large stationary machines like those typically found in gyms.

Free weights: You can use free-weight equipment such as dumbbells, barbells, medicine balls, kettlebells, resistance bands, and weighted ropes to perform strength-training exercises.

Pilates or yoga: Pilates and yoga sessions are excellent workouts for muscle lengthening and muscle strengthening.

Personal workouts: You can use your own body weight as a source of resistance and create your own strength-training workouts. Create a personal workout by blending basic strength-building exercises such as sit-ups, push-ups, pull-ups, planks, and so on, and design the intensity and duration of each exercise according to your level of fitness. Include upper-body, lower-body, and core exercises in your workout. Perform your personal routine for some or all your strength-training workouts.

SAMPLE

The following is a sample personal strength-training workout that uses personal body weight as resistance.

Practice each of the following exercises, concentrating on proper form, prior to engaging in a workout.

IN-OUT ABS

muscle focus: abdominal muscles

Intensity Level 1

Sit on a cushioned surface with your elbows flat on the ground slightly behind your hips. Keeping your knees bent, lift both legs until they are parallel to the ground. Extend your legs straight out in front of you and then return to the bent-knee position.

In-out abs: Intensity Level 1

Intensity Level 2

Sit on a cushioned surface with your hands flat on the ground slightly behind your hips. Keeping your knees bent, lift both legs until they are parallel to the ground. Extend your legs straight out in front of you and then return to the bent-knee position.

Intensity Level 3

Sit on a cushioned surface with your arms held straight above your head. Keeping your knees bent, lift both legs until they are parallel to the ground. Extend your legs straight out in front of you and then return to the bent-knee position.

In-out abs: Intensity Level 2

In-out abs: Intensity Level 3

FORWARD LUNGES

muscle focus: glutei maximi, hamstrings, and quadriceps

Intensity Level 1

Perform alternate forward lunges. Start with your feet together. Step 1 foot forward and bend your knee as low as you comfortably can. Do not exceed a 90-degree angle. Return to the starting position and then repeat the exercise with your other leg.

Intensity Level 2

Perform alternate forward lunges. Start with your feet together. Step 1 foot forward and bend your knee to a 90-degree angle. Return to the starting position and repeat the exercise with your other leg.

Intensity Level 3

Start with your feet together. Step your right foot forward and bend your knee to a 90-degree angle. Go back to the starting position. Continue lunging with your right foot until you have completed the repetitions. Next, lunge by stepping forward with your left foot until you complete the repetitions.

Forward lunges: Intensity Level 1

Forward lunges: Intensity Level 2

Forward lunges: Intensity Level 3

RIGHT-ANGLE PUSH-UPS

muscle focus: pectoralis majors, deltoids, triceps, biceps, and abdominal muscles

Intensity Level 1

Perform knee push-ups. Kneel on a cushioned surface with your back straight and your hands on the ground under your shoulders. Bend your elbows 90 degrees and then return to the straight-arm position, or plank position.

Intensity Level 2

Lie on your stomach. Place your hands under your shoulders. Straighten your arms to lift up your body. Make sure that your back and legs are straight from head to toe. Lower your body by bending your elbows as far as you can without exceeding 90. Straighten your arms to lift your body back up to the plank position, keeping your back and legs straight.

Right-Angle Push-ups: Intensity Level 1

Right-Angle Push-ups: Intensity Level 2

Intensity Level 3

Lie on your stomach. Place your hands under your shoulders. Straighten your arms to lift up your body. Make sure that your back and legs are straight from head to toe. Lower your body by bending your elbows 90 degrees. Straighten your arms to lift your body back up to the plank position, keeping your back and legs straight.

Right-Angle Push-ups: Intensity Level 3

ALTERNATE 6 INCHES

muscle focus: abdominal muscles

Intensity Level 1

Lie on your back on a cushioned surface. Pull 1 knee toward your chest. Extend your other leg straight out in front of you and parallel to the floor. Hold your extended leg 6 to 10 inches above the ground for 3 seconds. Switch legs.

Intensity Level 2

Lie on your back on a cushioned surface. Extend 1 leg up toward the ceiling with your knee bent. Extend your other leg straight out in front of you and parallel to the floor. Hold your extended leg 6 to 10 inches above the ground for 6 seconds. Switch legs.

Intensity Level 3

Lie on your back on a cushioned surface. Extend 1 leg straight up toward the ceiling. Extend your other leg straight out in front of you and parallel to the floor. Hold your extended leg 6 inches above the ground for 6 seconds. Switch legs.

Alternate 6 inches: Intensity Level 1

Alternate 6 inches: Intensity Level 2

Alternate 6 inches: Intensity Level 3

SQUATS

muscle focus: glutei maximi, hamstrings, and quadriceps

Intensity Level 1

Stand with your legs shoulder-width apart and your hands on your hips. Lower your body by bending your knees and hips as low as you comfortably can. Do not lower your hips below knee level.

Intensity Level 2

Stand with your legs shoulder-width apart and your arms extended out in front of you at shoulder height. With your legs apart, lower your body by bending your knees and hips until your hips are even with your knees.

Intensity Level 3

Perform ¼-squat jumps. Standing with your legs shoulder-width apart, lower your body by bending your knees and hips until your hips are even with your knees. Jump to the right, making a quarter turn and landing gently in a squat position. Continue until you are back to the starting position. Repeat the exercise to the left.

Squats: Intensity Level 1

Squats: Intensity Level 2

Squats: Intensity Level 3

TRICEPS PUSH-UPS (NARROW PUSH-UPS)

muscle focus: pectoralis majors, pectoralis minors, deltoids, triceps, biceps, and abdominal muscles

Intensity Level 1

Perform knee push-ups. Kneel on a cushioned surface with your back straight and your hands on the ground inside your shoulders. Bend your elbows 90 degrees and return to straight arms.

Intensity Level 2

Lie on your stomach. Place your hands on the floor close to your body at chest level. Lift your body up with your triceps until you return to the straight-arm position. Make sure that your back and legs are straight from head to toe. Lower your body by bending your elbows as far as you can without exceeding 90 degrees. Return to the straight-arm position.

Intensity Level 3

Lie on your stomach. Place your hands on the floor close to your body at chest level. Lift your body up with your triceps until you return to the straight-arm position. Make sure that your back and legs are straight from head to toe. Lower your body by bending your elbows 90 degrees. Return to the straight-arm position.

SIT-UPS

muscle focus: abdominal muscles

Intensity Level 1

Perform fitness curl-ups. Lie on a cushioned surface with your knees flexed and your feet about 12 inches from your buttocks. With your arms at your sides, slide your fingertips 3 to 4 inches forward along the ground, simultaneously lifting your head and shoulders off the ground. Slowly lower your head and shoulders back to the ground.

Intensity Level 2

Perform sit-ups. Lie on a cushioned surface with your knees flexed and your feet about 12 inches from your buttocks. A partner may hold your feet. Cross your arms, placing your hands on opposite shoulders and holding your elbows close to your chest. Raise your body until your elbows touch your thighs; then, lower your body until your shoulder blades touch the ground.

Intensity Level 3

Perform sit-ups. Lie on a cushioned surface with your knees flexed and your feet about 12 inches from your buttocks. Cross your arms, placing your hands on opposite shoulders and holding your elbows close to your chest. Raise your body until your elbows touch your thighs; then, lower your body until your shoulder blades touch the ground.

Triceps push-ups

Triceps push-ups: Intensity Level 1

Right-Angle Push-ups: Intensity Level 2

Right-Angle Push-ups: Intensity Level 3

Sit-ups: Intensity Level 1

Sit-ups: Intensity Level 2

Sit-ups: Intensity Level 3

STEP-BACK LUNGES

muscle focus: glutei maximi, hamstrings, and quadriceps

Intensity Level 1

Perform alternate step-back lunges. Start by standing with your feet together and your hands on your hips. Step back with 1 foot and lower your knee as low as you comfortably can. Go back to the starting position and repeat this with your other leg.

Step-back lunges: Intensity Level 1

Intensity Level 2

Perform alternate step-back lunges with high arms. Start by standing with your feet together and your arms extended straight above your head. Step back with 1 foot and lower your knee as far as you comfortably can. Return to the starting position and repeat this with your other leg.

Step-back lunges: Intensity Level 2

Intensity Level 3

Start by standing with your feet together. Step back with your right foot and lower your knee as far as you comfortably can. Return to the starting position and continue lunging back with your right foot until you have completed the repetitions. Next, step back with your left foot until you complete the repetitions. Your hands may remain on your hips or remain extended.

Step-back lunges: Intensity Level 3

WIDE PUSH-UPS

muscle focus: pectoralis majors, deltoids, triceps, biceps, and abdominal muscles

Wide push-ups

Intensity Level 1

Kneel on a cushioned surface with your back straight and your hands on the ground outside your shoulders. Bend your elbows 90 degrees. Return to the straight-arm position.

Wide push-ups: Intensity Level 1

Intensity Level 2

Lie on your stomach. Place your hands outside your shoulders. Lift your body up to a straight-arm position. Make sure that your back and legs are straight from head to toe. Lower your body by bending your elbows as far as you can without exceeding 90 degrees. Return to the straight-arm position.

Wide push-ups: Intensity Level 2

Intensity Level 3

Lie on your stomach. Place your hands outside your shoulders. Lift your body up to a straight-arm position. Make sure that your back and legs are straight from head to toe. Lower your body by bending your elbows 90 degrees. Return to the straight-arm position.

Wide push-ups: Intensity Level 3

Have a trusted adult or friend evaluate you for correct form for the previous exercises. Did you respond positively to the feedback?

Reciprocate and evaluate your friend. Were you able to provide feedback in a positive manner?

How to Use Your Body Weight in a Strength-Training Workout

- Warm up before your workout. Cool down after your workout.
- Choose the appropriate level of intensity for you.
- Perform each exercise 2 to 3 days per week.
- Begin with 1 set of 10 repetitions of each exercise. Increase sets and repetitions when the exercise becomes easy for you.
- Your goal should be to reach 3 sets of 15 repetitions of each exercise.

Write down an excuse that you have used to avoid strength training and how you overcame or will overcome that obstacle.

My Excuse for Not Exercising	What I Did to Overcome That Excuse

RESEARCH INTEGRATION

Research and participate in yoga, Pilates, or tai chi as an alternative way to improve strength and flexibility and to reduce stress. You can enroll in a class or follow a workout from a DVD or app.

RESISTANCE EXERCISE: FITNESS BALL

Including a fitness ball (or exercise ball) in your exercise routine is a fun, efficient way to improve muscular strength, muscular endurance, flexibility, and balance. Your core muscles work to balance on an unstable ball while exercising a variety of muscle groups.

⚠ **CAUTION: Do not overinflate the ball.**

FITNESS BALL EXERCISES
TIPS FOR USING A FITNESS BALL

- Exercises done on a firmer ball are more challenging.
- A beginner should start with a slightly-deflated ball.
- When you are seated on the ball, your feet should be flat on the floor.

Practice each of the following exercises, concentrating on proper form, prior to engaging in a workout.

BASIC ROLLOUTS

muscle focus: abdominal muscles

- Sit perfectly upright on the ball with your arms behind your head.
- Sit perfectly upright on the ball with your arms behind your head.
- Walk your feet out slowly.
- Holding your head still, tighten your abdominal muscles as you continue to walk your feet out. Keep your buttocks up as your feet leave the ball.
- Once the ball has reached your shoulders, walk your feet back to the starting position.
- Keep your body parallel to the ground during this exercise.

Basic rollouts

SIT-UPS

muscle focus: abdominal muscles

- Lie on your back on the ball. The middle of your back should be on the ball. Place your hands behind your head.
- Keep your elbows flat and in line with your head as you raise your upper body and back off the ball. You should end up almost in a sitting position.
- Lower your body slowly back to the starting position.

Sit-ups

PLANKS

muscle focus: abdominal muscles

- Place the ball on a flat surface on the ground. Place your forearms on the ball.

Planks

- Extend your legs straight out behind you and place them shoulder-width apart with your toes on the ground.
- Push yourself up on the ball so that your chest is not resting on your forearms. Only your forearms should be on the ball.
- Hold this position for 30 seconds.

LEG EXTENSIONS

muscle focus: quadriceps, hamstrings, and glutes

- Sit on the ball with both feet firmly on the ground.
- Lift your right leg so that your calf is parallel to the ground.
- Lower your right leg slowly back to the starting position.
- Lift your left leg so that your calf is parallel to the ground.
- Lower your left leg slowly back to the starting position.
- Continue to alternate legs until the exercise is complete.

Leg extensions

LEG RAISES

muscle focus: abdominal muscles, quadriceps, hamstrings, and glutes

- Lie flat on your back on the ground, squeezing the middle of the ball tightly between your feet and ankles.
- From this position, keep your upper back and shoulders on the ground and slowly raise your legs about 6 inches off the ground.
- Bring the ball slowly down without resting it on the ground.

Leg raises

Have a trusted adult or friend evaluate you for correct form for the previous exercises. Did you respond positively to the feedback?

Reciprocate and evaluate your friend. Were you able to provide feedback in a positive manner?

The following is a suggested use of the fitness ball in a strength-building workout. Exercise to your level of fitness.

- Warm up and cool down.
- Perform each exercise 2 to 3 days per week.
- For the basic rollouts, sit-ups, planks, leg extensions, and leg raises, begin with 1 set of 10 repetitions. Increase sets and the number of repetitions when the current number is easy for you to complete. Hold each plank for 20 to 30 seconds.
- For the basic rollouts, sit-ups, planks, leg extensions, and leg raises, your goal should be to reach 3 sets of 10 to 15 repetitions. Your goal for each plank should be to hold it for 30 to 60 seconds.

RESEARCH INTEGRATION

Research the benefits of using an exercise ball as a replacement for a desk chair.

CROSS-TRAINING CARDIOVASCULAR AND STRENGTH CIRCUIT

For a combination cardiovascular and strength workout, you can do a cross-training circuit. This cross-training circuit alternates strength exercises with aerobic movements. Cross-training saves time by giving you 1 workout that has both strength and aerobic benefits. It is important for you to set your own goals based on your ability level and determine your intensity and duration based on your individual target heart rate zone.

The purpose of this lesson is to encourage you to create and implement a cross-training circuit workout. The workout would be included in the recommended 60 minutes of daily physical activity and would count as both an aerobic and strength workout. **The Cardiovascular Endurance section of this manual includes the target heart rate zone formula and the Borg Rating of Perceived Exertion Scale to help you to determine if you are exercising for heart health.** You can also use available technology to monitor your pulse rate and workout intensity.

⚠️ **CAUTION: Do not overinflate the ball.**

CROSS-TRAINING CIRCUIT WORKOUT: CARDIOVASCULAR, STRENGTH, AND FLEXIBILITY

Review the following example and use the information to establish a workout regimen that fits into your schedule. Adhere to the FITT principle (frequency, intensity, time, and type of exercise). This workout requires a jump rope and a fitness ball. You should have a mat or cushioned surface for sit-ups and push-ups.

SAMPLE CROSS-TRAINING CIRCUIT WORKOUT

Build cardiovascular endurance, strength, and flexibility in a cross-training circuit workout using exercises from the appropriate sections of your PE Manual: Cardiovascular Endurance, Muscle Strength, Muscle Endurance, and Flexibility. Review the 7th-grade Aerobics, 8th-grade Jump Rope, 8th-grade Strength Training, and 8th-grade Fitness Ball sections in your PE Manual to practice correct forms for the skills.

Warm-up: Perform 5 to 10 minutes of light cardio to increase your heart rate, breathing rate, and body temperature. Do some dynamic stretches to increase flexibility.

Perform each exercise for 30 seconds. Rest and hydrate when necessary.

1. jumping jacks
2. sit-ups
3. high knees
4. fitness ball leg extensions
5. jump rope
6. right-angle push-ups
7. burpees
8. fitness ball plank
9. jog in place
10. squats
11. jump rope
12. triceps push-ups (narrow push-ups)
13. ¼-squat jumps
14. fitness ball sit-ups
15. knee tucks
16. forward lunges
17. jump rope
18. wide push-ups

Repeat for an 18-minute workout.

Cool-down: Walk slowly until your heart rate, breathing rate, and body temperature have returned to baseline. Do some static stretches to increase flexibility.

Use the cross-training information to create your personal circuit workout.

RATE YOUR ENJOYMENT OF A CROSS-TRAINING CIRCUIT

On a scale from 1 to 4, where 1 is not enjoyable and 4 is very enjoyable, rate this activity.

1	It was not enjoyable, and I will not participate again.
2	It was not enjoyable, but I will participate again for exercise.
3	It was enjoyable, and I will complete a cross-training circuit again.
4	It was very enjoyable, and I will create more cross-training routines outside of PE class.

Explain to a trusted adult or friend how you can make your cross-training workout more enjoyable.

RESEARCH INTEGRATION

Review the appropriate sections in your manual to practice the correct forms for basic locomotor skills before creating your movement sequence.

HEALTH INTEGRATION

Use available technology to monitor your pulse rate and workout intensity. Apply the results to your overall fitness plan.

SPORTS-RELATED AND SKILL-RELATED ACTIVITIES

FITNESS TIP: Prior to beginning your physical education activities, read the following safety information that applies to every lesson, review the timeline, and review the assessment rubric.

SAFETY ALERT: Before you exercise, make sure that you are properly warmed up and have enough room to perform each activity. Wear proper equipment and follow activity-specific safety rules. Stay hydrated and take breaks as needed. Exercise only if you are healthy, and always exercise at your own pace. If an exercise starts to hurt, if you feel dizzy, or if you feel light-headed, stop the exercise completely and get help. Upon completion of any workout, cool down and stretch.

TIMELINE

Review all of the activity information before beginning. Use the scoring rubrics as assessment tools. You may ask a trusted adult or friend to observe your performance and provide feedback. Progress according to your skill level. The time that it takes you to complete a module will depend on your personal progress.

- **Practice and assess the first skill until competent.**
- **Continue to progress until you have practiced and assessed each skill until competent.**
- **Apply skills in a game situation.**

ASSESSMENT RUBRIC

You will find a rubric assessment tool following some of the basic skills. Use this tool to evaluate and score your progress in learning the elements of a new skill.

SKILL	PROGRESSING	COMPETENT	PROFICIENT
skill 1	1 or 2 of the elements	3 or 4 out of 5 elements	all elements met

FLOOR HOCKEY

Floor hockey is played by 2 opposing teams each made up of 6 players on a rectangular court. A point is scored when the puck or hockey ball goes into a goal. It is a fast, energetic sport that does not permit physical contact with other players. Playing floor hockey helps you develop hand-eye coordination, balance, agility, and physical fitness. Many people choose to complete aerobic workouts by playing in fun pick-up games like floor hockey.

The purpose of this lesson is for you to participate in aerobic exercise and in skill-building activities. Game participation will depend upon the availability of a facility and players. When you are playing floor hockey, be sure to follow game rules, communicate with teammates in a positive and effective manner, and exhibit appropriate behavior with your team and the opposing team.

⚠ **CAUTION: Keep 2 hands on the hockey stick. Keep the stick below waist level. Do not body check or otherwise contact anyone.**

FLOOR HOCKEY SKILLS

GRIP

- Place your dominant hand lower on the hockey stick and your non-dominant hand near the top of the stick. Now, switch hands so that your non-dominant hand is lower on the stick and your dominant hand is near the top of the stick. You may use the hand position that is most comfortable for you.
- Face your palms up like you are shaking hands with someone. Place your hands 6 to 8 inches apart on the stick. Bend your elbows and keep them loose. Let your arms hang loose and ready to play.
- Always keep the tip of the stick below your waist.
- Your bottom hand is the pivot, and your top hand is the control.

STICKHANDLING

- Stay in place and move the puck from side to side or from front to back.

SIDE TO SIDE

- Your feet should be slightly wider than shoulder-width apart.
- Move the puck from right to left using both sides of the stick to softly tap the puck.
- Keep the blade of the stick on the floor.
- The puck should remain slightly in front of your feet.
- Keep your head up.

SKILL	PROGRESSING	COMPETENT	PROFICIENT
side to side	1 or 2 of the elements	3 or 4 out of 5 elements	all elements met

Copyright 2024 © Lincoln Learning Solutions. All rights reserved.

FRONT TO BACK

- Your feet should be staggered so that 1 is forward and 1 is back.
- Push the puck forward with the front of the blade (the side facing away from you) and then backward with the back of the blade using soft taps and not pushing the puck beyond your toes.
- Keep the blade on the floor.
- Transfer your weight from your front foot to your back foot.
- Keep your head up.
- Switch your feet so that the other foot is forward and repeat the exercise.

SKILL	PROGRESSING	COMPETENT	PROFICIENT
front to back	1 or 2 of the elements	3 or 4 out of 5 elements	all elements met

DRIBBLING ON THE MOVE

- The puck should stay in contact with the stick blade on 1 side only.
- Practice moving the puck on both the right and left sides of the stick.
- Move the puck forward with short taps or pushes.
- Tilt the stick blade slightly over the puck for better control.
- Keep the puck in the middle of the blade.
- Hold your head up as you move.
- To switch direction, move the puck in front of you rather than to the side. Use short taps while pushing the puck from side to side in the middle of the blade.

SKILL	PROGRESSING	COMPETENT	PROFICIENT
dribbling on the move	1, 2, or 3 of the elements	4 or 5 out of 6 elements	all elements met

SHOOTING THE PUCK

There are 2 types of shots: wrist shots and slap shots. Wrist shots are used for shorter distances and quick execution, while slap shots are used for moderate to long distances.

WRIST SHOT

- Touch the puck with the stick blade before you shoot the puck.
- Look toward the target.
- When you are shooting, move your lower hand down the stick for better control.
- Follow through your shot with the stick ending no higher than your hips.

SKILL	PROGRESSING	COMPETENT	PROFICIENT
wrist shot	1 or 2 of the elements	3 out of 4 elements	all elements met

SLAP SHOT

- When you are approaching the puck, move your lower hand slightly down the stick for better control.
- Keep your eyes on the puck.
- Swing the stick behind you to about waist level and in line with the target.
- Swing the stick quickly forward and hit through the puck.
- Follow through your shot with the stick ending no higher than your hips. Finish with all your weight on your front foot.

SKILL	PROGRESSING	COMPETENT	PROFICIENT
slap shot	1 or 2 of the elements	3 or 4 out of 5 elements	all elements met

PASSING AND RECEIVING THE PUCK

PASSING

Keep the stick blade upright.

Use your lower hand to execute a smooth, sweeping motion.

Do not raise the stick above your waist during the backswing or forward swing.

Pass slightly ahead of your receiver on their stick side. This is called a lead pass.

Aim the puck to where the receiver will be able to intercept it.

SKILL	PROGRESSING	COMPETENT	PROFICIENT
passing	1 or 2 of the elements	3 or 4 out of 5 elements	all elements met

RECEIVING

Track the puck with your eyes.

Move into position to receive the puck.

Intercept the puck by placing your stick blade over the puck to trap it.

Cushion the pass by allowing the stick blade to give during impact (let the stick move slightly backward to keep control of the puck).

SKILL	PROGRESSING	COMPETENT	PROFICIENT
receiving	1 or 2 of the elements	3 out of 4 elements	all elements met

PRACTICE THE SKILLS

Practice each skill until you are competent.

- Shoot a stationary puck at a wall or other target. Use the wrist shot with forehand and backhand shooting.
- Dribble and shoot toward a target using a forehand and backhand wrist shot.
- Shoot a stationary puck at a wall or other target using the slap shot.

- Pass with a partner while both of you are stationary. Pass the puck quickly back and forth. Trap the puck with the blade of the stick and pass it immediately back to your partner.
- While standing still, pass the puck to your partner while your partner is on the move. Your partner should stop, trap the puck, and pass it back to you. Repeat this 5 times and switch roles.
- Pass the puck back and forth while you and your partner are moving forward. Try short passes and long passes.

OFFENSIVE AND DEFENSIVE SKILLS

Quick, fast, agile footwork is an essential component of a floor hockey game. Practice footwork skills to improve your offensive and defensive play.

OFFENSIVE SKILLS

FAKE

The purpose of the fake is to lead your opponent in a different direction.

- Look in 1 direction, and then pass or move in another direction.
- Stay on the balls of your feet.
- Move quickly.

SKILL	PROGRESSING	COMPETENT	PROFICIENT
fake	1 of the elements	2 out of 3 elements	all elements

GIVE AND GO

The purpose of the give and go in a hockey game is to for you to pass the puck to a teammate and to quickly relocate so that you can receive a pass.

- Pass the puck to a teammate.
- Move quickly to relocate and support your offense.
- Indicate (call out) that you are ready and open to receive the puck.
- Receive the puck.

SKILL	PROGRESSING	COMPETENT	PROFICIENT
give and go	1 or 2 of the elements	3 out of 4 elements	all elements

DEFENSIVE SKILLS

READY POSITION FOR DEFENSE

The purpose of the ready position is to keep you on the balls of your feet and ready to react as appropriate.

- Bending your knees, stand with your feet shoulder-width apart.
- Keep your head up and your weight on the balls of your feet.
- Hold your hockey stick with both hands, letting the edge of the stick rest on the floor.

SKILL	PROGRESSING	COMPETENT	PROFICIENT
ready position	1 of the elements	2 out of 3 elements	all elements met

DEFENSIVE SLIDES

The purpose of defensive slides in floor hockey is to keep up with your opponent and to legally take the puck or legally disrupt the opponent's pass or shot.

- Place your weight on the balls of your feet.
- Slide to the side or diagonally backward with quick steps.
- Do not cross your feet.
- Keep your knees bent.
- Face your hips toward your opponent.
- Hold your stick with both hands in front of you and keep the tip of the blade near the floor.
- Anticipate and react quickly to your opponent's movements.

SKILL	PROGRESSING	COMPETENT	PROFICIENT
defensive slides	1, 2, or 3 of the elements	4, 5, or 6 out of 7 elements	all elements met

PRACTICE OFFENSIVE AND DEFENSIVE SKILLS

Practice each skill until you are competent.

- Practice the **give and go** with a partner and a defender. Pass the puck, quickly relocate, and then receive the pass, avoiding the defender.
- Practice the **fake** independently. Set up a cone as a decoy. Fake the pass toward the cone and then pass to your partner until you feel comfortable with the movement.
- Practice the **fake** with a partner defending you. Dribble, fake, and move in another direction to get around the defensive player. Do this until you feel comfortable with the fake.
- Practice the **defensive slide** with a partner. As your partner dribbles, defensive slide to try to prevent them from making a successful pass or shot. Do this until you feel comfortable with the defensive slide.

FACING OFF

A face-off starts a hockey game. It is also used to restart the game after each point is scored.

- Stand facing your opponent in the center of the court, about a stick-length apart. Face the goal your team is trying to score in. Place the stick blades on the floor so they are almost touching. Slide your lower hand down the shaft of your stick for more power and control.
- The referee will drop the puck between you and your opponent. Once the puck hits the floor, try to gain control of the puck.

PLAYING THE GAME

- You should play in a large gym or on a rectangular court. Play begins in the center of the court. You may play off the walls, but tape off the goalie area for safety.
- Each goal that is scored is worth 1 point.
- A floor hockey team consists of 1 goalie, 2 defensive backs, and 3 forwards.
- A face-off between the 2 center forwards starts the game and restarts it after a goal is scored. After every goal, the center forward should switch with 1 of the other forwards.
- Play an even number of minutes for halves with a 2-minute halftime to switch sides of the court. If there are extra players, swap so that everyone gets a chance to play.

- A goalie may use their hands, stick, or feet to stop the puck inside their own goal area. They must release the puck within 3 seconds of catching it. A goalie cannot throw or shoot the puck toward their opponent's goal.
- Defensive players cannot cross the center line.
- Center forwards may play the entire floor.
- Wing forwards may play from their start position and go forward, staying out of the back-court area.
- If the puck gets trapped under bleachers or against a wall, a face-off takes place at the nearest X spot (the spot away from the bleachers or walls often marked with tape) or the game can be restarted close to where the puck was lost.
- If any of the fouls listed below are made, the puck will be given to the opposite team at the place where the foul occurred. The opposite team is then allowed a penalty shot, which means that the team gets a free shot where the foul was made. Defensive players must stay 15 feet away when the puck is put back into play.
    - touching the puck with your hands
    - swinging the stick above your shoulders
    - having a player other than the goalie inside the goalie box
    - having guards and forwards out of position
    - stepping on, holding, or lying on the puck
- If any of the personal fouls listed below are made, the player who made the foul will be given a 2-minute penalty.
    - tripping someone with a stick or foot
    - pushing or body checking
    - checking someone with a stick
    - using bad language

Insert hockey court from Getty images # 1008822910

Prior to playing a pick-up game, establish and review the game rules so that all participants understand them. If problems arise, while self-officiating, work as a group to solve them in a positive and effective manner. Appreciate different players' abilities. Consider the number of participants, the facility, the amount of equipment, and other variables to establish game rules for your personal situation. An example of a rule that you may want to implement is to switch positions after a certain period of time so that everyone can play both offense and defense.

Below are our game rules for safety and fairness.
1.
2.
3.
4.
5.

RATE YOUR ENJOYMENT OF FLOOR HOCKEY

On a scale from 1 to 4, where 1 is not enjoyable and 4 is very enjoyable, rate this activity.

1	It was not enjoyable, and I will not participate again.
2	It was not enjoyable, but I will participate again for exercise.
3	It was enjoyable, and I will play again.
4	It was very enjoyable, and I will initiate future games.

RESEARCH INTEGRATION

Research the official rules and regulations of ice hockey and compare them to the rules for floor hockey presented in this lesson.

HEALTH INTEGRATION

Count your pulse during and after playing floor hockey to determine if you are exercising in your personal target heart rate zone. Predict and then compare the difference between your heart rate after playing in the goalie position and your heart rate after playing in a running position. Apply your results to your overall fitness plan.

JUGGLING

Juggling improves focus and coordination, and it increases the range of motion in your arms and shoulders. Juggling requires intense concentration, which can help relieve stress because it requires your mind to stay focused on the task. Juggling is a workout that you can take almost anywhere and that requires little space. Juggling is unique and adds variety to your 60 minutes of daily activity and regular aerobic workouts.

The purpose of this lesson is for you to participate in juggling in and outside of PE class.

JUGGLING PROGRESSIONS

1-CUBE JUGGLE

- Hold 1 juggling cube in your dominant hand.
- Throw the cube in an arc pattern from your dominant hand to your non-dominant hand. Do not throw the cube high; rather, throw it at eye level.
- Throw the cube at eye level in an arc pattern from your non-dominant hand back to your dominant hand.
- Continue tossing the cube from 1 hand to the other until it feels comfortable. Make sure that you throw in an arc pattern, not a circle.

SKILL	PROGRESSING	COMPETENT	PROFICIENT
1 cube juggling	1 or 2 of the elements	3 out of 4 elements	all elements met

2-CUBE JUGGLE

Do not toss the cubes at the same time. Wait for 1 cube to reach eye level before tossing the other cube. It may help to say to yourself, "Toss, toss, catch, catch."

- Hold a cube in each hand.
- Toss 1 cube in an arc pattern from your dominant hand to your non-dominant hand.
- After the cube tossed from your dominant hand has reached eye level, toss the cube in your non-dominant hand in an arc pattern to your dominant hand.
- Catch the cube tossed from your dominant hand with your non-dominant hand. Then, catch the cube tossed from your non-dominant hand with your dominant hand.

SKILL	PROGRESSING	COMPETENT	PROFICIENT
2-cube juggle	1 or 2 of the elements	3 out of 4 elements	all elements met

Challenge: Toss 2 cubes, beginning by tossing with your non-dominant hand first.

3-CUBE JUGGLE

- Place 2 cubes in your dominant hand and 1 cube in your non-dominant hand.
- Toss the first cube from your dominant hand in an arc pattern to your non-dominant hand.
- After the cube tossed from your dominant hand has reached eye level, toss the cube in your non-dominant hand in an arc pattern to your dominant hand.

- Catch the first cube tossed from your dominant hand with your non-dominant hand.
- After the cube tossed from your non-dominant hand has reached eye level, toss the second cube in your dominant hand in an arc pattern to your non-dominant hand.
- Catch the cube tossed from your non-dominant hand with your dominant hand. Then, catch the second cube tossed from your dominant hand with your non-dominant hand.

SKILL	PROGRESSING	COMPETENT	PROFICIENT
3-cube juggle	1, 2, or 3 of the elements	4 or 5 out of 6 elements	all elements met

After you are proficient in juggling the cubes, start the exercises from the beginning and use the juggling balls.

RATE YOUR ENJOYMENT OF JUGGLING

On a scale from 1 to 4, where 1 is not enjoyable and 4 is very enjoyable, rate this activity.

1	It was not enjoyable, and I will not participate again.
2	It was not enjoyable, but I will participate again for exercise.
3	It was enjoyable, and I will juggle again.
4	It was very enjoyable, and I will include juggling in my regular orkout schedule.

RESEARCH INTEGRATION

1. Research the origin of juggling.
2. Research how to juggle with a partner.

HEALTH INTEGRATION

Count your heart rate during and after juggling to determine if you are exercising in your personal target heart rate zone. Apply the results to your overall fitness plan.

PICKLEBALL

Pickleball is a popular game that is enjoyed by players of all ages. Pickleball is a paddle sport that combines elements of badminton, tennis, and table tennis. It is played with a paddle, a pickleball ball, and a low net on a hard court. This striking activity helps you develop concentration, hand-eye coordination, footwork, and fitness.

The purpose of this lesson is for you to participate in aerobic exercise and in skill-building activities. Game participation will depend upon the availability of a facility and players. When you are playing pickleball, be sure to follow game rules, communicate with teammates in a positive and effective manner, and exhibit appropriate behavior with your team and the opposing team.

CAUTION: Make sure that nobody is close to you before you swing the paddle. Do not walk into the path of another person who is swinging a paddle.

PICKLEBALL SKILLS

STROKES

READY POSITION

- Wait for the ball, keeping your paddle in front of the middle of your chest. This way, you are ready to return the ball from wherever it goes.
- Bend your knees and stand with your feet shoulder-width apart.
- Keep your head up and your weight on the balls of your feet.
- Hold the paddle in your dominant hand.

HANDSHAKE GRIP

- Hold the paddle in your dominant hand away from your body and at waist height.
- Placing the head of the paddle vertical to the ground, point the handle toward your belly button.

UNDERHAND STROKE

- Hold the paddle so that the head is facing the ground and is positioned under the ball.
- Flick your wrist to hit the ball with the center of the paddle.
- Rotate your forearm so that it faces upward on contact.
- Follow through to your target.

SKILL	PROGRESSING	COMPETENT	PROFICIENT
underhand stroke	1 or 2 of the elements	3 out of 4 elements	all elements met

OVERHAND STROKE

- Bend your elbow slightly and position the paddle under the ball.
- Flick your wrist to hit the ball with the center of the paddle.
- Extend your arm when you make contact.
- Follow through to your target.

SKILL	PROGRESSING	COMPETENT	PROFICIENT
overhand stroke	1 or 2 of the elements	3 out of 4 elements	all elements met

FOREHAND STROKE

- The paddle should be on the same side of your body as your dominant hand.
- Face the palm of your hand forward.
- Extend your arm and flick your wrist to hit the ball.
- Point the face of the paddle up to get the ball over the net.
- Follow through to your target.

SKILL	PROGRESSING	COMPETENT	PROFICIENT
forehand stroke	1 or 2 of the elements	3 or 4 out of 5 elements	all elements met

BACKHAND STROKE

- Rotate the paddle and extend it across your body.
- Rotate your feet and shoulders in the same direction as the paddle.
- Face the back of your hand (your knuckles) forward.
- Flick your wrist as you hit the ball with the center of the paddle.
- Follow through to your target.

OPTION: 2-HANDED BACKHAND STROKE

- Place your non-dominant hand below your dominant hand.
- Rotate the paddle.
- Rotate your feet and shoulders in the same direction as the paddle.
- Flick your wrists as you hit the ball with the center of the paddle.
- Follow through to your target.

SKILL	PROGRESSING	COMPETENT	PROFICIENT
backhand stroke	1 or 2 of the elements	3 or 4 out of 5 elements	all elements met

UNDERHAND SERVE

- Hold the paddle in your dominant hand. Hold the ball in your non-dominant hand.
- Hold the head of the paddle down toward the ground.
- Step forward with your non-dominant foot.
- Drop the ball slightly below your waist.
- Hit the ball with the center of the paddle. Flick your wrist as you make contact.
- Follow through to your target.
- Serve successfully 70 percent of the time.

SKILL	PROGRESSING	COMPETENT	PROFICIENT
underhand serve	1, 2, 3, or 4 of the elements	5 or 6 out of 7 elements	all elements met

PRACTICE THE STROKES

- Practice each stroke by hitting the ball against a wall with the paddle.
    - Allow the ball to bounce before striking it.
    - Volley the ball against the wall. This means that you should not allow the ball to bounce off the ground.
- Strike the ball toward the wall using various levels of force.
- Aim and strike the ball to the left of the target.
- Aim and strike the ball to the right of the target.
- Hit the ball back and forth with a partner. How many times can you hit it back and forth?

SHOTS

DINK SHOT

The most effective short-hand shots, or dinks, are those that bounce in front of the no-volley line (the area 7 feet from the net, where volleying is not allowed). Dinks should be short and low.

LOB

A lob is high and pushes your opponent to the rear of the court. This slows down the game to give you a chance to get ready for your opponent's shot.

DRIVE

A drive is a hard, fast hit that is difficult to return.

PRACTICE THE SHOTS

Practice the shots independently by bouncing or tossing the ball at the appropriate height for each shot. Practice with a net set up.

- Practice the dink shot forward and crosscourt.
- Practice the lob shot.
- Practice the drive shot.
- Describe a shot and then execute it. Do this for the 3 shots.
- Have a partner toss the ball for you. Practice each shot and then switch roles. Be supportive and encouraging to your partner.

PLAYING A GAME

- Pickleball is a singles game with 2 players or a doubles game with 4 players.
- Start by serving the ball underhand from the right side of the court. Serve diagonally to your opponent on the left. Stand behind the serving line when you start your serve.
  - If a point is scored, the server then serves from the left side of the court. Continue this side-to-side pattern until the serve is lost. In a doubles game, the other teammate then serves. Once the second teammate loses the serve, the opposing team serves.
- The ball must land in the opponent's section of the court.
- Your opponent must let the ball bounce once before returning the serve.
- After each team hits the ball once, you may either let the ball bounce once or hit it. This starts the game.
- Points are only scored when a player is serving.
- Games are played to 11 points. A team must win by 2 points.
- Faults include the following.
  - hitting the ball out of bounds
  - serving faults
  - allowing the ball to bounce more than once
  - hitting the ball on the fly in the non-volley zone
  - hitting the ball to the wrong service court

PICKLEBALL OPTIONS

- Play at picnics and group outings.
- Make a net by tying jump ropes together and then tying the jump ropes to the tops of chairs. If there are 2 trees in your playing area, tie the jump ropes to the trees. You may also go to a park with a tennis court and set smaller boundaries on the tennis court.

DEMONSTRATE POSITIVE GAME BEHAVIOR

- Follow the rules.
- Call for a shot, when appropriate, to identify that you are going to hit it. This is for safety and game efficiency.
- Be supportive and encouraging to your teammate.
- Treat your opponents with respect.

SKILL	PROGRESSING	COMPETENT	PROFICIENT
game behavior	1 or 2 of the elements	3 out of 4 elements	all elements met

RATE YOUR ENJOYMENT OF PICKLEBALL

On a scale from 1 to 4, where 1 is not enjoyable and 4 is very enjoyable, rate this activity.

1	It was not enjoyable, and I will not participate again.
2	It was not enjoyable, but I will participate again for exercise.
3	It was enjoyable, and I will play again.
4	It was very enjoyable, and I will initiate future games.

RESEARCH INTEGRATION

Research pickleball's country of origin and who invented the game.

HEALTH INTEGRATION

Count your pulse during and after playing pickleball to determine if you are exercising in your personal target heart rate zone. Apply the results to your overall fitness plan. Many people choose to complete aerobic workouts by playing in casual games with friends.

PLAYGROUND BALL GAME

SPEED BALL: INDOOR BASKETBALL VERSION

Speed ball is a game that is played by 2 teams of 7 players and is a combination of basketball, soccer, and team handball. It is played with a playground ball on a basketball court. There are 2 goals at each end of the court—a basketball hoop and a soccer goal placed beneath the hoop. The object of the game is to shoot the ball through the basketball hoop and kick or throw the ball into the soccer goal to score.

Playing the game utilizes and improves the skill-related components of agility, balance, coordination, speed, power, and reaction. Playing speed ball is an aerobic workout. The game also provides the opportunity to work as a team to develop offensive and defensive strategies as well as the ability to transition quickly between them.

The purpose of this lesson is for you to participate in aerobic exercise and in skill-building activities. Game participation will depend upon the availability of a facility and players. When you are playing speed ball, be sure to follow game rules, communicate with teammates in a positive and effective manner, and exhibit appropriate behavior with your team and the opposing team.

⚠ **CAUTION: Do not overinflate the ball.**

SPEED BALL SKILLS

Speed ball utilizes skills from basketball, soccer, and team handball. Practicing skills from these 3 sports will enhance your ability to play each of those sports as well as lead to better performance in speed ball. You can find a full description of each of the 3 sports in the 7th-grade section of your PE Manual.

BASKETBALL SKILLS USED IN SPEED BALL: USE A PLAYGROUND BALL

HAND DRIBBLING

- Using your dominant hand, spread your fingers and push the ball down gently toward the ground with your finger pads. Do not slap the ball.
- Let the ball bounce on the ground and come back to your hand. Do not let the ball bounce higher than your waist.
- Flex your wrist and push the ball back to the ground with your finger pads. This is a continuous movement; do not catch the ball after every bounce.
- Dribble with your head up.
- Keep your eyes looking forward, not watching the ball.
- Repeat dribbling the ball with your non-dominant hand.

SKILL	PROGRESSING	COMPETENT	PROFICIENT
right-handed dribble	1 or 2 of the elements	3 or 4 out of 5 elements	all elements met
left-handed dribble	1 or 2 of the elements	3 or 4 out of 5 elements	all elements met

PRACTICE HAND DRIBBLING

- See how many times you can dribble the ball with your dominant hand without losing control of it.
- Push the ball down with different amounts of force to make it bounce at different levels.
- Try pushing the ball with a soft force so that it bounces at a low level.
- Try pushing the ball with a hard force so that it bounces at a high level.
- Dribble with your dominant hand.
- Dribble with your non-dominant hand.
- Dribble from 1 hand to the other.
- Dribble from 1 hand to the other while moving.
- Dribble while moving, increasing and decreasing your speed.
- Dribble while moving and change directions.

BASIC SHOOTING

- Stand facing the hoop with your feet shoulder-width apart and your knees slightly bent.
- Place your dominant hand on the back of the ball and bend your wrist. Place your non-dominant hand on the side of the ball.
- Place the ball on the finger pads of your dominant hand.
- Use your non-dominant hand as your guide.
- Position your elbow so that it is behind the ball, not out to the side.
- Look at the target—the front of the rim.
- Push your dominant hand toward the target while straightening your legs to give you more power to shoot.
- Shoot the ball toward the target and follow through with your arm and wrist. Snap your wrist as the ball leaves your hand.
- Remember BEEF.
    - **Balance** the ball in your dominant hand.
    - Place your **elbow** behind the ball, not out to the side.
    - Keep your **eyes** on the target.
    - **Follow** through with a snap of your wrist.

SKILL	PROGRESSING	COMPETENT	PROFICIENT
BEEF elements	1 or 2 of the elements	3 out of 4 elements	all elements

PRACTICE SHOOTING

- Shoot from a variety of spots inside the 3-point line.

TEAM HANDBALL SKILLS USED IN SPEED BALL: USE A PLAYGROUND BALL

OVERHAND PASS

- Grip the ball with your hands.
- Step toward your target and transfer your weight to your front foot.
- Move your arms forward in the direction of your target.
- Snap your wrists.
- Aim and pass to your target by releasing the ball, using the appropriate force to reach your target.

SKILL	PROGRESSING	COMPETENT	PROFICIENT
passing	1 or 2 of the elements	3 or 4 out of 5 elements	all elements met

RECEIVING

- Spread your fingers to catch the ball.
- Catch the ball firmly using only your hands.
- Gain control of the ball.
- Maintain your balance throughout the catch.
- Make the necessary pass or run with the ball after the catch.

SKILL	PROGRESSING	COMPETENT	PROFICIENT
receiving	1 or 2 of the elements	3 or 4 out of 5 elements	all elements met

RECEIVING WHILE RUNNING

- Keep your eyes on the ball.
- Anticipate the throw. Change your speed and direction to accommodate the throw.
- Use speed and direction to create an opening.
- Catch the majority of throws.

SKILL	PROGRESSING	COMPETENT	PROFICIENT
receiving while running	1 or 2 of the elements	3 out of 4 elements	all elements met

PRACTICE THROWING AND CATCHING

- Throw the ball against a wall and catch it.
- Throw and catch the ball with a partner.

SOCCER SKILLS USED IN SPEED BALL: USE A PLAYGROUND BALL

FOOT DRIBBLING

Use your peripheral vision, or your side vision, to watch the ball as you dribble it. Dribbling is a series of small, controlled touches that you complete in order to move with the ball in your possession. Dribble the ball with the insides and outsides of your feet as well as with the tops of your feet, where your shoelaces lay. Do not dribble the ball with your toes, otherwise, you risk losing control of the ball.

- Start with the ball positioned in front of you on the ground.
- Dribble forward, keeping the ball close—no more than 3 to 5 feet in front of you.
- Move the ball with the insides, outsides, and/or tops of both of your feet.
- Keep your head up.
- Match your speed to your skill.
- Change directions.

SKILL	PROGRESSING	COMPETENT	PROFICIENT
foot dribbling	1, 2, or 3 of the elements	4 or 5 out of 6 elements	all elements

PRACTICE FOOT DRIBBLING

- Practice dribbling by placing discs in various locations around your practice area. As you are dribbling, weave in and out of the discs.

PASSING

Players pass the ball to each other in order to keep the other team from gaining control of the ball and to progress the ball toward the other team's goal.

- Start with the ball on the ground, next to the inside of your dominant foot.
- Position the inside of your kicking foot behind the middle of the ball.
- Establish your non-kicking foot slightly behind you.
- Swing your kicking leg back, keeping it straight throughout your entire kick.
- Contact the middle of the ball with the inside of your foot. Follow through your kick with your foot and leg.
- Use appropriate force and direction to keep your pass on target.

SKILL	PROGRESSING	COMPETENT	PROFICIENT
passing	1, 2, or 3 of the elements	4 or 5 out of 6 elements	all elements

PRACTICE PASSING

- Set up 2 discs about 3 feet apart. Aim to pass the ball between the discs.
- Pass back and forth with a partner.

TRAPPING: OPTION 1

Trapping is a way of stopping the ball, receiving a pass, or gaining control of the ball.

- Start with the ball positioned in front of you on the ground.
- Place your dominant foot on top of the ball. To do this, lift your foot slightly off the ground, keeping your ankle locked and your toes up.
- Repeat this with your non-dominant foot.

SKILL	PROGRESSING	COMPETENT	PROFICIENT
trapping: option 1	1 of the elements	2 out of 3 elements	all elements

TRAPPING: OPTION 2

Trapping is also a way to stop the ball in order to quickly gain control and transition to your next move.

- When the ball comes toward you, turn the ankle of whichever foot you are trapping with so that your instep, or the inside of your foot, is facing forward.
- Cushion the ball with your foot as you stop it lightly, as if you were catching an egg.
- Repeat this with your other foot.

SKILL	PROGRESSING	COMPETENT	PROFICIENT
trapping: option 2	1 of the elements	2 out of 3 elements	all elements

SHOOTING ON GOAL

The purpose of shooting is to get the ball into your opponent's goal by striking it with your foot.

- Stand so that your dominant leg, or kicking leg, is pulled back behind you.
- Place your non-kicking foot alongside the ball, with your toes pointing at your goal.
- Bend the knee of your kicking leg by pulling your foot back. Then, in a single motion, swing your leg forward, straightening your leg and pointing your toes to kick the ball with the top of your foot. Kick the center of the ball with the laces of your shoe, pointing your toes down. You do not want to kick the ball with your toes.
- Follow through your kick, making sure that you finish with your toes pointing toward the goal.

SKILL	PROGRESSING	COMPETENT	PROFICIENT
shooting on goal	1 or 2 of the elements	3 out of 5 elements	all elements

PRACTICE TRAPPING AND SHOOTING ON GOAL

- Place 2 disc cones about 4 feet apart to use as your goal. Place them 10 to 20 feet away from you.
- Toss the ball slightly up in the air, trapping it with your foot and guiding it to the ground just in front of you.
- Dribble the ball toward the goal.
- When you get to about 5 feet away from the goal, shoot the ball through the discs.

OFFENSIVE AND DEFENSIVE SKILLS

OFFENSIVE SKILLS

OFFENSIVE READY POSITION

Being in the ready position allows you to move quickly in any direction. This position is used for both offense and defense.

- With your elbows out, hold the ball with both hands to the dominant side of your chest.
- Bend your knees to keep your body low.
- Stand with your feet shoulder-width apart.
- Keep your head up and your weight on the balls of your feet.

SKILL	PROGRESSING	COMPETENT	PROFICIENT
offensive ready position	1 or 2 of the elements	3 out of 4 elements	all elements met

FAKE

SOCCER

BASKETBALL

- Look 1 direction, but pass or move in another direction.
- Stay on the balls of your feet.
- Move quickly.

SKILL	PROGRESSING	COMPETENT	PROFICIENT
fake	1 of the elements	2 out of 3 elements	all elements

GIVE AND GO

The purpose of the give and go is for you to pass the ball to a teammate and quickly relocate so that you can receive a pass.

SOCCER

BASKETBALL

- Pass the ball to a teammate.
- Move quickly to relocate and support your offense.
- Indicate (call out) that you are ready and open to receive the ball.
- Catch the ball.

SKILL	PROGRESSING	COMPETENT	PROFICIENT
give and go	1 or 2 of the elements	3 out of 4 elements	all elements

PIVOT

The purpose of the pivot in a speed ball game is for you to look around and decide to dribble, pass, or shoot.

- Plant 1 foot, which will be your pivot foot, in place on the ground.
- Place your weight on the balls of your feet.
- Slide your non-pivot foot and rotate your body 180 degrees.
- Repeat this exercise with your other foot.

SKILL	PROGRESSING	COMPETENT	PROFICIENT
pivot	1 of the elements	2 out of 3 elements	all elements

DEFENSIVE SKILLS

DEFENSIVE READY POSITION

Being in the ready position allows you to move quickly in any direction. This position is used for both offense and defense.

- Bend your knees to keep your body low.
- Stand with your feet shoulder-width apart.
- Keep your head up and your weight on the balls of your feet.
- Hold your arms extended out above waist height so that they are ready to receive the ball.
- React quickly.
- Anticipate direction.

SKILL	PROGRESSING	COMPETENT	PROFICIENT
defensive ready position	1, 2, or 3 of the elements	4 or 5 out of 6 elements	all elements met

DEFENSIVE SLIDES

The purpose of defensive slides in speed ball is to keep up with your opponent and to legally take the ball or legally disrupt the opponent's pass or shot.

- Place your weight on the balls of your feet.
- Slide to the side with quick steps.
- Do not cross your feet.
- Keep your knees bent.
- Face your hips toward your opponent.
- Hold your hands up at chest level.
- Keep your eyes on your opponent's waistline.
- Stay with your opponent.
- Anticipate and react quickly to your opponent's movements.

SKILL	PROGRESSING	COMPETENT	PROFICIENT
defensive slides	1, 2, 3, 4, or 5 of the elements	6, 7, or 8 out of 9 elements	all elements met

PRACTICE OFFENSIVE AND DEFENSIVE SKILLS

- Practice the **pivot** by planting your right foot and rotating your left foot until you feel comfortable with the movement.
- Practice the **pivot** by planting your left foot and rotating your right foot until you feel comfortable with the movement.
- Practice the **give and go** with a partner and a defender. Pass the ball, quickly relocate, and then receive the pass, avoiding the defender.
- Practice the **fake** independently. Set up a cone as a decoy. Fake the pass toward the cone and then pass to your partner until you feel comfortable with the movement.
- Practice the **fake** with a partner defending you. Dribble, fake, and move in another direction to get around the defensive player. Do this until you feel comfortable with the fake.
- Practice the **defensive slide** with a partner. As your partner dribbles, defensive slide to try to prevent them from making a successful pass or shot. Do this until you feel comfortable with the defensive slide.

SPEED BALL GAME
OBJECT OF THE GAME

Speed ball is a combination of basketball, soccer, and team handball. A player is allowed 3 steps when they are in possession of the ball. They can take 3 steps then throw, hand dribble 3 steps then pass, or foot dribble 3 steps then pass. If the ball is on the floor, the ball is moved like in soccer; if the ball is in the players' hands, the ball is moved like in basketball. The players continue to move the ball until a goal is made, the ball is turned over to the other team, or a penalty occurs.

SPEED BALL SETUP

- It is recommended to have a trusted adult supervise the game.
- Play on a basketball court.
- Set up a soccer goal under each basketball hoop.
    - You can use nets or cones to mark off the goals.
- Use a playground ball to play the game.
- Establish 2 teams of 7 players each.
    - The number of players on each team can be adjusted according to the number of available players. This means that you have the option of playing a 3-on-3 game, a 4-on-4 game, and so on.

RULES OF THE GAME

- Establish the time of your game or the total points to reach in your game.
- Begin the game at mid-court with a jump ball. Have a neutral person toss the ball between 2 designated opposing players.
- In the event where there is nobody to toss the ball, perform a coin toss to decides which team has first possession of the ball.
- After a score, the opposing team throws the ball in.
- A player can hold onto the ball for 3 seconds before moving or passing.
- A player can take 3 steps before throwing the ball.
- Bounce passes are not allowed.
- A player is allowed 3 hand or foot dribbles before passing the ball.
- A turnover occurs when an incomplete pass or an interception is made.
- A dropped ball turns the game to soccer.
- A player can flip the ball from the floor from feet to hands (soccer to basketball).
- A player can be in possession of the ball for only 30 seconds.
    - No physical contact is allowed.
    - Defensive physical contact is a penalty that results in a basketball foul shot for the offensive player.
    - Offensive physical contact results in a turnover, or a change in possession of the ball between teams.

SCORING

1 point: Throw the ball into the goal from outside the 3-point line.
- You cannot throw the ball into the goal from inside the 3-point line.

2 points: Soccer kick the ball into the goal from inside the 3-point line.
- You cannot kick the ball into the goal from behind the 3-point line.

3 points: Shoot a basket from inside the 3-point line.
- The 3-point line is the arc line.

Prior to playing the game, establish and review the game rules so that all participants understand them. If problems arise, work as a group to solve them in a positive and effective manner. Appreciate different players' abilities. Provide game options and variations to fit your circumstances; for example, if you want to play a version of the game on an outdoor field, eliminate the hand dribble and basketball basket.

Below are our game rules for safety and fairness.
1.
2.
3.
4.
5.

RATE YOUR ENJOYMENT OF SPEED BALL

On a scale from 1 to 4, where 1 is not enjoyable and 4 is very enjoyable, rate this activity.

1	It was not enjoyable, and I will not participate again.
2	It was not enjoyable, but I will participate again for exercise.
3	It was enjoyable, and I will play again.
4	It was very enjoyable, and I will initiate future games.

RESEARCH INTEGRATION

1. Research the basic skills for speed ball in the 7th-grade sections for basketball, team handball, and soccer in your PE Manual.
2. Research the game of 4 square in the 7th-grade section of your PE Manual for another playground ball activity option.

HEALTH INTEGRATION

Count your pulse during and after playing speed ball to determine if you are exercising in your personal target heart rate zone. Apply the results to your overall fitness plan. Many people complete aerobic workouts by playing in team games like speed ball.

TENNIS

Tennis is a sport that is played by striking a ball with a racket over a net. It is played against a single opponent or as a doubles game. This striking activity helps you develop concentration, hand-eye coordination, and footwork. You may play tennis as a competitive sport or as an opportunity for social play.

The purpose of this lesson is for you to participate in aerobic exercise and in skill-building activities. Game participation will depend upon the availability of a facility and players. When you are playing tennis, be sure to follow game rules, communicate with teammates in a positive and effective manner, and exhibit appropriate behavior with your team and the opposing team.

⚠️ **CAUTION: Make sure that nobody is close to you before you swing the racket. Do not walk into the path of another person who is swinging a racket.**

RACKET SKILLS

READY POSITION

The ready position allows a player to move quickly in any direction.

- Bend your knees and stand with your feet shoulder-width apart.
- Keep your head up.
- Keep your weight on the balls of your feet.
- Hold the racket in your dominant hand.

SKILL	PROGRESSING	COMPETENT	PROFICIENT
ready position	1 or 2 of the elements	3 out of 4 elements	all elements met

HANDSHAKE GRIP

- Hold the racket in your dominant hand like you are about to shake someone's hand.
- Place your 4 fingers around the racket, and then wrap your thumb around the racket.
- Hold the racket so that the head is vertical to the ground. Make sure that the strings on the racket head are facing front and back.
- Point the handle toward your belly button.

SKILL	PROGRESSING	COMPETENT	PROFICIENT
handshake grip	1 or 2 of the elements	3 out of 4 elements	all elements met

FOREHAND STROKE

- Begin in the ready position.
- Pivot to bring the racket back on the same side of your body as your dominant hand.
- Face the palm of your hand forward.

- Shift your weight from your back foot to your front foot while stepping forward and swinging the racket with your dominant hand.
- Extend your arm and flick your wrist to hit the ball, pointing the face of the racket up to get the ball over the net.
- Follow through to your target.

SKILL	PROGRESSING	COMPETENT	PROFICIENT
forehand stroke	1, 2, or 3 of the elements	4 or 5 out of 6 elements	all elements met

BACKHAND STROKE

- Begin in the ready position.
- Rotate the racket and extend it across your body.
- Rotate your feet and shoulders in the same direction as the racket.
- Face the back of your hand (the side that your knuckles are on) forward.
- Step forward with your non-dominant foot while swinging the racket.
- Flick your wrist when hitting the ball with the center of the racket.
- Follow through to your target.

SKILL	PROGRESSING	COMPETENT	PROFICIENT
backhand stroke	1, 2, 3, or 4 of the elements	5 or 6 out of 7 elements	all elements met

2-HANDED BACKHAND STROKE

- Place your non-dominant hand below your dominant hand on the racket handle.
- Rotate the racket and extend it across your body.
- Rotate your feet and shoulders in the same direction as the racket.
- Flick your wrists when you are hitting the ball with the center of the racket.
- Follow through to your target.

OVERHAND STROKE

- Bend your elbow slightly and position the racket under the ball.
- Flick your wrist to hit the ball with the center of the racket.
- Extend your arm as you make contact.
- Follow through to your target.

SKILL	PROGRESSING	COMPETENT	PROFICIENT
overhand stroke	1 or 2 of the elements	3 out of 4 elements	all elements met

SERVES

Every game starts with a serve

PUNCH SERVE

Stand behind the service line at a 45-degree angle to the net. A punch serve is an excellent stroke to use as a beginner.

- If you are right-handed, place your left foot forward; if you are left-handed, place your right foot forward. Put your weight on your back foot.
- Hold the racket with a forehand grip in your dominant hand. Raise the racket over your head and slightly back.
- Hold the ball with your fingertips in your non-dominant hand.
- Toss the ball slightly in front of you and high above the racket. Look up at the ball.
- As the ball comes back down, hit it up and forward with the racket. Extend your arm and the racket while you are hitting the ball.
- Follow through to your target. Swing out, across, and down.

SKILL	PROGRESSING	COMPETENT	PROFICIENT
punch serve	1 or 2 of the elements	4 out of 6 elements	all elements met

OVERHAND SERVE

- Hold the racket with your dominant hand.
- Place your non-dominant foot toward the opposite post of the net and your dominant foot parallel to the court.
- Toss the ball into the air just above your head.
- Bring your dominant arm back with the head of the racket pointing toward the sky.
- Watch for the ball to begin to fall.
- Extend your arm up over your head and contact the ball with the head of the racket.

SKILL	PROGRESSING	COMPETENT	PROFICIENT
overhand serve	1, 2, or 3 of the elements	4 or 5 out of 6 elements	all elements met

PRACTICE

AGAINST A WALL

- Practice the various strokes and serves by hitting the ball against a wall with the racket. Catch the ball each time and repeat.
- Allow the ball to bounce before hitting it against the wall.
- Volley against the wall, aiming at and hitting certain spots.

WITH A PARTNER

You can use a jump rope to separate each side if a net is unavailable.

- Have a partner stand on 1 side of the net and toss the ball toward your forehand. Return with a proper forehand stroke.
- Have a partner stand on 1 side of the net and toss the ball toward your backhand. Return with a proper backhand stroke.
- Have a partner stand on 1 side of the net and toss the ball, mixing up forehand and backhand shots. Return with a proper forehand stroke or backhand stroke.
- Use the various strokes to hit the ball back and forth with a partner. Stand 15 feet away from your partner when you are volleying back and forth.

Have your partner evaluate you for correct form for the partner exercises. Did you respond positively to the feedback?

Reciprocate and evaluate your partner. Were you able to provide feedback in a positive manner?

GAME

OFFICIAL SINGLES GAME

- You will need traditional tennis balls for this game.
- Start with an overhand serve from the right side of the court. Serve from behind the baseline to your opponent on the left.
- Get the ball into your opponent's service box. You have 2 tries to get the ball into the service box. If you hit the ball into your opponent's service box and your opponent cannot return it, you win that volley and get a point.
- Serve from the left side of the court next. When your score is an even number, serve from the right side of the court. When your score is an odd number, serve from the left side of the court.
- Continue serving the ball until the game is over. The receiver becomes the server during the next game.
- You may only hit the ball 1 time on each side.
- You score if your opponent does not have a successful serve, fails to return a serve, or hits the ball out of bounds.
- You lose a volley if you or the racket touch the net.

SCORING

- The server's score is always announced first.
- The point system is as follows.
    - no points or love = 0 points
    - 1 point = 15 points
    - 2 points = 30 points
    - 3 points = 40 points
    - 4 points = win
- To win a game, you must lead by at least 2 points.
- If the score is tied at 40 points (a deuce), you must earn 2 consecutive points (an advantage point) to win the game.
- You must win at least 6 games in a set. You must lead by 2 sets to win a match.

DEMONSTRATE POSITIVE GAME BEHAVIOR

- Follow the rules.
- There is to be no intentional hitting of an opposing player with the ball. You forfeit a point if you hit the opposing player with a ball.
- Be supportive and encouraging to your teammate.
- Treat your opponents with respect.

SKILL	PROGRESSING	COMPETENT	PROFICIENT
game behavior	1 or 2 of the elements	3 out of 4 elements	all elements met

RATE YOUR ENJOYMENT OF TENNIS

On a scale from 1 to 4, where 1 is not enjoyable and 4 is very enjoyable, rate this activity.

1	It was not enjoyable, and I will not participate again.
2	It was not enjoyable, but I will participate again for exercise.
3	It was enjoyable, and I will play again.
4	It was very enjoyable, and I will initiate future games.

RESEARCH INTEGRATION

1. Research proper tennis etiquette.
2. Attend a tennis game or watch a tennis game on television.

HEALTH INTEGRATION

Count your pulse to determine if you are exercising in your personal target heart rate zone. Count your pulse after practicing skills and after playing in a game. Apply the results to your overall fitness plan. Many people choose to complete aerobic workouts by playing in games with friends.

VOLLEYBALL

The official game of volleyball is played by 2 teams of 6 players on an indoor volleyball court. Another popular version of volleyball is beach volleyball, which is played by 2 teams of 2 to 6 players on a sand surface. The object of the game is to strike a ball over a net onto the ground so that the opposing team cannot return it.

You may play volleyball as a competitive sport or as an opportunity for social play. Casual games of volleyball can be played by as few as 2 players and set up in a yard, park, beach, or gym.

The purpose of this lesson is for you to participate in aerobic exercise and in skill-building activities. When you play volleyball, be sure to follow the rules, communicate with teammates in a positive and effective manner, and exhibit appropriate behavior with your team and the opposing team.

CAUTION: Do not overinflate the ball.

VOLLEYBALL SKILLS

The following striking skills will not only help to improve your volleyball game, but they may also enhance skills used in other sports and activities.

READY POSITION

The ready position will enable you to react quickly.

- Stand with your legs shoulder-width apart.
- Balance on the balls of your feet.
- Bend your knees slightly.
- Hold your shoulders rounded and slightly forward.
- Hold your arms in front of you and ready to react.

SKILL	PROGRESSING	COMPETENT	PROFICIENT
ready position	1 or 2 of the elements	3 or 4 out of 5 elements	all elements met

FOREARM GRIP

Try both of the following grips to decide which works better for you.

1. Right-handed players: Make a fist with your left hand, wrap the fingers of your right hand around your left hand, and line up your thumbs side by side on top. Left-handed players: Make a fist with your right hand, wrap the fingers of your left hand around your right hand, and line up your thumbs side by side on top.

2. Place 1 hand out flat with your palm up. Place the other hand underneath with the palm up. Curl your thumbs until they are next to each other, centered, and pointing down.

FOREARM PASS (BUMP)

- Stand in the ready position.
- Use the correct grip.
- Contact the ball with your forearm platform.
- Follow through toward your target.

SKILL	PROGRESSING	COMPETENT	PROFICIENT
forearm pass	1 or 2 of the elements	3 out of 4 elements	all elements met

FOREARM PASS (BUMP) PRACTICE

- Forearm pass and catch: Toss the ball to yourself to begin. Pass it back up with your forearm platform, reaching toward your target and catching it. Do not allow your swing to be out of control.
- Forearm pass: Toss the ball to yourself to begin, then continue to pass it. How many times can you pass in a row?
- Wall forearm passes: Toss the ball to yourself to begin, then pass it against a wall. How many times can you pass in a row?
- Partner wall forearm passes: Take turns passing against a wall with a partner.
- Partner toss, forearm pass, and catch: Toss the ball to your partner. Your partner passes it back to you. You catch it. Switch roles.
- Partner forearm passes: How many times can you pass back and forth with a partner?

OVERHAND PASS (SET)

- Stand in the ready position.
- Hold your hands level with your forehead with your elbows bent. Form the size and shape of the ball with your fingers and thumbs.
- Contact the ball with your finger pads, not tips.
- Use a soft touch near your forehead and extend your elbows to push the ball up into the air.

SKILL	PROGRESSING	COMPETENT	PROFICIENT
overhand pass	1 or 2 of the elements	3 out of 4 elements	all elements met

OVERHAND PASS (SET) PRACTICE

- Set and catch: Toss the ball to yourself to begin, set it back up with your finger pads, and catch it.
- Set: Toss the ball to yourself to begin, then continue to set it. How many times can you set in a row?
- Wall sets: Toss the ball to yourself to begin, then set it against a wall. How many times can you set in a row?
- Partner wall sets: Take turns setting against a wall with a partner.
- Partner toss, set, and catch: Toss the ball to your partner. Your partner sets it back to you. You catch it. Switch roles.
- Partner sets: How many times can you set back and forth with a partner?

UNDERHAND SERVE

- Put your non-dominant foot forward.
- Hold the ball on the palm of your non-dominant hand. Position that arm across your body at waist height.
- Make a fist with your striking hand.
- Bring your striking arm back and then forward, striking the ball with the heel of your hand.
- Shift your weight to your front foot.
- Serve successfully 70 percent of the time.

SKILL	PROGRESSING	COMPETENT	PROFICIENT
underhand serve	1 or 2 of the elements	4 or 5 out of 6 elements	all elements met

UNDERHAND SERVE PRACTICE

- Wall serves: Practice serving toward a wall.
- Partner serves: Serve to a partner and volley back and forth using the set and bump skills.

CHALLENGING VOLLEYBALL SKILLS

The following advanced skills are for students who have mastered the basic skills. The challenge level is recommended if you want to further explore the volleyball activity.

OVERHAND SERVE

- Put your non-dominant foot forward.
- Turn the non-dominant side of your body slightly toward the net or target.
- Hold the ball in your non-dominant hand.
- Bend your striking arm with your hand cupped near your ear.
- Contact: Toss the ball 2 to 3 feet in the air, placing your weight on your back foot. Shift your weight to your front foot as you strike the ball approximately 12 inches above your head.
- Follow through in the direction of the ball.

SKILL	PROGRESSING	COMPETENT	PROFICIENT
overhand serve	1 or 2 of the elements	3, 4, or 5 out of 6 elements	all elements met

OVERHAND SERVE PRACTICE

- Wall serves: Practice serving toward a wall.
- Partner serves: Serve to a partner and volley back and forth using the set and bump skills.

OVERHAND HITTING (SPIKE)

1 player: Follow the overhand serve techniques.

2 players: A teammate hits the ball up high near the net.

- As a hitter, approach from behind using a 4-step approach.
- Place your dominant foot forward.
- Step forward with your non-dominant foot, then quick step with your dominant then non-dominant foot. For example, if you are right-handed, you would start with your right foot forward, step left, then right, then left.
- Begin with your arms at waist height in front of your body. Swing them backward then forward until both of your arms are reaching high with your dominant arm slightly forward.
- Strike the ball with the fleshy part of your dominant hand.
- Follow through, facing the direction in which you want the ball to go.

SKILL	PROGRESSING	COMPETENT	PROFICIENT
overhand hit (spike)	1 or 2 of the elements	3, 4, or 5 out of 6 elements	all elements met

EXTENSION

If you have an available outdoor wall or garage door and permission from your parent or guardian, you can place a horizontal line of tape or chalk mark 7 feet 4½ inches from the ground to represent the height of a net. Begin approximately 10 feet back and practice the underhand and overhand serves. When you are successful, move back farther. Continue this until you are able to serve from 30 feet back, which is the official serving distance.

VOLLEYBALL GAMES

REGULATION VOLLEYBALL GAME

- There are 6 people on a team: 3 front row players and 3 back row players.
- Players rotate in order to reach the serving position.
- The players from the same team all rotate 1 position clockwise when it is their team's turn to serve.
- The serving position is behind the end line. Most players will serve from the right end line; however, for left-handed servers, you may serve from anywhere behind the end line.
- The objective is to serve the ball across the net into the opponent's court within the boundaries. The ball can hit the net on the way over and still be playable.
- Each team is allowed 3 hits, but no player can hit the ball twice in a row.
- A player may not make contact with any part of the net.
- A ball contacting the net is considered playable.

SCORING

- The serve starts the game.
- When the serving team wins the rally, a point is scored.
- If the rally is won by the non-serving team, that team gets a point and a chance to serve.
- The first team to score 25 points and be ahead by at least 2 points wins the game.
- A match consists of either winning 2 out of 3 games or 3 out of 5 games.

ALTERNATIVE: A COOPERATIVE SCORING GAME

- You will need at least 2 players.
- Toss a coin to see which side serves first.
- There will be 1 person or team on each side of the net. You may use a jump rope or disc cones to separate each side if a net is unavailable.
- Rally back and forth.
- Count each time the ball goes over the net except for the serve.
- There are unlimited hits per side, but a point is scored only when it goes over the net.
- Continue until the ball is not in play.
- Indicate the score.
- Rotate sides and players for each serve.
- Count again and try to beat your previous score.

DEMONSTRATE POSITIVE GAME BEHAVIOR

- Follow the rules.
- Call out when you are attempting to strike the ball to avoid collisions.
- Be supportive and encouraging to your teammates.
- Treat your opponents with respect.

SKILL	PROGRESSING	COMPETENT	PROFICIENT
game behavior	1 or 2 of the elements	3 out of 4 elements	all elements met

RATE YOUR ENJOYMENT OF VOLLEYBALL

On a scale from 1 to 4, where 1 is not enjoyable and 4 is very enjoyable, rate this activity.

1	It was not enjoyable, and I will not participate again.
2	It was not enjoyable, but I will participate again for exercise.
3	It was enjoyable, and I will play again.
4	It was very enjoyable, and I will initiate future games.

RESEARCH INTEGRATION

1. Research who invented the game of volleyball, including the rules and regulations.
2. Attend a volleyball game or watch a volleyball game on television and compare the skills you have practiced for the game of volleyball with the skills the players use.

HEALTH INTEGRATION

Count your pulse to determine if you are exercising in your personal target heart rate zone. Count your pulse after practicing skills and after playing in a game. Apply the results to your overall fitness plan.

ANATOMY
SECTION

ANATOMY

The study of Anatomy is an excellent way to learn important things about your body. It is important to learn proper terminology of the body parts. Use this section as a reference when learning the muscles that are used during the exercises shown in this physical education workbook.

SKELETAL SYSTEM

The skeletal system consists of 206 bones. They are connected by tendons, ligaments and cartilage. The skeletal system supports the body, aids in movement, and protects internal organs.

Impact exercises and eating healthfully—especially foods high in calcium—help to keep your bones strong.

- Skull
- Mandible
- Cervical vertebrae
- Clavicle
- Scapula
- Humerus
- Sternum
- Rib
- Ulna
- Radius
- Thoracic vertebrae
- Lumbar vertebrae
- Ilium
- Sacrum
- Ischium
- Femur
- Patella
- Tibia
- Fibula
- Carpals
- Phalanges
- Metacarpals
- Tarsals
- Metatarsals
- Phalanges

MUSCULAR SYSTEM

The **muscular system** is made up of over 600 muscles. Inside this system are thousands of thin, long cells called muscle fibers. These fibers allow our muscles to relax and contract in order for us to move around. The muscles in our body are all shapes and sizes and help us have strength, balance, posture, movement, and heat.

Types of Muscles

- Skeletal Muscles - these are the muscles we use to move around. They cover our skeleton and move our bones. These muscles are voluntary because we control them directly with signals from our brain. Sometimes they are called striped muscles because they come in long, dark bands of fiber and look striped. Opposing muscles, or antagonistic muscles, work in pairs to pull on bones to create movements and should be equally trained (for example, triceps and biceps or quadriceps and hamstrings are antagonistic muscles).

- Smooth Muscles - these are special muscles that don't connect to bones, but control organs in our body. These organs include the esophagus, stomach, intestines, bladder, blood vessels, respiratory system, and uterus (female). Smooth muscles are involuntary and are controlled by the nervous system, so you do not have to think about controlling them.

- Cardiac Muscle - this is a special muscle that pumps our heart and blood through our body. It can stretch like a smooth muscle and contract like a skeletal muscle. Like the smooth muscle, cardiac muscle is involuntary.

CIRCULATORY SYSTEM

The **circulatory system** allows blood to circulate throughout the body and transport nutrients, oxygen, carbon dioxide, hormones, and blood cells. Arteries carry oxygen rich blood from the heart to the rest of the body. Veins carry deoxygenated blood back to the heart.

Your heart is a muscle that is about the size of your fist. It pumps blood throughout your body by way of your blood vessels. A child's heart pumps blood through approximately 60 thousand miles of blood vessels (2 ½ times around Earth). Your heart is a part of your circulatory system, which also includes blood, blood vessels, and lungs.

Your blood contains important nutrients and oxygen for your body's cells. Your body is made up of cells that require nutrients and oxygen. Cardiovascular exercise, also referred to as aerobic exercise, helps to keep your heart muscle pumping strong. Exercise almost every day to keep your heart strong.

Your heart is made up of four chambers: the right atrium, right ventricle, left atrium, and left ventricle. The **right atrium** and **right ventricle** receive "waste" blood by way of your veins. This blood collects a waste called carbon dioxide gas, which needs to be sent to your lungs so you can breathe it out. The blood then picks up oxygen and enters the **left atrium** and **left ventricle**. Your blood is now filled with fresh oxygen and nutrients and is ready to be pumped to your body's cells.

Circulatory System

- The blood that returns to the heart, flows into the right atrium through the vena cava.
- Blood from the left ventricle into the aorta ejected.
- The blood goes to the lungs through the pulmonary artery.
- The blood that returns to the heart, is going in the right atrium.
- Oxygenated blood returns from the lungs.
- Left atrium
- Blood from the right ventricle into the pulmonary artery is pushed.
- Left ventricle
- Valves allow blood to flow in only one direction.
- The partition that separates the two halves of the heart.
- The largest of veins – inferior vena cava.
- The largest artery – Aorta.

RESPIRATORY SYSTEM

Your lungs are part of your **respiratory system**, which also includes your nose, mouth, trachea (windpipe), and diaphragm (muscle). An exchange of gases occurs when you breathe. You breathe in oxygen and breathe out carbon dioxide, which is a waste gas.

Regular exercise is important for clear, healthy lungs. Exercise makes you breathe in more air than usual, helping to clear out carbon dioxide.

NERVOUS SYSTEM

Your brain is part of your **nervous system**, which also includes your nerves and spinal cord. Messages travel between your nerves and brain. Your brain controls just about everything you think, do, and feel. It coordinates and controls body systems that involve movement, personality, thinking, heartbeat, breathing, and more.

Research has connected exercise to a healthy brain. Compared to the rest of your body, your brain is small; however, it uses a quarter of the oxygen you breathe in. The increased blood flow from exercise brings important oxygen and nutrients to your brain. Regular exercise is associated with improved learning.

DIGESTIVE SYSTEM

Your stomach is part of your **digestive system**, which also includes your mouth, esophagus, and intestines. When food enters your mouth, the digestive process begins with your saliva and the chewing of the food. Your tongue pushes the chewed food into your esophagus, which is attached to your stomach.

Healthful eating is very important to a healthy body. Your body needs the nutrients and vitamins from healthful foods to work at its best. Proper nutrition and regular exercise should be lifelong commitments.

CAREERS

CAREERS RELATED TO PHYSICAL EDUCATION

ARE YOU INTERESTED IN PHYSICAL ACTIVITY AND HOW IT RELATES TO HEALTH AND SPORTS? IF SO, YOU MAY BE INTERESTED IN THE FOLLOWING CAREER OPPORTUNITIES:

Sports medicine: a doctor who helps to treat and prevent sport injuries

Sports psychologist: a trained professional who helps athletes improve their mental skills for better sport performance

Sports nutritionist: a dietician who educates athletes about proper nutrition for better sport performance

Sports manager: a trained professional who organizes and budgets sports and sport activities

Physical therapist: a trained professional who works with patients to improve their health and mobility

Physical education teacher: a trained professional who teaches students about exercise and its connection to health

Fitness trainer: a certified trainer who helps people improve their fitness levels

Coach: a person with a sport background who leads players in a sport at the high school, college, or professional level

Chiropractor: a health care professional who treats back, joint, and muscle problems

PHYSICAL ACTIVITY JOURNALS

PHYSICAL ACTIVITY JOURNALS

Activity journals are a wonderful way to express fitness progress and ideas. Keeping a journal can help you record the progression of your fitness goals and achievements. In addition, these journals help to promote proper writing, spelling, and math skills. Parents are encouraged to check the Physical Activity Journals as a way of monitoring the development of these skills. **** *Please note that these journals are for personal use only and are not required to be submitted for course credit.* ****

FITNESS WORKOUT JOURNAL

The fitness workout journal is used to record progress in your cardiovascular fitness. The electronic movement band is a great tool to help with record this progress. This journal can be helpful if you want to walk or run in a 5K race or any race of significant distance. As you progress, you can see the changes in your time and distance by utilizing the fitness workout journal. *Please note that this journal is for personal use only and is not required to be submitted for credit.*

PHYSICAL EDUCATION JOURNAL

The Physical Education journal is a tool that you can use weekly to record each day that you are active. Using the journal, record the date, nature of activity, and amount of time used to complete the activity. At the end of each week, you can can total the minutes of activity completed and covert the time (minutes) into hours. *Please note that this journal is for personal use only and is not required to be submitted for credit.*

Copyright 2024 © Lincoln Learning Solutions. All rights reserved.

FITNESS WORKOUT JOURNAL

The Fitness Workout Journal is used to record progress in your cardiovascular fitness. The electronic movement band is a great tool to help with recording this progress. This journal can be helpful if you want to walk or run in a 5K race or any race of significant distance. As you progress, you can see the changes in your time and distance by utilizing the Fitness Workout Journal. *Please note that this journal is for personal use only and is not required to be submitted for credit.*

Date	Activity	Distances/Strides	Time	Heart Rate
09-01	Walking	10,000 Steps	1.5 hours	90 bpm

PHYSICAL EDUCATION JOURNAL

	AEROBIC EXERCISE	STRENGTH EXERCISE	FLEXIBILITY OR OTHER PHYSICAL ACTIVITY	TOTAL TIME PER DAY
Monday	Activity	Activity	Activity	Time
Tuesday	Activity	Activity	Activity	Time
Wednesday	Activity	Activity	Activity	Time
Thursday	Activity	Activity	Activity	Time
Friday	Activity	Activity	Activity	Time
Saturday	Activity	Activity	Activity	Time
Sunday	Activity	Activity	Activity	Time

TOTAL WEEKLY TIME: _____

Fitness experts recommend 1 hour per day of physical activity.
Exercise only if you are healthy.

It is recommended that you complete no more than two activity hours per day.

Make copies of this page as needed to complete your physical education course and for future workouts. Please note that this journal is for personal use only. You must submit the electronic form for grading.

GLOSSARY OF TERMS

PHYSICAL EDUCATION GLOSSARY OF TERMS

Abductors - muscles that pull the arm or leg away from the midline of the body.

Adductors - muscles that pull the arm or leg toward the midline of the body.

Aerobic - physical activity or exercise done at a steady pace for an extended period of time so that the heart can supply as much oxygen as the body needs (e.g., walking, running, swimming, cycling).

Agility - a component of physical fitness that relates to the ability to rapidly change the position of the body in space with speed and accuracy.

Anaerobic - physical activity or exercise done in short, fast bursts that cause the heart to not be able to supply oxygen as fast as the body needs (e.g., sprinting, weightlifting).

Anterior - front side of the body.

Artery - a blood vessel that carries blood away from the heart.

Balance - a skill related component of physical fitness that relates to the maintenance of equilibrium while stationary or moving.

Blood Pressure - the force of circulating blood on the walls of the arteries.

Body Mass Index (BMI) - the measurement of body fat based on height and weight.

Body Alignment - body control using such skills as balance, coordination, spatial judgments, and postural efficiency.

Body Composition - a health-related component of physical fitness that relates to the percent of fat tissue and lean tissue in the body.

Body Systems - anatomically or functionally related to parts of the body (e.g., skeletal, muscular, circulatory).

Calorie - the unit of measuring the energy produced by food when oxidized in the body.

Cardiorespiratory - relating to both the heart and respiratory system.

Cardiorespiratory Fitness - a health related component of physical fitness relating to the ability of the circulatory and respiratory systems to supply oxygen during sustained physical activity.

Cardiovascular Endurance - the body's ability to use oxygen to meet energy demands of muscles through aerobic exercise.

Carotid Artery - main artery located in the neck.

Circuit Training - exercise program, similar to an obstacle course, in which the person goes from one place to another doing a different exercise at each place.

Circulatory System - the heart and system of blood vessels in the body, including arteries, capillaries, and veins.

Conditioning - engaging in regular physical activity or exercise that results in an improved state of physical fitness.

Continuous - two or more repetitions of the same skill such as dribbling in basketball or soccer.

Contract - muscle shortens.

Cool-down - brief, mild exercise done after vigorous exercise to help the body safely return to a resting state.

Coordination - a skill related component of physical fitness that relates to the ability to use the senses together with body parts in performing motor tasks smoothly and accurately.

Dehydration - excess fluid loss from the body.

Directions - forward, backward, left, right, up, down.

Dynamic Balance - equilibrium used when in motion, starting, and stopping.

Dynamic Flexibility - is the ability to move quickly or at normal speed into a stretched position.

Effort - this concept defines how the body moves. It consists of three components: *time* (faster or slower), *force* (harder or softer), and *flow* (bound or free).

Equilibrium - state at which there is no change in the motion of the body.

Exercise - physical activity that is planned, structured, repetitive, and results in the improvement or maintenance of personal fitness.

Extend - muscle lengthens or becomes longer.

External Oblique - muscles located on the anterior side of the abdomen or stomach area.

Fitness - capability of the body of distributing inhaled oxygen to muscle tissue during increased physical activity.

FITT - is an acronym for Frequency, Intensity, Time, and Type, which are four key ways that activity can be manipulated to create a desired fitness outcome.

Flex - muscle shortens.

Flexibility - the elasticity of muscles and connective tissues, which determines the range of motion of the joints.

Frequency - the amount of time you repeat an exercise.

Goal - something that you want to achieve in your physical activities. A predetermined plan of action.

Health-Related Fitness - components of physical fitness that have a relationship with good health. Components are cardiorespiratory endurance, muscular strength, muscular endurance, flexibility, and body composition.

Heart - muscle that pumps blood throughout the body.

Heart Rate - the number of heartbeats occurring within a specified length of time.

Individual Sport - a sport with one participant, such as archery, cycling, golf, running, swimming, tennis.

Individuality - the training principle that takes into account that each person begins at a different level of fitness. Each person has personal goals and objectives for physical activity and fitness.

Intensity - the level of effort exerted during a workout, measured with target heart rate.

Interval Training - an anaerobic exercise program that consists of runs of short distance followed by rest.

Journal - written record of activities or events.

Kinesthetic - the sense perception of movement, the muscular sense.

Kinetic - energy that an object possesses because it is moving, such as a pitched baseball or person running.

Learning Stages - Three Stages:
Cognitive Stage - the first stage of motor learning when the participant requires intense concentration with no distraction.
Associative Stage - the second and intermediate stage. Skill is used in combination with other skills when the learner is improving the quality of performance.
Automatic Stage - the final stage. Advanced, proficient and dynamic, skill is used in combination with other skills in an open environment.

Levels - positions of the body (e.g., high, medium, low).

Lifelong Activity - a non-impact physical activity that you can enjoy into adulthood. Walking, hiking, biking, golf, tennis, etc.

Linear Movement - movement which occurs in a straight path.

Locomotor Movement - movement producing physical displacement of the body by weight transfer of feet. Basic locomotor steps are walk, run, hop, skip, slide, gallop, and jump.

Manipulative Skills - a skillful movement done to or with objects such as throwing a ball, striking a soccer ball, catching a Frisbee, or juggling.

Maximum Heart Rate - the highest number of times the heart can beat in one minute. Generally calculated by subtracting a person's age from 220.

Moderate Physical Activity - sustained, repetitive, large muscle movements (e.g., walking, running, cycling) done at less than 60% of maximum heart rate for age.

Motor Skills - non-fitness abilities that improve with practice and relate to one's ability to perform specific sports and other motor tasks (e.g. tennis serve, shooting a basketball).

Muscular Endurance - a health related component of physical fitness that relates to the ability to contract your muscles repeatedly without excessive fatigue.

Muscular Strength - a health related component of physical fitness that relates to the maximal force that you can exert when you contract your muscles.

Muscular System - is an organ system consisting of skeletal, smooth, and cardiac muscles. It permits movement of the body, maintains posture, and circulates blood.

Non-locomotor - movement in the space that the body or its parts can reach without traveling away from starting point.

Non-manipulative Skills - skillful movements done with the body like turning, twisting, or rolling.

Nutrient - a basic component of food that nourishes the body. There are six nutrients: carbohydrates, lipids, proteins, vitamins, minerals, and water.

Obesity - a condition in which the body has excessive adipose (fat) tissue.

Pathways - patterns of travel while performing locomotor movements (e.g., straight, curved, zigzag).

Physical Activity - body movement that is produced by the contraction of skeletal muscles.

Physical Education - a planned, sequential, movement-based program of curricula and instruction that helps the students to develop knowledge, motor skills, and self-management skills needed to maintain a physically active life.

Physical Fitness - a level of physical ability to perform daily tasks effectively with enough energy for additional recreational activities and physical challenges.

Posterior - back side of the body.

Power - a skill-related component of physical fitness that relates to the ability to move your body parts swiftly while at the same time applying maximum force on your muscles.

Progression - a rate at which you change the frequency, intensity, and time of your exercise.

Psychomotor - physical activity relating to fitness and skill.

Pulse - the rhythmical throbbing of arteries produced by the regular contraction of the heart. Common areas to check pulse are the wrist and neck.

Radial Artery - main artery located on the anterior wrist.

Range of Motion (ROM) - varying degrees of motion around a joint.

Reaction Time - a skill related component of physical fitness that relates to the time elapsed between stimulation and the beginning of the response to it.

Recovery Time - time or rest between exercises.

Repetition - number of times a skill is repeated.

Resistance - opposition of some force to another.

Respiratory System - system in the body that takes in and distributes oxygen during the breathing process.

Rubric - a scoring tool that lists the criteria for a fitness test.

Self-space - all the space that the body or its parts can reach without traveling from a starting position.

Serial - two or more different skills performed with each other, such as fielding a ball and throwing it to a target, or dribbling a basketball and shooting it.

Set - a group of several repetitions.

Skeletal System - internal framework of bones; helps provide the body with shape and support, protects vital organs, and produces blood cells.

Skilled-related Fitness - consists of components of physical fitness that have a relationship with performance in sports and motor skills. The components are agility, balance, power, reaction time, and speed.

Speed - a skill related component of physical fitness that relates to the ability to perform a movement or cover a distance in a short period of time.

Static Balance - maintaining equilibrium while holding a pose or remaining motionless.

Strength - the quality of being strong, such as body or muscle power.

Strength Training - the use of resistance to muscular contraction to build the strength, anaerobic endurance, and size of skeletal muscles.

Target Heart Rate - a figure used to represent the number of heart beats per minute required to reach during exercise in order to achieve desired positive results.

Team Sports - includes any sport which involves players working together to win the contest. (e.g., basketball, volleyball, football, soccer, lacrosse, etc.).

Torque - a turning, or rotary force.

Warm-up - a variety of low intensity activities designed to prepare your body for more vigorous activities.

Vigorous Physical Activity - sustained, repetitive, large muscle movements (e.g., running, swimming, soccer) done at 60% or more of maximum heart rate for age. Activity makes person sweat and breathe hard.

SHAPE AMERICA NATIONAL STANDARDS FOR PHYSICAL EDUCATION

Standard 1: *Demonstrates competency in a variety of motor skills and movement patterns.*
Standard 2: *The physically literate individual applies knowledge of concepts, principles, strategies and tactics related to movement and performance.*
Standard 3: *The physically literate individual demonstrates the knowledge and skills to achieve and maintain a health-enhancing level of physical activity and fitness.*
Standard 4: *The physically literate individual exhibits responsible personal and social behavior that respects self and others.*
Standard 5: *The physically literate individual recognizes the value of physical activity for health, enjoyment, challenge, self-expression and/or social interaction.*

NATIONAL STANDARD OUTCOMES FOR PHYSICAL EDUCATION

Each outcome is fully defined in the online program.

Primary Outcomes
Embedded Outcomes (Secondary Outcomes)

STANDARD OUTCOMES FOR THE FRONT INFORMATIONAL SECTIONS

Section: Physical Education Requirements
S3.M116.6
S3.M8.7
S3.M8.8
S3.H4.L1
S4.M7.7
S4.M2.8
S4.M7.8

Section: PE Log
S3.M3.6
S3.M5.6
S3.M6.6
S3.M16.7
S3.M16.8

Section: Organized or Team Sports Verification Log
S4.M1.6
S4.M2.6
S4.M2.7
S4.M2.8

Section: Essentials of Fitness
S3.M7.6
S3.M8.6

S5.M2.6
S5.M3.6
S5.M4.6
S3.M7.7
S3.M7.8
S3.M1.8
S5.M1.7
S5.M1.8
S5.M2.7
S5.M4.7
S5.M2.8
S5.M4.8

Section: Principles of Fitness
S3.M11.6
S3.M15.6
S3.M11.7
S3.M11.8
S3.M15.7
S3.M15.8

Section: Planning and Preparing: Warm-Up and Cool-Down
S3.M9.6
S3.M12.6
S3.M9.7
S3.M9.8

S3.M10.8
S3.M12.7
S3.M12.8
S3.M18.7

Section: Planning and Preparing: Weather Precautions
S2.M13.6
S2.M13.7
S2.M13.8
S4.M7.6
S4.M7.7
S4.M7.8

Section: Measuring Fitness
S3.M15.6
S3.M15.7
S3.M15.8
S3.M16.8
S5.M3.8
S5.M6.8

Section: Health-Related Fitness Components: Body Composition
S3.M1.6
S3.M10.7

S3.M17.8

Section: Health-Related Fitness Components: Cardiovascular Endurance
S3.M10.6
S3.M13.6
S3.M8.6
S4.M7.6
S5.M1.6
S5.M2.6
S3.M10.7
S3.M13.7
S3.M13.8
S3.M8.7
S3.M8.7
S4.M7.7
S4.M7.8
S4.M2.7
S5.M1.7
S5.M2.7
S5.M1.8

Section: Health-Related Fitness Components: Flexibility
S3.M9.6
S3.M9.7

S3.M9.8

Section: Health-Related Fitness Components: Muscular Strength
S3.M8.6
S3.M10.6
S4.M7.6
S3.M3.7
S3.M4.7
S3.M6.7
S3.M6.8
S4.M7.7
S4.M7.8

Section: Muscular Endurance
S3.M8.6
S3.M10.6
S4.M7.6
S3.M3.7
S3.M4.7
S3.M6.7
S3.M6.8
S4.M7.7
S4.M7.8

STANDARDS AND STANDARD OUTCOMES FOR GRADES 6-8 PE EQUIPMENT KIT SECTION

WARM-UP AND COOL-DOWN GRADES 6–8

Module: Warm-Up
S3.M9.6
S3.M12.6
S3.M9.7
S3.M12.7

S3.M9.8
S3.M10.8
S3.M12.8
S5.M1.7
S5.M1.8

Module: Cool-Down
S3.M9.6
S3.M12.6
S3.M9.7
S3.M12.7

S3.M17.7
S3.M9.8
S3.M10.8
S3.M12.8
S5.M1.8

SIXTH GRADE PE EQUIPMENT KIT

Module: Aerobic Exercise
S2.M1.6
S3.M3.6
S3.M6.6
S3.M8.6

S3.M10.6
S3. M11.6
S4.M1.6
S4.M7.6
S5.M1.6
S5.M3.6
S5.M5.8

Module: Agility Ladder
S2.M1.6
S3.M6.6
S3.M7.6
S4.M7.6
S5.M3.6

Module: Dance
S1.M1.6
S2.M12.6
S3.M2.6
S3.M6.5
S4.M6.6

S5.M4.6
S5.M5.6

Module: Jump Rope
S1.M24.6
S3.M2,6

S3.M5.6
S3.M6.6
S3.M8.6
S4.M1.6
S4.M3.6
S4.M7.6
S1.M24.6
S3.M5.6
S3.M6.6
S3.M8.6
S4.M5.6
S4.M7.6
S5.M3.6
S5.M5.6
S5.M6.6

Module: Strength Training

S3.M2.6
S3.M6.6
S3.M8.6
S3.M10.6
S3.M11.6
S3.M15.6
S4.M1.6
S4.M3.6
S4.M7.6
S5.M1.6
S5.M3.6

Module: Resistance Bands

S3.M2.6
S3.M6.6
S3.M8.6
S3.M10.6
S3.M11.6
S3.M14.6
S3.M15.6
S4.M1.6
S4.M3.6
S4.M7.6
S5.M1.6
S5.M3.6

Module: Exercise Stations

S1.M24.6
S2.M1.6
S3.M3.6
S3.M5.6
S3.M6.6
S3.M7.6
S3.M8.6
S3.M10.6
S3.M11.6
S3.M14.6
S3.M15.6
S4.M1.6
S4.M3.6
S4.M7.6
S5.M1.6
S5.M3.6
S5.M5.6

Module: Basketball

S1.M2.6
S1.M5.6
S1.M6.6
S1.M7.6
S1.M8.6
S1.M9.6
S1.M10.6
S1.M24.6
S2.M1.6
S2.M2.6
S2.M3.6
S2.M4.6
S2.M5.6
S2.M6.6
S2.M9.6
S2.M13.6
S3.M2.6
S3.M9.6
S4.M1.6
S4.M2.6
S4.M3.6
S4.M4.6
S4.M5.6
S4.M6.6
S4.M7.6
S5.M4.6

S5.M5.6
S5.M6.6

Module: Soccer

S1.M2.6
S1.M6.6
S1.M7.6
S1.M10.6
S1.M11.6
S1.M22.6
S2.M1.6
S2.M2.6
S2.M3.6
S2.M4.6
S2.M6.6
S2.M10.6
S2.M13.6
S3.M2.6
S3.M5.6
S4.M1.6
S4.M2.6
S4.M3.6
S4.M4.6
S4.M5.6
S4.M6.6
S4.M7.6
S5.M4.6
S5.M6.6

Module: Volleyball

S1.M11.6
S1.M12.6
S1.M13.6
S1.M15.6
S1.M17.6,
S2.M7.6
S2.M8.6
S2.M9.6
S2.M10.6
S3.M2.6
S3.M5.6
S4.M1.6
S4.M2.6.
S4.M3.6
S4.M5.6
S4.M6.6

S4.M7.6
S5.M3.6
S5.M4.6
S5.M5.6
S5.M6.6

Module: Playground Ball Games Four Square and Two Square

S1.M12.6
S1.M13.6
S1.M15.6
S3.M2.6
S4.M1.6
S4.M5.6
S4.M6.6
S4.M7.6
S5.M3.6
S5.M6.6

Kickball Games

S1M22.6
S1.M24.6
S2.M1.6
S2.M10.6
S3.M5.6
S4.M1.6
S4.M5.6
S4.M6.6
S4.M7.6
S5.M6.

Module: Flying Disc

S1.M2.6
S1.M3.6
S1.M4.6
S1.M5.6
S1.M10.6
S3.M5.6
S4.M1.6
S4.M5.6
S4.M6.6
S4.M7.6
S5.M6.6

Module: Pickleball

S1.M12.6
S1.M13.6
S1.M14.6
S1.M15.6
S1.M16.6
S1.M17.6
S2.M1.6
S2.M6.6
S2.M7.6
S2.M8.6
S2.M9.6
S2.M10.6
S2.M13.6
S3.M2.6
S3.M5.6
S4.M1.6
S4.M3.6
S4.M4.6
S4.M7.6
S5.M3.6
S5.M4.6
S5.M6.6

Module: Wiffle® Ball

S1.M2.6
S1.M3.6
S1.M6.6
S1.M20.6
S1.M21.6
S1.M22.6
S2.M9.6
S2.M10.6
S2.M11.6
S2.M13.6
S3.M5.6
S4.M1.6
S4.M2.6
S4.M4.6
S4.M6.6
S4.M7.6
S5.M3.6
S5.M4.6
S5.M6.6

SEVENTH GRADE PE EQUIPMENT KIT

Module: Aerobic Exercise

S1.M1.7
S1.M1.8
S2.M12.7
S3.M1.7
S3.M2.7
S3.M6.7
S3.M8.7
S3.M10.7
S3.M12.7
S3.M18.7
S3.M2.8
S3.M3.8
S3.M5.8
S3.M8.8
S3.M12.8
S3.M13.8
S3.M14.8
S3.M16.8
S4.M2.7
S4.M7.
S4.M1.8
S4.M2.8
S4.M7.8
S5.M2.7
S5.M4.7
S5.M5.7
S5.M2.8
S5.M4.8
S5.M5.8

Module: Dance

S1.M1.7

S2.M12.7
S3.M2.7
S3.M6.7
S4.M2.7
S4.M6.7
S5.M1.7
S5.M4.7
S5.M5.7
S5.M6.7

Module: Jump Rope

S1.M24.7
S3.M2.7
S3.M5.7
S3.M6.7
S3.M7.7
S4.M1.7
S4.M2.7
S4.M3.7
S4.M7.7
S5.M1.7
S5.M3.7
S5.M5.7
S5.M6.7

Module: Strength Training

S3.M1.7
S3.M2.7
S3.M3.7
S3.M4.7
S3.M6.7
S3.M8.7
S3.M10.7

S3.M12.7
S3.M14.7
S4.M7.7
S5.M1.7
S5.M2.7
S5.M4.7
S5.M5.7

Module: Resistance Bands

S3.M2.7
S3.M3.7
S3.M4.7
S3.M6.7
S3.M8.7
S3.M10.7
S4.M3.7
S4.M7.7
S5.M1.7

Module: Badminton

S1.M11.7
S1.M12.7
S1.M13.7
S1.M14.7
S2.M1.7
S2.M6.7
S2.M7.7
S2.M8.7
S2.M9.7
S2.M10.7
S2.M12.7
S3.M5.7

S3.M12.7
S3.M14.7
S4.M7.7
S4.M3.7
S4.M4.7
S4.M6.7
S4.M7.7
S5.M4.7
S5.M5.7

Module: Basketball

S1.M2.7
S1.M5.7
S1.M6.7
S1.M7.7
S1.M8.7
S1.M9.7
S1.M10.7
S1.M24.7
S2.M1.7
S2.M2.7
S2.M3.7
S2.M4.7
S2.M5.7
S2.M6.7
S2.M9.7
S2.M13.7
S3.M1.7
S3.M2.7
S4.M1.7
S4.M2.7
S4.M3.7
S4.M4.7
S4.M5.7
S4.M6.7

S4.M7.7
S5.M1.7
S5.M4.7
S5.M5.7
S5.M6.7

Module: Golf

S1.M19.7
S1.M22.7
S1.M24.7
S2.M8.7
S2.M9.7
S2.M10.7
S2.M13.7
S3.M5.7
S4.M2.7
S4.M6.7
S4.M7.7
S5.M1.7
S5.M4.7
S5.M5.7

Module: 4 Square (Playground Ball Games)

S1.M11.7
S1.M12.7
S1.M13.7
S1.M15.7
S1.M16.7
S1.M22.7
S2.M1.7
S2.M2.7
S2.M8.

S2.M9.7
S2.M10.7
S2.M13.7
S4.M1.7
S4.M2.7
S4.M3.7
S4.M4.7
S4.M5.7
S4.M6.7
S4.M7.7
S5.M3.7
S5.M4.7
S5.M5.7
S5.M6.7

Module: Team Handball (Playground Ball Games)

S1.M2.7
S1.M3.7
S1.M5.7
S1.M6.7
S1.M7.7
S1.M10.7

S1.M11.7
S1.M21.7
S1.M22.7
S2.M1.7
S2.M2.7
S2.M3.7
S2.M4.7
S2.M5.7
S2.M6.7
S2.M13.7
S3.M2.7
S3.M5.7
S4.M1.7
S4.M2.7
S4.M3.7
S4.M4.7
S4.M5.7
S4.M6.7
S4.M7.7
S5.M3.7
S5.M4.7
S5.M5.7
S5.M6.7

Module: Soccer

S1.M2.7
S1.M4.7
S1.M6.7
S1.M7.7
S1.M10.7
S1.M11.7
S1.M22.7
S2.M1.7
S2.M2.7
S2.M3.7
S2.M4.7
S2.M6.7
S2.M10.7
S2.M13.7
S3.M1.7
S3.M2.7
S3.M5.7
S4.M1.7
S4.M2.7
S4.M3.7
S4.M4.7
S4.M5.7
S4.M6.7

S4.M7.7
S5.M4.7
S5.M5.7
S5.M6.7

Module: Short-Handled Racket Tennis

S1.M13.7
S1.M15.7
S1.M16.7
S1.M17.7
S2.M1.7
S2.M6.7
S2.M8.7
S2.M9.7
S2.M10.7
S2.M12.7
S2.M13.7
S3.M5.7
S4.M1.7
S4.M2.7
S4.M3.7
S4.M4.7
S4.M6.7

S4.M7.7
S5.M4.7
S5.M5.7
S5.M6.7

Module: Wiffle® Ball

S1.M20.7
S1.M21.7
S1.M22.7
S2.M8.7
S2.M9.7
S2.M10.7
S2.M11.7
S2.M13.7
S3.M5.7
S3.M14.7
S4.M1.7
S4.M2.7
S4.M4.7
S4.M6.7
S4.M7.7
S5.M4.7
S5.M5.7
S5.M6.7

EIGHTH GRADE PE EQUIPMENT KIT

Module: Aerobic Exercise

S1.M1.8
S3.M2.8
S3.M3.8
S3.M5.8
S3.M8.8
S3.M12.8
S3.M13.8
S3.M14.8
S3.M16.8
S4.M1.8
S4.M2.8
S4.M7.8
S5.M2.8
S5.M4.8
S5.M5.8

Module: Hip-Hop Dance

S1.M1.8
S2.M12.8
S3.M2.8
S3.M3.8
S3.M5.8
S4.M1.8
S4.M2.8
S4.M5.8
S4.M6.8
S5.M2.8
S5.M4.8
S5.M5.8
S5.M6.8

Module: Jump Rope

S1.M1.8
S1.M24.8
S2.M12.8
S2.M13.8
S3.M2.8
S3.M7.8
S3.M16.8
S4.M1.8
S4.M3.8
S4.M7.8
S5.M2.8
S5.M4.8

S5.M5.8
S5.M6.8

Module: Strength Training

S3.M1.8
S3.M2.8
S3.M9.8
S3.M11.8
S3.M12.8
S3.M18.8
S4.M1.8
S4.M2.8
S4.M7.8
S5.M5.8
S5.M6.8

Module: Fitness Ball

S3.M2.8
S4.M1.8
S4.M2.8
S4.M7.8
S5.M6.8

Module: Cross-Training Circuit

S1.M1.8
S3.M1.8
S3.M2.8
S3.M4.8
S3.M6.8
S3.M8.8
S3.M9.8
S3.M11.8
S3.M12.8
S3.M13.8
S3.M16.8
S4.M1.8
S4.M7.8
S5.M4.8
S5.M5.8

Module: Floor Hockey

S1.M4.8
S1.M6.8
S1.M7.8
S1.M9.8
S1.M10.8
S1.M15.8
S1.M19.8
S2.M1.8
S2.M2.8
S2.M3.8
S2.M4.8
S2.M5.8
S2.M6.8
S2.M7.8
S2.M8.8
S2.M9.8
S2.M10.8
S2.M11.8
S3.M5.8
S4.M2.8
S4.M4.8
S4.M5.8
S4.M6.8
S4.M7.8
S5.M4.8
S5.M5.8
S5.M6.8

Module: Juggling

S1.M24.8
S3.M2.8
S3.M18.8
S4.M1.8
S4.M7.8
S5.M4.8
S5.M5.8

Module: Pickleball

S1.M12.8
S1.M13.8
S1.M14.8
S1.M16.8
S1.M17.8
S2.M1.8
S2.M6.8

S2.M7.8
S2.M8.8
S2.M9.8
S2.M11.8
S2.M12.8
S2.M13.8
S3.M5.8
S4.M2.8
S4.M3.8
S4.M6.8
S4.M7.8
S5.M4.8
S5.M5.8
S5.M6.8

Module: Speed Ball: Basketball Version

S1.M2.8
S1.M5.8
S1.M6.8
S1.M7.8
S1.M8.8
S1.M9.8
S1.M11.8
S1.M18.8
S1.M21.8
S2.M1.8)
S2.M2.8
S2.M3.8
S2.M4.8
S2.M5.8
S2.M6.8
S2.M9.8
S2.M10.8
S2.M11.8
S3.M2.8
S3.M5.8
S4.M1.8
S4.M2.8
S4.M3.8
S4.M4.8
S4.M5.8
S4.M7.8
S5.M4.8
S5.M5.8

Module: Tennis

S1.M13.8
S1.M14.8
S1.M15.8
S1.M17.8
S1.M19.8
S1.M20.8
S1.M22.8
S2.M1.8
S2.M6.8
S2.M7.8
S2.M8.8
S2.M9.8
S2.M13.8
S3.M2.8
S3.M5.8
S4.M1.8
S4.M2.8
S4.M3.8
S4.M4.8
S4.M7.8
S5.M4.8
S5.M5.8
S5.M6.8

Module: Volleyball

S1.M12.8
S1.M13.8
S1.M17.8
S2.M7.8
S2.M8.8
S2.M9.8
S3.M2.8
S3.M5.8
S4.M1.8
S4.M2.8
S4.M3.8
S4.M5.8
S4.M6.8
S4.M7.8
S5.M4.8
S5.M5.8
S5.M6.8

STANDARD OUTCOMES FOR THE ANATOMY, JOURNALS, AND GLOSSARY SECTIONS

Section: Careers

S3.H5.L2
S4.H3.L2

Section: Anatomy

S3.M14.7
S3.M14.8
S3.H9.L2

Section: Journals

S3.M16.7
S3.M16.8
S4.M2.7
S4.M2.8
S3.H6.L1

S3.H11.L2

Section: Glossary

S2.H1.L1

LINCOLN EMPOWERED PE

PHYSICAL EDUCATION
Grades 6 to 8